Praise for *Building a Life Worth Living*

"In *Building a Life Worth Living*, Marsha Linehan shares her experience of depression and suicide to help others who may be experiencing this themselves or in someone they love. Since using what happens to us to help others is the final stage of healing, this book is a victory on both sides of the page."

—GLORIA STEINEM,
New York Times bestselling author of *My Life on the Road*

"A brilliant memoir by one of the greatest pioneers in psychotherapy history . . . Marsha Linehan holds absolutely nothing back, making good on the vow she made as a young woman to escape hell and help others do the same. This book—with its fierce honesty and, for the careful reader, practical advice—will help anyone who has struggled to build a life worth living."

—ANGELA DUCKWORTH,
New York Times bestselling author of *Grit*

"To read this book is to understand how a life is built. In dark, there is light. Everything in Marsha Linehan's life and remarkable memoir uncovers the dark—the hell of the unhappy self and the hell of inadequate help—and brings us into the light, with humor and detail in her grappling and growth, and in her courage and vision of how to create a treatment for even the most unhappy of us."

—AMY BLOOM,
New York Times bestselling author of *White Houses*

"Shocking and heart-wrenching on one end, triumphant on the other, and an inspiration of hope all the way through."

—Goop.com

"Powerful and intimate . . . Linehan ably guides readers along her roller-coaster life as she conquers the male-dominated world of academia while hiding her physical and emotional scars. . . . Readers looking to overcome their past will find inspiration in this dramatic, heartfelt narrative."

—*Publishers Weekly*

"Practical and engaging . . . Linehan leads readers through her life and details how key moments brought her to develop DBT [Dialectical Behavior Therapy], bringing mindfulness into psychotherapy. Weaving the instructive with the personal, she alternates anecdotes with universal tools for approaching life with a combination of acceptance and motivation to change."

—*Booklist*

"Gripping . . . An inspiring account of healing and helping."

—*Kirkus Reviews*

BY MARSHA M. LINEHAN

Building a Life Worth Living

*Cognitive-Behavioral Treatment
of Borderline Personality Disorder*

*Skills Training Manual for
Treating Borderline Personality Disorder*

DBT Skills Training Manual

DBT Skills Training Handouts and Worksheets

Building a Life Worth Living

Building a Life Worth Living

A MEMOIR

Marsha M. Linehan

RANDOM HOUSE
NEW YORK

2021 Random House Trade Paperback Edition

Published in the United States by Random House, an imprint and division of
Penguin Random House LLC, New York.

RANDOM HOUSE and the HOUSE colophon are registered trademarks of Penguin
Random House LLC.

Originally published in hardcover in the United States by Random House, an
imprint and division of Penguin Random House LLC, in 2020.

LIBRARY OF CONGRESS CATALOGING-IN-PUBLICATION DATA
Names: Linehan, Marsha M., author.
Title: Building a life worth living : a memoir / Marsha M. Linehan.
Description: New York : Random House, 2020. | Includes index.
Identifiers: LCCN 2018043513 | ISBN 9780812984996 | ISBN 9780812994629
(ebook)
Subjects: LCSH: Linehan, Marsha M.—Mental health. | Teenagers—Suicidal
behavior—United States—Biography. | Psychotherapists—United States—
Biography. | Suicidal behavior—Treatment. | Dialectical behavior therapy.
Classification: LCC RJ506.S9 L56 2020 | DDC 618.92/8914—dc23
LC record available at https://lccn.loc.gov/2018043513

Printed in the United States of America on acid-free paper

randomhousebooks.com

9

Book design by Simon M. Sullivan

To my brother Earl, sister, Aline, and daughter, Geraldine

To my patients—I carry you in my heart
and I wish you *skillful means*

If I can do it, you can do it.

Foreword

MARSHA LINEHAN HAS personally treated hundreds of the most difficult patients, but her very first was by far the toughest. This was a troubled and troubling teenage girl who had been hospitalized for more than two years, much of it spent isolated in seclusion. Her life had reduced itself to a repetitive cycle of self-harm from burning, cutting, violent head-banging, and suicide attempts. High doses of every conceivable medication, alone and in combination, and multiple trials of shock treatment had no effect. Psychotherapy appeared impossible, because the girl was so bitterly angry and mistrustful. Her hospital record revealed how much helplessness, desperation, frustration, and anger she provoked in the staff. She was described as the most incurable patient they had ever seen and was unceremoniously discharged, uncured.

But things worked out quite differently than anyone might have expected. The chaotic young girl matured into a highly successful woman, became a psychotherapist and therapy researcher, and went on to invent a remarkable behavioral therapy that has helped hundreds of thousands of people all over the world. She was, of course, Marsha Linehan. Marsha found a way out of her own personal hell that allowed her to lead others out of theirs. She developed practical ways of taming her own self-destructive and provocative behaviors that could easily be learned and widely taught.

Only a few of us knew Marsha's past before she revealed it in a speech that was given prominent coverage in *The New York Times* a few years ago. It took great courage to "go public"—to share the most painful and private moments, ones that anyone might naturally want to forget and protect. My esteem for Marsha, already profound, deepened much further. Marsha has never been timid in anything she has done, and this bold act was not just personally liberating but, more important, it was liberating for everyone suffering from similar problems—past, present, and future. There is always hope—seemingly "incurable" people routinely get cured. Marsha has walked the walk; she has lived it, not just talked it. This is an inspiration for patients and therapists never to give up, even when the future looks unrelievedly bleak and giving up seems the only remaining option.

The therapy Marsha created is called Dialectical Behavior Therapy. DBT is the most effective treatment for highly suicidal and self-destructive people, often people diagnosed with borderline personality disorder (a terrible term, but we seem to be stuck with it). These are people who suffer greatly, and also cause great suffering around them—to family and friends, and to therapists. They have the highest incidence of completed suicide and suicide attempts. And they often tie therapists in therapeutic knots because of their complex, unpredictable, and sometimes emotionally and physically violent behaviors.

Before Marsha developed DBT, therapists often gave up on treatments that seemed futile and going nowhere, and patients often ended up in the hospital or dead. It was hard to find the damsel in distress hidden under the threatening dragon. This is no longer true. During the past two decades, 10,000 therapists worldwide have been trained in DBT, bringing emotional relief to hundreds of thousands of the most deeply disturbed psychiatric patients. And in 2011, the editors of *Time* magazine named DBT one of the 100 most important new science ideas of our time.

In the past half century there have been just two really influential clinical innovators in the field of mental health. One is Aaron "Tim" Beck, who developed cognitive therapy in the 1960s. The other is Marsha. That she has made this major contribution to psychology, a field previously dominated mostly by men, is testament not only to her intellectual creativity but also to her determination to overcome all obstacles.

And there were more than a few. I first met Marsha in the early eighties, when I was on the committee of the National Institute of Mental Health that decided which psychotherapy studies to fund. Research on BPD is a hard sell. The studies have many potential fatal flaws that can give critics an excuse to blackball. And Marsha was blackballed. But she stuck to her guns and kept on submitting better and better grant proposals, and she finally convinced even the most ardent of naysayers.

Many people come up with good ideas but don't have what it takes to get them into the world. Marsha has the charisma, energy, commitment, and organizational skills to turn dream into reality.

In myths the world over, heroes must first descend into the underworld, where they are faced with a series of epic challenges to be overcome before they can prevail in their heroic life journey. Once they succeed, they return to their country bearing some special new secret of life. Marsha was plunged into an unbelievably challenging journey of self-discovery, far away from family support, and returned bearing precious insights to help turn abject misery into lives worth living.

Thank you, Marsha, for being you, for courageously sharing your story, and for imparting the wisdom gained from your life of suffering, discovery, and love.

Dr. Allen Frances
Professor Emeritus of Psychiatry and Behavioral Sciences
Duke University

Contents

FOREWORD by Dr. Allen Frances — xi

PART ONE

ONE   Building a Life Experienced as Worth Living   3

TWO   Descent into Hell   13

THREE   I Will Prove Them Wrong   30

FOUR   A Traumatic Invalidating Environment   46

FIVE   A Stranger in a Strange Land   65

SIX   I Had to Leave Tulsa   75

PART TWO

SEVEN   On My Way to Chicago   81

EIGHT   Intellectual and Spiritual Transformations   88

NINE   The Path to Thinking Like a Scientist   97

TEN   My Enlightenment Moment in the Cenacle Chapel   101

ELEVEN   I Have Proved My Point!   107

TWELVE   Love That Came and Went, Came and Went   120

THIRTEEN	A Suicide Clinic in Buffalo	124
FOURTEEN	The Development of Behaviorism and Behavior Therapy	130
FIFTEEN	Fitting In at Last: Small Fish in a Big Pond	133
SIXTEEN	What Have I Done?	140
SEVENTEEN	Finding a Nurturing Community	148
EIGHTEEN	Like a Fish on a Hook	156
NINETEEN	Finding a Therapist, and an Ironic Twist	161

PART THREE

TWENTY	A Thumbnail Sketch of DBT	167
TWENTY-ONE	Finding My Feet in Seattle and Learning to Live an Anti-Depressant Life	174
TWENTY-TWO	My First Research Grant for Behavior Therapy and Suicide	192
TWENTY-THREE	Science and Spirituality	196
TWENTY-FOUR	My Fight for Tenure	207
TWENTY-FIVE	The Birth of Dialectical Behavior Therapy	212
TWENTY-SIX	Dialectics: The Tension, or Synthesis, Between Opposites	226
TWENTY-SEVEN	Learning Acceptance Skills	234
TWENTY-EIGHT	Not Just Acceptance—*Radical* Acceptance	247
TWENTY-NINE	Good Advice from Willigis: Keep Going	255
THIRTY	Becoming a Zen Master	273

THIRTY-ONE   Trying to Put Zen into Clinical Practice   277

THIRTY-TWO   Mindfulness: We All Have Wise Mind   280

THIRTY-THREE   DBT in Clinical Trial   289

PART FOUR

THIRTY-FOUR   The Circle Closes   311

THIRTY-FIVE   A Family at Last   314

THIRTY-SIX   Going Public with My Story:
The Real Origins of DBT   323

AFTERWORD   333

ACKNOWLEDGMENTS   337

APPENDIX: REASONS FOR LIVING INVENTORY BY SUBSCALE   341

INDEX   345

Part One

CHAPTER ONE

Building a Life Experienced
as Worth Living

IT WAS A beautiful summer's day, toward the end of June 2011. I was standing in front of an audience of about two hundred in a large auditorium at the Institute of Living, a renowned psychiatric institution in Hartford, Connecticut.

Uncharacteristically for me, I was anxious about giving my talk. I was there to tell the story of how, more than two decades earlier, I had developed a type of behavioral treatment for highly suicidal people, known as Dialectical Behavior Therapy (DBT for short). It was the first successful treatment for this population of people who experience their lives as being in hell, so miserable that death seems to them a reasonable alternative.

A lot of people were at the institute to hear me talk that June day. There were people from all around the world who had been trained in the therapy, people who knew me or knew of my research, former students and colleagues, my family. I'd given talks about DBT many, many times before. When I did, I usually titled the talk "DBT: Where We Were, Where We Are, and Where We Are Going." I would describe how I had developed the therapy through several years of exploratory research, often involving trial and error. I would describe its impact on suicidal people, what other conditions it was proving to be beneficial for, and so on.

But my talk that June day was going to be different. I was going to tell people for the first time how I *really* came to develop DBT. Not just the years of research and trials that went into it, but my personal journey, too. "Writing this talk has been one of the most difficult things I have done in my life," I began.

I Didn't Want to Die a Coward

I have done many hard things in my life, most prominent of which was having to come to terms with a totally unexpected complete and devastating breakdown of *me*, of who I was in the world, which you will get a glimpse of shortly. As a result of that episode, I had to fight to rebuild my high school education, which required me to go to night school while doing a day job to support myself. It was a day-job-and-night-school life again for me as I then strove to be a university undergraduate. By this time I had spent a lot of time living in small rooms in YWCAs in different cities. Most of the time I was friendless. And at almost every step of the way, I faced rejection after rejection that might easily have derailed me on my journey. Later, in my professional life, I had to battle to have my radical ideas and approach to therapy accepted by my peers and by the world of psychiatry more generally, and struggle as a female in male-dominated academia.

I had been working on the talk for three months. Many times, I rued the fact that I had put myself into this predicament. I had to compress my life into the space of ninety minutes. Another problem was that I have almost complete amnesia of my life before my twenties, and up to twenty-five, for reasons I will explain. What I have instead are "lightbulb memories," bright moments of recollection sparsely scattered across a dark canvas. It's like looking at the night sky in the city, where you see points of light from planets and stars here and there, but mostly it is unbroken blackness. I therefore had to turn to family, friends, and colleagues to help me reconstruct my life story, drawing on their vastly superior memories of my past. It was a difficult process—and, more than that, I was about to reveal publicly for the first time extremely intimate details about my life that for decades I had kept a carefully guarded secret, outside of a few very close friends and my family. So why did I want to do this?

Because I didn't want to die a coward. Continuing to keep quiet about my life seemed to me a cowardly thing to do.

Could I Make It Through the Talk Without Tears?

The Institute of Living had been an important part of my life, and I therefore thought it would be a good venue for me to give the talk I was planning. I had called David Tolin, who was director of the institute's Anxiety Disorders Center, and said I wanted to give an important talk on the East Coast and thought the IOL would be a good place to give it. He was thrilled, until I told him I wanted to give the talk in one of the large rooms, because I knew it would draw a big audience. He agreed, but only if I would tell him why. I did.

Now that I was there, in front of several hundred people, I wondered, "What have I gotten myself into?" I was worried that I would not be able to make it through the talk without tears, and I absolutely did not want to cry.

I began by telling the audience that, when I give talks about the development of DBT, I usually say that it began in 1980, when I was awarded a grant from the National Institute of Mental Health. The grant was for me to conduct research on the efficacy of behavior therapy for individuals diagnosed with borderline personality disorder. "But this wasn't when my passion for getting people out of hell started," I said.

I looked at the audience for a few seconds, casting my eyes here and there at the gathering of so many wonderful people in my life—friends, colleagues, students and former students. I knew that my sister, Aline, would be there, and I had especially wanted my brothers, John, Earl, Marston, and Mike, to be there, but I wasn't sure Aline would be able to get them to come. Yet there they were, sitting in the front row. Right behind them were Geraldine, my Peruvian daughter, and her husband, Nate, with whom I have lived ever since they were married. Geraldine's brother and his partner were also there. I thanked them and everyone else for coming. In this very emotional moment, I was on the edge of tears. Fortunately, none showed up.

The Real Beginnings of DBT

"In reality, the seeds of DBT were planted in 1961," I continued, "when, at age eighteen, I was admitted here, to the Institute of Living."

I had been a happy-go-lucky, confident high school girl, popular among my classmates, often the one to initiate activities—organizing concerts, for example, or simply getting together a group of us to go to the drugstore for ice cream. I was always careful to make sure everyone's needs were met, that no one was left out of the action. In my junior year I was nominated to be class Mardi Gras queen. My popularity extended beyond having a lot of friends to being elected and nominated to important class roles in junior year and senior year. I was the kind of girl who might be voted "most popular" or "most likely to succeed."

But then, as my senior year progressed, this confident girl began to disappear.

I did not know what had happened to me. No one knew. My experience at the institute was one of descending into hell, an out-of-control storm of emotional torture and absolute anguish. There was no escape. "God, where are you?" I whispered each day, but got no answer. I find the pain and turmoil hard to describe. How do you adequately describe what it is like being in hell? You can't. You can only feel it, experience it. And I did. I felt this inside myself, and it came out finally as suicidal behavior.

But I survived. And toward the end of my time at the institute, I made a promise to God, a vow, that I would get myself out of hell—and that once I did, I would find a way to get others out of hell, too.

DBT was, and is, my best effort to date at keeping that vow. This vow has controlled most of my life. I was determined to find a therapy that would help these people, people who were so often deemed beyond saving. And I did. I have felt the pain that my clients feel as they wrestle the emotional demons that tear at their souls. I understand what it is like to feel terrible emotional pain, desperately wanting to escape by whatever means.

A Journey Full of Surprises

When I embarked on my quest to fulfill my vow to God, I had no notion that the journey would be as complex and surprising as it turned out to be, or that the goal (an effective treatment for highly suicidal people) would be so completely different from existing therapies. All I had at the beginning was an unshakable conviction that I would develop a behavior therapy that would help highly suicidal people live lives worth living. That's all. And a good measure of naïveté, as I was to discover.

I had no idea, for instance, that one day I would walk into my chairman's office and say that I needed to spend time in a Zen monastery in order to learn the practice of acceptance. Very Zen. But I did. I had no idea, either, that, when fully developed, the treatment program would require a complete twelve months, not the three months I had expected at first. And I had never even heard the word "dialectical."

Two things make DBT unique. The first is the dynamic balance between acceptance of oneself and one's situation in life, on the one hand, and embracing change toward a better life, on the other. (That is what "dialectics" means—the balance of opposites and the coming to a synthesis.) Traditional psychotherapy focuses primarily on helping people change their behaviors, replacing negative behaviors with positive behaviors.

I discovered very early on in developing DBT that if I focused on helping clients change their behavior (which is what behavior therapy typically aims for), clients would protest, saying something like "What? You're telling me I am the problem?" If, on the other hand, I focused on teaching clients how to tolerate their life, that is, accept it, they would protest again: "What? You aren't going to help me?"

The solution I arrived at was to find a way to balance both acceptance and change, a dynamic dance between the two: back and forth, back and forth, back and forth. This balance between pursuing change strategies and pursuing acceptance strategies is a basis of DBT, and unique to DBT. This emphasis on acceptance as a counterbalance to change flows directly from the integration of Eastern (Zen) practice, as I experienced it, and Western psychological practice.

The second aspect of DBT that makes it unique is the inclusion of mindfulness practice as a therapeutic skill, a first in psychotherapy. This, too, came from my experience with Zen practice. At the time (the mid-1980s), mindfulness was something of an arcane subject, often dismissed as too "New Agey" to be taken seriously, particularly in academic circles. Now, as I'm sure you know, mindfulness is everywhere, not only in psychotherapy but also in health care, business, education, sports, even the military.

Who Benefits from Dialectical Behavior Therapy?

The goal of any behavior therapy is to help individuals change behaviors, in particular behavior patterns that significantly disrupt their lives at home and in the workplace, and to replace those with more effective behavioral alternatives. Dialectical Behavior Therapy is a type of behavior therapy—but, as I just explained, it is very different from traditional behavior therapy.

I designed DBT to help individuals who are at very high risk for suicide, who are difficult to treat, have multiple other serious psychological and behavioral problems, and often are on the "no admit" lists of hospitals. Principal among these disorders is borderline personality disorder (BPD), a notoriously challenging condition to deal with. The criteria for BPD include extreme emotional swings, explosive anger, impulsive and self-destructive relationships, fear of abandonment, and self-loathing, among other things. Borderline personality disorder is extremely distressing for the patient, often making life unbearable, and also for those around her, her family and friends. It is also a huge challenge for therapists, who often find themselves the target of a client's anger. As a result, many therapists simply refuse to take BPD individuals as clients.

DBT Skills Are Life Skills

DBT is a behavioral treatment program, not so much an individual psychotherapy approach. It is a combination of individual psychotherapy sessions, group training, telephone coaching, a therapist consultation team, and the opportunity to help change the client's social or family situation as well (for example, with family interventions). Other forms of behavior therapy include some of these components, but not all. That's another way in which DBT is special.

Learning skills is central to the effectiveness of DBT: skills that help a client find a way to transform a truly miserable life into one that is worth living and in which the client is effective in her life. I have been privileged enough to witness this transformation many, many times.

But these same skills are extraordinarily important to each and every one of us in our daily lives. And, as such, you could call them life skills. They help us navigate relationships we have with loved ones, friends, colleagues at work, and the world in general, and they help us manage our emotions and overcome fears. They are important in how well we manage in the practical realm, such as doing a job well.

In all these skills, the emphasis is on being effective in one's life, in the social and practical realms. Some people are more adept than others at these skills. Some people find it easier to navigate the ups and downs and the practical challenges that are the stuff of everyday life.

The Dalai Lama said everybody wants to be happy. I believe he's right about that. All of my clients want to be happy, so my job is to help figure out how they can get themselves there, or at least to a life experienced as worth living. By this I mean that when you wake in the morning, there are sufficient positive things in prospect—activities you enjoy, people you like being with, walking the dog—that you want to get out of bed and experience them. It doesn't mean that there is nothing negative in your life, because for many of us there are routinely things that happen, or emotions we have, that are not pleasant. This is particularly the case for my clients. I teach my clients life skills that help them, first, to accept the problems in their lives so that they can then change the way they are in the world, to seek out the positive and tolerate the negative.

We, as behaviorists, never believe that a person chooses to be miserable. We believe that their state of misery is caused—that it is caused by something in their history, their environment. Nor do we believe that anybody doesn't want to change. We assume that everyone wants a happy life. In psychodynamic therapy, which is a form of in-depth therapy that seeks to open a window on a person's unconscious mind, therapists never tell a client what to do. I tell clients what to do all the time. This is another way in which DBT is different.

My stance toward each client is this: "You know what you need in your life, but you don't know how to get what you need. Your problem is you might have good motives, but you don't have good skills. I will teach you good skills."

A Story of the Power of Persistence and Love

Like the speech I gave at the Institute of Living that June day, this book is the story of my time at the institute, how I came to make that vow, how I managed to climb out of hell myself—and how I managed to find ways to help others get out of hell, too.

My life is something of a mystery because, to this day, I have no idea how I descended into hell so swiftly and completely, at the age of eighteen. I hope that my success in getting out of hell and staying out will bring hope to those who are still in hell. My basic belief is that if I can do it, others can do it, too.

My story has four threads, woven closely together.

The first is what I know of my descent into hell, and how that led to the vow to get out of hell and then to get others out.

The second is my spiritual journey—the journey that saved me. It is the story of how I ultimately became a Zen master, a path that profoundly influenced my approach to developing DBT, most particularly as it led to my bringing mindfulness into psychotherapy.

The third is my life as a research professor—how that shaped my ability to reach my goal, and the difficulties I faced all along the way to overcome the mistakes I made and the multiple rejections I experienced.

The fourth is the story of the enormous power of love in my life, of how love affairs both put me on top of the world and later caused one of the deepest sorrows of my life. The power of accepting the kindness and love of so many people who were always ready to pull me up. And, in turn, the power of loving others, which pulled me up from falling in its own way. Part of this story is how I became one with my sister again, how we reached forgiveness after so many years of distance and pain. And how I became a mom and now a grandma.

My story is also a story of both faith and how important luck can be. It is a story of never giving up. It is a story of failure after failure, but of somehow always getting up (or being pulled up) again and again, and carrying on. It is a story of persistence, of acceptance—a big part of DBT is saying yes.*

---

* You may be wondering why, as I tell you about my life and work, I don't include any stories of the lives of my clients. Well, the good person that I am believes that telling these stories would be unethical and outside of what I believe to be right.

....

CHAPTER TWO

Descent into Hell

Marsha is known for her various activities, such as YCS [Young Christian Society] and her willingness to help others. Her laughter can be heard echoing around the halls as she performs another good-natured prank. The high esteem for Marsha has led her to be Junior Mardi Gras Queen candidate and Senior Class Council Secretary. She will long be remembered for her high ideals, spirit and sense of humor.

1961 yearbook, Monte Cassino School, Tulsa, Oklahoma

THIS DESCRIPTION IN my high school yearbook is accompanied by a black-and-white photograph of me, my blond hair coiffed in the style of the times, with a smile apparently full of life and optimism. It is the physical embodiment of the verbal depiction. Under the picture is a quote by me: "If it be right, do it boldly."

At the time, I was one of six siblings of a highly respected, upper-middle-class family in Tulsa that, in many ways, from my perspective and those of many others, was a wonderful family. My father, John Marston Linehan, was vice president of the Sunoco oil company and a pillar of Tulsa society, known for his steel-trap integrity and trustworthiness. He came home to be with our family for dinner every evening, often stopping at church on the way home to say prayers or calling in on his mom and dad. After dinner, sometimes he returned to his office to catch up on work, and sometimes he took walks with me to pick up a newspaper and ice cream.

My mother, Ella Marie (known to everybody as Tita), was Louisiana Cajun (and proud of it). She was outgoing and uninhibited in just about any situation, and very active in volunteering. With six young children to manage, she and about twenty other moms started a weekly sewing club (mending socks, underwear, clothes, etc.) that expanded over time into a social club that ultimately became part of all the children's lives. The women in sewing club brought food when needed, were there to take in visitors when too many were coming to someone's house, helped out with weddings, birthdays, and illnesses, and planned and managed funerals and any other situations that called for extra help. (How Mom also pitched in with all this, with six children, is still beyond me.) She was beautiful and fun and had an aura that could dominate any social space she was in.

Mother, too, went to church almost every day, usually before anyone else was up. Mom could buy a piece of cloth from the thrift store and make it look like something from Dior. She was very creative. After she died, we were shocked when we discovered that the pictures she had framed, which we had assumed had been done by skilled artists, were in fact hers. She was the artist. The Tulsa newspaper once put her picture on the front page and named her one of the most beautiful women in Tulsa.

My brothers John and Earl (both older than me) and Marston and Mike (both younger) were good-looking, accomplished, and popular; and my sister, Aline, who is eighteen months younger than me, was and still is slim and very beautiful. Aline was the model daughter somehow without effort, it seemed to me, being the kind of person Mother approved of. According to Aline, we were not friends when we were young.

My father's success in the corporate world made the family reasonably well-off. We lived in a big, beautiful, white Spanish-style house on the 1300 block of Twenty-sixth Street, a neighborhood with many children (at one point it had more children than any other block in Tulsa) and within walking distance of our schools. Our yard was landscaped with care by Mother, with perennial beds, flowering bushes, and magnolia trees that she worked on every spring. Mom put as much emphasis on making the inside of the house beautiful as she did the outside. To this day, I have never forgotten her belief and teaching that beauty is worth the effort it takes. I also learned from her that beauty requires talent and effort far more than it does money. Alas, although I love making things beautiful in our home, it really did take me a long time to get even close to Mother's and Aline's talent.

I Was Different

And then there was me. The bottom line is that I did not fit in at home or, frankly, anywhere else. When I was younger, I had a good friend who lived down the block from our house. I was invited to stay overnight with her many times and loved going. Her parents were nice, and were friends with my parents. But at some point during almost every sleepover, I got homesick and her parents had to call my dad to come and get me. Eventually, they told my dad that I could not come again to sleep over until I stopped getting so homesick. And that was that.

When the family went to play golf, I didn't go, because I didn't like golf. (My dad insisted it was because I wasn't good at it. Not true.) When we took long driving vacations or flew somewhere in my dad's company plane, I seemed to always get motion sickness, bad enough one time that I even had to be dropped off at an aunt's house halfway through the trip. When we went for a weekend to a friend's house on a beautiful lake, which we did often, I was without exception the only one who never got up on water skis. I also couldn't sit on the deck of the boat with everyone else because it hurt my bottom too much.

I was the only child in our family who was pretty consistently overweight, given the expectations of the times in Tulsa. I wasn't slim like Mother and Aline, and somehow I could not fix my hair in a way that Mom approved of. I had the heavier build of my grandfather on my father's side. When I now look at contemporary photographs, I can see that my weight wasn't a complete disaster. It did not help, of course, that both of my good-looking older brothers had very good-looking, slim, and sophisticated girlfriends. Although we were friends—I used to give one of my brothers back rubs when he came home from playing football, and I helped another brother tuck his shirt into the back of his pants whenever he had a date in high school—I was not close enough with my brothers to cry on their shoulders when I was upset and get some soothing and positive regard from them. I don't remember them ever saying, "Wow, Marsha! You look great!" On the other hand, I don't remember any negative statements from them, except the usual teasing that tends to happen among siblings. It also didn't help that when Aline and I applied to be cheerleaders for the football team at the boys' school down the street, Aline was accepted, but I was not.

My sister says that the bottom line was that, at some point in time, I simply could not please my mother no matter what I did. Mother's efforts to transform me into a girl who was cute, good-looking, and socially appropriate in Tulsa society somehow always backfired.

I Was the Problem

During all of this, I was the target of what was probably meant as playful teasing from my brothers, but it was painful to hear: "Marsha, Marsha, Million-Ton Motor Mouth." Not only was I not as attractive as other girls, but I also had an impulsive mouth that rarely shut up, a problem I have fought unsuccessfully all my life, and one that was not acceptable in a family like mine, which encouraged socially sophisticated interactions.

As I moved into my teens, Mother's continuing efforts to improve how I presented myself must have deflated, at least somewhat, my approval of myself. If a person said something mean to me, my mother's immediate response was to figure out how to change me so they would like me more. She never asked what was wrong with those people; I never even thought of that as a possibility until much later, when I was visiting my sister-in-law Tracey, wife of my brother Marston. When people said mean things to her daughter, Tracey's response was to defend her daughter from such character attacks. Tracey's and my mother's reactions were opposites in this same situation. I wonder how I might have been had Mother been like Tracey. But they were both doing their best, as they saw it.

A Popular Girl

Although my incessant need to talk didn't sit well at home, it made me popular at school. According to my cousin Nancy, when I was in fourth grade I was "the life and soul of the party, always a moving force, always initiating something, always playing pranks, always a dominant presence." I have no recollection of this "me" of the time, but I assume that this was probably the real me, right up through junior year. Nancy also said this of me recently: "At fifth or sixth grade, I decided that Marsha was the deepest and most profound thinker I knew, always willing to tackle any kind of questions. She always had an interesting way of looking at things."

In junior year, I was nominated to be the class Mardi Gras queen. I didn't get to be queen, because the senior class collected more newspapers for recycling than the junior class did. The queen's crown goes where the most money is made, from selling the newspapers. It was almost always the senior class nominee who went on to wear the crown. But the fact that I was junior class nominee, elected by a student vote, says something about my popularity among my classmates. And at the beginning of senior year, I was elected class council secretary, as noted in the yearbook blurb at the beginning of this chapter.

Although I was popular in my classes and I was friends with all the older girls, not just when I was a senior but before, just about every girl I knew had a steady boyfriend, and I did not. I occasionally had a boyfriend, but never a serious, longer-term relationship. As high school was coming to a close and my friends all were paired up with boys, I ended up in my room at home, depressed, refusing to come out.

A Rapid Descent into Hell

By the time the yearbook was in the hands of my classmates, in May 1961, the girl who "will long be remembered for her high ideals, spirit and sense of humor" had been admitted to the Institute of Living in Hartford, Connecticut. In no time, I was an inmate in Thompson Two, a secure, double-locked unit that was home to the most disturbed patients in the institution. I was drowning in an ocean of self-loathing and shame, of feeling unloved and unlovable, and of indescribable emotional agony, so much so that I wanted to be dead.

The mystery of my story is how could such sadness have happened to that high-functioning, well-liked, happy-go-lucky girl? And, given that, how did I manage to get myself out of the hell that I had fallen into and over time create a life experienced as worth living?

Entering the Institute of Living—and Beginning Cutting

When I was admitted to the IOL on April 30, 1961—weeks before I was supposed to graduate from high school—my main complaint, according to my clinical notes, was "increased tension and social withdrawal." I had also been assaulted by increasingly excruciating headaches, sometimes so bad that I had to call Mother from the pay phone at school and beg her to come take me home. I'm not sure if she always believed me, but she did come to get me. I began seeing a local psychiatrist, Dr. Frank Knox. (I would assume this was after my family doctor could not find a medical disorder, but I figured out that he had no idea what caused the headaches.) Dr. Knox eventually recommended that I go to the Institute of Living for what we were told would be two weeks of diagnostic evaluation.

I have just a single sliver of a memory of that first full day alone at the institute. It is of me sitting on the back steps of what must have been an open unit, looking across at a landscape of lawns and trees. That's it. I don't remember who took me there or anything of the admissions process. I don't even know how I felt about being there.

I do know that within a few days I somehow discovered cutting, but I have no memory of how or why. These days, most people have heard about cutting. But when I was a teen, cutting was off the radar screen, and I feel sure I knew nothing about it before I went to the institute.

This is how it is described in my clinical notes: "She broke the lens from her eye glasses and inflicted superficial lacerations on her left wrist." The notes imply that I broke the lens deliberately, in order to cut my wrist. But it's possible that breaking the lens was an accident. It's a mystery to me. The research literature on self-cutting indicates that it is highly contagious in institutions, and that cutters often find the act virtually pain-free and emotionally calming. Family members of cutters view the behavior as a major problem. Cutters see it as a solution to emotional pain. And from a medical point of view, we now know that when a person cuts themselves like this, endorphins, which can be thought of as natural opiates, are often released in the blood, and their effect is to reduce stress and induce a sense of well-being.

Whatever my motives, the result of that initial cutting event was that within a few days of admission to that open unit I was transferred to the most secure unit in the institution, Thompson Two. And, most likely, I was put on various psychoactive drugs that apparently were increased over time. (From my perspective today, I'd say it's too bad they did not transfer me back home, because I've now seen that institutionalization can sometimes do more harm than good.) The staff were not bad people, just young and without the knowledge we have now about how to treat people with the problems I had.

My one friend from the institute, Sebern Fisher, tells me that I probably got to Thompson Two via a series of acrid-smelling, scary underground tunnels, carried by two nurses up to the second floor of the Thompson Building suspended in a canvas restraint bag, hauled like bagged venison. Sebern was a fellow inmate. After losing touch with each other for many years, we later reconnected and still to this day are good friends.

Life in Thompson Two

Sebern describes Thompson Two at that time as being "the Bellevue of the Institute of Living," with a constant smell of urine, fecal smearing, and psychotic patients screaming, getting naked, and fighting. I remember few of those details, but I do recall one skinny older woman who sat in her chair all day long, and if you walked close to her she'd kick you with her big, black, heavy boots. And then there was Nancy, white-haired, psychotic Nancy, who endlessly sang a tune from *Minnie the Mermaid:*

Oh what a time I had with Minnie the Mermaid
Down at the bottom of the sea.
Down among the bubbles I forgot my troubles.
Gee but she was awful nice to me.
And every night when the starfish came out
I'd hug and kiss her, gee.
There every night when the starfish were bright
I used to love her so
Oh what a time I had with Minnie the Mermaid.

I am pretty sure she didn't get all the words right, but I can still hear that chorus.

Once I was in Thompson Two, I continued self-cutting, much more seriously than in that initial, tentative venture, breaking windows and using knife-like shards to slice my arms and thighs. I began self-burning, using cigarettes (thank the Lord they let us smoke in those days). I'd get so completely out of control, sometimes breaking things other than windows, that I was often put in cold packs to calm down, and sometimes put into seclusion, once for a period of three months.

I have no way to describe what happened to me when I got to the institute. In my mind, it has always been as if I just went crazy. Somehow I lost all ability to regulate not only my emotions but my behavior as well. The highly functional girl from Monte Cassino high school had disappeared. She had morphed into what my clinical notes describe as "one of the most disturbed patients in the hospital." This was not that popular girl from Tulsa, Oklahoma.

It was an alarmingly rapid and complete descent into hell. I lost control. I lost myself. In my decades of work, I have never seen anyone become so quickly and relentlessly out of control as I was. I cannot say what brought it on, or what the staff could have done to prevent it. I simply have no understanding of those early days at the institute.

Looking back, it's as if it wasn't me doing all these things. It was someone else trying to harm me. I would be sitting quietly, not necessarily thinking dark thoughts, and out of nowhere I would suddenly know I was going to do something. I was going to cut myself, burn myself, attempt to break something. And I'd often tell the nurses that I knew I was going to do it, and begged them to stop me. But I was faster than they were, so they couldn't stop me. I felt as if I was being pursued relentlessly by this other menacing person; it was like being chased down an alley by a would-be assailant and I knew he or she would always catch me. I kept running and running, but never fast enough. This other person would make me break a window and savagely slash my thigh before a nurse could stop me.

Even when I was in the seclusion room—with just a bed bolted to the floor, a chair, an iron-barred window, and the ever-present gaze of a nurse—I could be up on the chair or on the bed and launch myself, in a swan dive, headfirst onto the floor before the nurse could stop me. I did this repeatedly, the impulse taking me over before I could stop it. I feel sure that this resulted in brain damage that contributed to my abysmal memory—that, along with two long series of electroconvulsive shock therapy, a procedure that these days would be considered barbaric. A well-known psychoanalytic psychiatrist, Dr. Zielinski, whom I saw for some time in the years after the institute, told me that I had multiple personalities. Which, for some reason, I feel sure I didn't.

I would stand in the middle of the room in Thompson Two for long periods of time, like a tin man, unable to move, totally empty on the inside, unable to communicate or say anything to anyone about the inside me, knowing that no one could help me. My psychiatrist at the institute, Dr. John O'Brien, did his very best to help me. Our sessions probably involved the standard psychiatric goal, at the time, of trying to uncover the unconscious basis of my aberrant behavior. I do remember a time—I must have had ground privileges—when I was standing outside of his office, wishing I could have a session.

As you will see in my letters to him, I apparently knew he cared for me. Many years later, after I left the IOL, he told me how much he had loved me and he said that it had caused some problems in his life. I wrote him many letters in between our sessions, trying to explain what was happening to me, sometimes venting anger and frustration. Given the absence of research at the time, there was little he could do to help me.

I was alone in hell.

Hell Is Like Being Trapped in a Small Room with No Way Out

I know what hell *feels* like, but even now I can't find words to describe it. Every word that comes to mind is so utterly inadequate to describe how terrible hell is. Even saying it is terrible communicates nothing about the experience. When I reflect on my life, I often realize that there is no amount of happiness in the universe that could ever balance the searing, excruciating emotional pain I experienced those many years ago.

What if God were to ask me to live my life over again? All of my life I have had a love affair with God, so how could I possibly say no? But on the other side, how could I say yes? I'd say yes only if I knew that my living would save others, I finally decided. "Thy will be done" has been my frequent prayer. Thank God I have not been asked.

To twiddle away the time that went by so slowly at the IOL, I sketched a lot and wrote poetry. I lost most of my journals in an apartment fire in Washington, D.C., some years back. My memories, gone up in smoke.

The following poem, which I wrote while in seclusion, is just a glimpse of my state of mind during those times:

They put me in a four-walled room
But left me really out
My soul was tossed somewhere askew
My limbs tossed here about

They put someone, a winsome one
They put her at the door
But even she could pick not up
My soul from off the floor

The room divided into three
A bed a wall a chair

I spent my time with each in turn
The room was wanton bare.

They put me in a four-walled room
But left me really out.

I wrote letters to my mother quite frequently, and Aline tells me that Mother would cry all night when she got them. My letters must have conveyed my unbearable emotional agony, including my self-injuries. I wrote that I wanted to come home and at the same time wanted to be dead. No wonder Mother was so upset.

When I teach clinicians how to understand what it is like for individuals who are suicidal, I often tell them the following story. It gives a glimpse into the world of the suicidal person and the hell that I experienced.

The suicidal person is like someone trapped in a small room with high walls that are stark white. The room has no lights or windows. The room is hot and humid, and the boiling heat of the floor of hell is excruciatingly painful. The person searches for a door out to a life worth living, but cannot find it. Scratching and clawing on the walls do no good. Screaming and banging bring no help. Falling to the floor and trying to shut down and feel nothing gives no relief. Praying to God and all the saints one knows brings no salvation. The room is so painful that enduring it for even a moment longer appears impossible; any exit will do. The only door out the individual can find is the door of suicide. The urge to open it is great indeed.

Dear Dr. O'Brien,
I feel so alone. Please help me. I realize you are trying to, I feel like
I'm in a row boat trying to row away from the Island but the boat
won't move. What am I to do? What a mess! I HATE this place but
hate myself even more. Wish I were dead.

Sincerely, Marsha

The Scenic Route

I am unable to chronicle most of my two-plus years at the institute, because of my almost total lack of memory and the loss of my diaries. The best I can do is offer some lightbulb moments, aided here and there by my friend Sebern's recollections.

Scattered among the repeated episodes of self-injury and constantly wanting to be dead as an exit from that white, windowless room were urges to get out of Thompson Two, the grim place of four walls, no sky, and no birdsong. I'd run to the pay phone and call home in desperation. "Mother, please come take me home," I pleaded. *"PLEASE!"* Her reply was always the same: "Your father will have you committed if you leave."

I had ceased to exist in the universe of my father's life the minute I went to the mental hospital in April 1961. As a very conservative Catholic man raised in Risingsun, Ohio, who almost died digging ditches during the Great Depression and then pulled himself up by the bootstraps to become president of DX Oil Company and vice president of Sunoco, my father had no understanding of what was happening to me. I suspect Dad thought I could shape up if I really wanted to, so it was silly to feel sorry for me. He couldn't tolerate my misery. He told Mother to quit worrying about me. I don't really know how he could say that to my mom, his wife. No wonder she was always calling Tante (Aunt) Aline, her surrogate mother, who assured her that I had a biological disorder and Mother should not blame herself. (Mother's mother died when Mother was quite young. We came to call Tante Aline "Grandma," which she liked.)

At desolate times, I occasionally tried to get myself out of the hospital. Sometimes we were allowed into a small enclosed courtyard attached to the Thompson Building. It was then that I'd make my break for freedom by climbing over the wall. At least that's how I remember it, but when I visited the institute recently, I saw that the walls looked to be twelve feet tall. I don't think I could have climbed them. But escape I did. Of course, I was always caught and hauled back in.

On one successful flight, I walked the short distance into town and went into a bar. I asked for a glass of water, drank it, went into the bathroom, smashed the glass, and cut my arm. Just like that. It wasn't a very big cut, but it was very bloody. When the bar owner discovered what I had done, he called the police. They came quickly and patched me up with bandages. "Please don't take me back," I begged one of the cops, but I knew they were going to, no matter what I said. He said, "Well, do you want to take the direct route back or do you want to take the scenic route?" I said, "I want to take the scenic route." They drove me around for quite a while before they took me back.

It was the sweetest thing, a simple, kindly act for a desperate girl who seemed so crazy. It touches me still when I think about it.

> *Dear Dr. O'Brien,*
> *I feel I can't express how I feel to you (or anyone else), but let me tell you one thing—I don't belong in this unit. If I do, I am as crazy as they are.*
>
> *I am depressed, dejected, deflated, and unhappy & I wish I had never been born. I hate this place so much. You could never realize how miserable I am. I wish I were dead, dead, dead, dead. I feel so lonely & that row boat just won't move. I am so alone. Even the idea of seeing Aline doesn't cheer me up. Why can't you help me? At home I could just cover all these feelings by staying on the go but here there is nothing to cover them with. They are coming into the open. It scares me.*
>
> *Sincerely, Marsha*

Cold Packs and Seclusion

There were about twenty of us in Thompson Two. Most of the women had individual bedrooms. They had behavioral disorders of various kinds, as we all did, but they weren't a danger to themselves, weren't likely to try to injure themselves. The patients who were a potential danger to themselves were under constant observation and slept at night in two rows of four beds arrayed in what felt like a corridor. There was very little privacy, and even visits to the bathroom had to be accompanied, with the door left open. (Think constipation.) For most of the time that I was in Thompson Two, I was one of these tortured souls. We were often the troublemakers, but the nurses had ways of bringing us to order. Namely, cold pack therapy.

Cold pack therapy involved being stripped naked, wrapped tightly in wet sheets that had been stored in a freezer, and strapped to the bed with restraints. You would lie there, immobile, for as long as four hours. The effect of the therapy is to make an agitated individual calm, and there are physiological data that show why it works. It induces a relaxation response, which, among other things, is the result of a lowering of heart rate and blood pressure. The initial cold can be intensely uncomfortable, almost painful, but this wears off as body heat slowly warms the sheets. Most people find the discomfort and physical constriction so unbearable that the mere threat of the therapy is sufficient to discourage problem behavior. The nurses had a simple but effective method of issuing such a threat. If we were talking instead of going to sleep, for instance, the nurses would rattle ice cubes in a metal container. That usually brought instant silence. (Cold pack therapy is rarely used in modern psychiatry.)

For me, however, the cold pack therapy was often a comfort, a means of controlling the demons that roiled me. I sometimes even asked to have the therapy if I felt out of control, if I felt the menacing person stalking me and I wanted to stop her.

Seclusion was the only place where I felt somewhat safe. The menacing person could not get me there. The rationale for putting a problem patient in seclusion was twofold. First, it was meant to keep them safe, usually from themselves. Second, it was assumed that the experience of being in seclusion would be negative and would therefore discourage problem behaviors. That second reason didn't work for me. I welcomed the feeling of being safe while in seclusion. In my clinical notes, there is mention of the fact that the more they tried to control me, the worse I got. Putting me in seclusion didn't discourage my problem behavior; it did the opposite.

Later, working as a therapist, I fell into the same trap. When you become afraid that a client might commit suicide, you become anxious, and as your anxiety increases, your urge to control the client increases, too. So for a while, my experience with clients was the same one the institute had with me. I eventually learned that trying to control a suicidal person often makes them worse, not better. Instead of reducing dysfunctional behavior, trying to control it can reinforce—or promote—the behavior. This insight became important in my work as a therapist.

> *Dear Dr. O'Brien,*
> *Here goes—*
>   *Two of the reasons I am unhappy are:*
>   *One—I am so overweight & ugly. I used to think I'd be completely happy if I were only thin like Aline & all my friends. Now I don't know if that is true or not.*
>   *The other is that I have never been very popular with boys, especially my senior year at School. Not one boy asked me out from last (a year ago last) May to the present. I think it is my weight but I think I am afraid that that is not what it is.*
>   *Sincerely, Marsha*

Looking at the letters I wrote at that point in my life, I am struck with how emotionally young I had become at the institute, so different from the high-functioning girl from Tulsa. I've seen this in many of the suicidal adolescent girls I have treated.

My Vow to God

Thompson Two had a piano at one end, an upright piano, and I spent a lot of time playing. I had been an accomplished pianist at school, and I hadn't yet lost that part of me on my descent into hell. Later, though, after I had multiple rounds of electroconvulsive therapy, in the days when it was not as safe as it is today, I lost my memory of just about everything and every person and, sadly, also my ability to read and remember musical notes and to play the piano. Playing the piano had always been a way to express my emotions. I still carry the hope that one of these days I will play again. It was at the piano that I later made my vow to God.

I typically spent a lot of time on constant observation during my more-than-two-year stay at the institute, but I wasn't on constant at this point, so I must have shaped up my behavior a little bit. I was back there at the piano one day and, as I did frequently, I was talking to God, much of it a desperate plea: "God, where are you?"

For most of my life, I had a visceral longing both to be with God and to please God by doing his will. I didn't want to please God so that I would get something out of it. The best way I can describe it is to say that it is a little bit like when you have someone whom you love and who loves you, and they especially like you in a particular dress, so you wear that dress because you know it makes them happy.

"God, where are you?" I cried. I also have a clear memory of standing in the seclusion room, at the iron-barred window, bereft, speaking the phrase "God, why have you abandoned me?"

The day when I was sitting in the piano room by myself, a lonely soul in the midst of other lonely souls on the unit, I am not sure what made me do what I did next. Whatever it was, there and then I made a vow to God that I would get myself out of hell and that, once I did, I would go back into hell and get others out. That vow has guided and controlled most of my life since then.

At that point, I didn't know what I would have to do to fulfill the vow. But I was determined, and that determination was crucial.

···

CHAPTER THREE

I Will Prove Them Wrong

WHEN I WAS at the Institute of Living, my brother Earl visited me occasionally, as did my sister, Aline (not that I remember any of their visits!). Their impressions of me were the same: that I had put on weight and that I was slow, zombie-like, the result of drugs and electroconvulsive therapy. Mother visited me, too, but I remember nothing about her visits, except for one occasion. During that visit, she suggested we go for a drive and got the requisite permission to do so. I couldn't have been happier, because, for me, being able to go outside was a big event. I had been locked up for so long, not being able to smell fresh air or look up at the sky. It was huge.

Shortly after my mother and I drove away from the institute, we pulled into a gas station and it started to rain. I jumped out of the car, stood in the rain, exhilarated, and probably twirled around, laughing out loud. Most of the details elude me, except that I had on a little seersucker dress and was as happy as could be.

My mother was stunned. "What are you doing?" she yelled immediately. "Get back in the car!"

Once I got back in the car, she said we had to go back to the hospital. I couldn't believe it. "What are you talking about?" I said as I got in the car. "I haven't been outside in so long. This is so wonderful." What to me was a visceral experience of freedom and exuberance looked to Mother as if I might be acting up like a crazed mental patient again. She took me back to the institute, probably terrified that I was suddenly getting worse. Poor Mother tried hard to do the right thing, but she simply couldn't for so much of the time.

The Punishment Was Worth the FUN

It's hard to convey the tedium of these long-term inpatient units for locked-up patients. It's paradoxical: There's so much internal drama of the sort I described earlier, and there's so much tedium, at the same time. Sebern has described it as "a frozen landscape that has volcanoes all through it. You're going to have an eruption here, an eruption there, but overall it's all pretty barren." The height of entertainment was the television in the group room. We all had to agree on a channel, which doesn't come easily to a gaggle of people of all ages on a unit like Thompson Two. In any case, we were often looking for some interesting diversion.

One teen on our unit was an accomplished lock picker. I don't know how she had learned that particular skill. Late one night toward the end of my time there, after the aide on our unit had gone to sleep, four of us—the lock picker, Sebern, one other teen, and I—decided it would be fun if we were to "escape." On the given night, we schemed not to take our sleeping medication. Around eleven o'clock, the lock picker deftly did her work, and the four of us wound up in an attic space that was littered with old prosthetic medical objects of some mysterious kind. From there we eventually found our way outside, standing in front of the imposing Center Building. I'm sure there was a lot of laughing, celebrating what we had done.

Then it was "Now what do we do?" We hadn't really intended to make an escape from the hospital; it was just a prank. Suddenly afraid of what would happen to us, the four of us, wearing our nightgowns and flimsy slippers, had to go through the admissions office building around midnight and pray nothing terrible would happen to us. We were probably punished somehow; I don't recall. But whatever the punishment, it was worth it for that insane moment of glory.

> *Dear Dr. O'Brien,*
> *What am I afraid of? I am afraid of never getting married, so I stay*
> *in here to give me a good reason. I'm afraid of being a social oddity,*
> *so I break windows to give me a good reason for being one. I am*
> *afraid being thin wouldn't solve my problems so I stay fat to avoid*
> *finding out. I'm afraid that Aline would still be more popular than*
> *me even if I were thin, so again I just stay fat. I'm afraid that*
> *mother wouldn't love me even if I were thin, so that again I stay fat.*

At this point in my life, I find a letter like the above to be extremely embarrassing. So I am giving myself many gold stars for including the letter in this book. The poem I showed you earlier reflects exactly how I felt at the time. I was crazy. I threw myself on my head repeatedly. Why? I have no idea. I know I didn't want to be there, in the institute, but I have no clear idea of my mental state at the time, other than the sentiment expressed so painfully in the poem. I feel now that I could cry for that girl. Maybe that's why I'm a good therapist: because I understand how my clients feel.

Sebern's Story

The ultimate outcome for highly out-of-bounds behavior—such as self-injury or obsession with suicide—was being sent to the seclusion room. It was supposed to provide four walls of external containment and safety that the patient herself couldn't provide internally, as well as provide a deterrent that would reduce further out-of-bounds behavior. I was a frequent occupant of the seclusion room, the last occasion being for twelve weeks, from early November 1962 to early February 1963, a length of time almost unthinkable, even in those days. I was forbidden to smoke in there, and I was supposed to have no contact with the other patients. It didn't work out quite like that.

It was during this period of incarceration that I met Sebern, who was a couple of years older than me. We instantly became good friends, forming strong bonds like comrades in a war zone. It was only much later that I learned about her earlier life.

Like many of my own clients, Sebern had a past that was many times more traumatic than mine. She was initially admitted to Thompson One, a relatively open unit at the institute, but about six months later she was sent down to Thompson Two.

Despite the ban on contact with other patients while in seclusion, I spent a lot of time talking with Sebern, that is, whenever she could sneak in without the nurses noticing. I sat on the edge of the bed, and she stood in the doorway, chatting with me and smoking. We had become close friends in part because we were equally troublesome. We were often featured together on the residents' morning report, which lists patients' transgressions.

I was a heavy smoker at that point—three packs a day. But smoking was banned in the seclusion room. Sometimes the nurse took pity on me and allowed Sebern to get close enough so that she could blow smoke from her cigarette into my mouth. Industrial-strength secondhand smoke!

A Supposed Punishment Was a Comfort to Me

The threat of being in the confinement unit was an effective deterrent to what was considered disturbed behavior. For most people on the unit, that is. But I often welcomed the safety of the seclusion room, for the same reason that I sometimes welcomed cold pack therapy.

As a behavior therapist, looking back at my earlier years at the institute, I have always thought that putting me in seclusion may have been reinforcing the behavior that got me there in the first place. It went like this: I behaved badly (broke something, caused a disruption); I was put in seclusion; I was supposed to feel distressed being in seclusion, punished, but instead I welcomed the feeling of safety; therefore I behaved badly some more, which got me more seclusion. The staff's response to my bad behavior (putting me in seclusion) reinforced my bad behavior. I don't believe this was a conscious strategy on my part; more an unconscious response. But no one saw this equation. (Today I have many clients whose suicidal behaviors have been reinforced by going to hospitals, because of the attention and care they got there—a similar unconscious link.)

Dear Dr. O'Brien,

All I want to do is cry, cry, cry. The trouble is I can't. I can't break a window because I am the only one on constant & they watch me too close. I feel like a bomb ready to explode & there is no way for it to explode. I'm wrapped up in a thousand sheets & there's no way to get free. Quite frankly I don't know what to do.

Dr. O'Brien, I just can't live this way. I've got to get out. I want to throw & break everything I can get my hands on. I just can't believe that I would feel the same if I were out of here.

I feel like I hate you but I kinda don't think I do. I do know that I want to go home & see Dr. Knox. Please let me go.

Sincerely, Marsha

A Moment Out of Control, a Moment of Self-Sacrificing Care

A few months before I was finally discharged, Sebern and I were both put on one of the Brigham units, which was more open than either of the Thompsons. Our behavior had been deemed to have improved sufficiently. I was thrilled, because it meant I could go outside and see the sky. I also remember standing on a chair, waving my arms in tune with my favorite Tchaikovsky, music that at one time I'd been able to play so well.

While I was in Thompson Two, I'd occasionally use smoldering cigarette butts to burn myself. I used to have a morbid sense of fascination as I watched my skin first redden, then crack and blister as a second-degree burn developed. It did hurt, but it didn't bother me enough to stop me. When the nurses saw what I was doing, I was usually given a cigarette "time-out" for a few weeks.

By the time I reached Brigham, I had stopped impulsive self-burning. Or so I thought. One day I burned myself in a quite deliberate way. I methodically constructed a complete ring of burns, like a bracelet, around my wrist. It was a deliberate act, but I was also watching it being done to me, as if by a different person.

I knew I would be in big-time trouble if the nurses were to see these burns. I would be sent back down to Thompson Two. My solution was to make myself a copper bracelet in metalwork class to hide the burns. It did—except, of course, the burns slowly became infected, turning a putrefying red and green and oozing. I needed to get some antiseptic cream, urgently but secretly.

Sebern, good soul that she is, snuck into town, got the cream from a drugstore, and then snuck back into our unit. My recollection was that she had climbed out a window to get out, and got back in the same way, to avoid being caught. But Sebern tells me now that she didn't have to do that, because she had grounds privileges. However, she did not have town privileges, so she would have been sent down to Thompson Two if someone discovered she had gone beyond the institute grounds. Either way, Sebern had taken a big risk to help me, a caring moment if ever there was one. The cream worked, the burns healed, and I was never found out.

I still have those bracelet scars on my wrist. There is no way (other than maybe major surgery) to get rid of them, no way to get rid of the many scars on my body from self-inflicted injuries. You can try to hide them, but there are many situations where it is impossible to hide scars: swimming, trying on new clothes, doctor appointments, etc. To this day, many people ask me what happened (even more than once in elevators!). My response to everyone is simply "Oh, it happened when I was young."

A Lapse of Judgment

Not long after this little episode, and about a month before I was scheduled to be discharged, Sebern and I became involved in what my clinical notes described as "a lapse of judgment." One very hot April day, Sebern and I and a few other girls decided we would have a picnic on the riverbank, which was less than a mile's walk. Although I didn't have permission to go off campus, I did have permission to be outside. There was a beach on the opposite bank of the river, which we could see clearly from our side. It looked very inviting. We bought some sandwiches and beer and headed over the Charter Oak Bridge. When we got to the other side, we discovered that in order to reach the beach, we had to trudge through a patch of stinking mud. We did it anyway.

We ate our sandwiches, drank some beer, enjoyed the sun for a while, and probably had a dip in the river. It must have been cold. When the time came for us to go back, Sebern said, "I don't want to go back through that muck. I'm going to swim." Terrific idea, I thought. We considered ourselves competent swimmers, and we thought it would be a lark, a lot of fun. Heck, we had been locked up for so long, it seemed absolutely the right thing to do. The two saner members of our party demurred, braving the polluted swamp and heading back over the bridge, carrying our belongings with them.

The Connecticut River was very wide at this spot, as we could see, but that didn't bother us. What we did not know was how very strong the current was. Sebern went in first and did a good job of staying close to the bridge. When she got to the first abutment, she held on and turned around to look for me. I had gone in right after her and immediately felt myself being swept along, almost out of control. I could hear Sebern yelling, "Go with the current, Marsha, go with the current!" It was all I could do just to stay afloat. I decided to swim sidestroke. It seemed to give me a bit more control. I could see the other bank and knew where I should try to land. "Swim! Swim! Swim!" I kept saying to myself. I was making some progress, but not enough. I started to feel myself being pulled under. I was terrified. I screamed to Sebern, "I'm drowning! I'm going under!"

I kept being pulled under the water, but I got myself back up each time. I could not give up, because in the direction the current was carrying me, there was a wall on the side of the river and I would not be able to climb out. It was me against the undercurrent. During my frantic efforts to keep swimming, I could see two guys standing by the edge of the river, watching me struggle. Eventually I made it across safely, way downstream from where I had intended. I clambered up the grassy bank and fell to the ground, exhausted. I looked up and saw the two guys still there, staring at me. "Why didn't you help me?" I asked. One of them laughed and said, "Well, every time you went under, you popped right back up."

Thanks a lot, I thought.

Sebern remembers that someone must have called the police. This little "lapse of judgment" had become a big deal. When Sebern and I arrived back at the institute, our shorts and T-shirts were dripping the foul waters of the Connecticut River. The police had informed the hospital of what had happened. We knew we were in big trouble. The staff were yelling at us, saying things like "How could you be so stupid?" and "You could die from the bacterial infections you probably picked up," and on and on.

We both had to have a slew of shots—tetanus, typhus, and several others—because the river was seriously polluted. I was threatened with not leaving the hospital as had been planned. And Sebern was forbidden from ever talking to me again. Sebern was forever being told not to talk to me because, they said, I was a bad influence on her.

I lost touch with Sebern when we both left the institute, but she tracked me down years later when I was an assistant professor at the University of Washington, in Seattle. She was a student in a social work program and had been assigned an article to read that had been written by me. She sent me a letter to see if I was the Marsha Linehan she remembered. We got together in Seattle; I clearly remember that she pulled out of her pocket one of the drugs that had been prescribed to both of us back at the institute. We laughed, and each of us decided to keep one for old times' sake. We have been good friends ever since, meeting each summer in Boston, not far from where she lives. Both of us are therapists, and both of us have written books on treatments we believe are important.*

> *Dear Dr. O'Brien,*
> *My veneer is pretty good at the moment but I am depressed about your statement as to how long I may be here. I talked to both my parents & got that straightened out. I am so mixed up as to how I feel. My bottom coat is so depressed, dejected, discouraged, hopeless & unhappy but my top coat keeps smiling. I feel like smashing, biting, breaking & ramming into something. I feel guilty about falling (did again) because I can't get over the feeling that I am doing it on purpose. Am I? I feel terrible, terrible, terrible but can't do anything about it.*
>
> *Marsha*

Dr. O'Brien's Love May Have Kept Me Alive, but It Wasn't Enough

The fact that I was placed in seclusion for an unheard-of period of twelve weeks indicates how very disturbed my behavior was. And

* Sebern's is *Neurofeedback in the Treatment of Developmental Trauma* (New York: W.W. Norton, 2014). Mine is *Cognitive-Behavioral Treatment of Borderline Personality Disorder* (New York: Guilford Press, 1993).

yet I was discharged a little over two months later. A miracle cure? Not exactly. Two practical issues factored into the timing of my discharge.

The first was that my psychiatrist, Dr. O'Brien, was due to leave the institute, and it would have been an enormous challenge for another psychiatrist to take me on at this juncture. Poor Dr. O'Brien: He had been a young resident in his late twenties when I arrived at the institute. According to clinic notes, I was "one of the most disturbed patients in the hospital," and I was also his first patient. I quickly became very attached to him and, as I later found out, he to me.

I continued writing to Dr. O'Brien for a year or two after I got out. Sometimes to express feelings I couldn't say face-to-face, sometimes simply to vent emotions, and sometimes just to tell him what was going on with me. I found some of the letters recently, and you've seen some of them in this book. It is very unnerving and more than a little humiliating for me to read them now, because I have no recollection of the person who wrote them. But I see that, even then, I understood a concept I later wrote about: "apparent competence." I'll elaborate on this below, but in short, it is when an individual appears to be in control of her life while inside she is in complete emotional turmoil and pain.

I was often experiencing intense inner pain and suffering while at the same time displaying a put-together self. In my letters to Dr. O'Brien, I called these two aspects of myself "top coat" and "bottom coat." At times I appeared to know that I was keeping my pain to myself. At other times, perhaps most of the time, I likely thought I was expressing my pain when I was not. People just didn't seem to see the real me, the person in pain. Many years later, I went to see the principal of my high school and I asked her, "Why didn't anyone do something to help me?" She responded, "Marsha, we did not know anything was wrong."

This can be common for people in desperate trouble. So many of my clients had the same behavioral pattern that I did. I once described it this way:

The tendency to appear competent and able to cope with every-day life at some times, and at other times to behave (unexpectedly to the observer) as if the observed competences did not exist.*

One of my clients used to tell me how much she dreaded coming into a session. When I asked why, she brought up something I had said in the previous session. It was very upsetting to her, but her upset hadn't been apparent to me. Sometimes she would start crying at the end of a session. She would tell me that something I had said to her earlier was invalidating.

I told her it was very hard for me to change my behavior if she did not tell me when I said or did something that was upsetting to her; her response was that she thought she had told me. A key part of treatment was getting her to practice telling me whenever I said or did something that hurt her feelings.

At the same time, we were working on how she could deal with her dad, who often said very invalidating, insensitive things to her and was the source of much misery. But it turned out that she was treating her dad exactly as she was treating me—that is, her dad had no idea how hurtful he was to his daughter.

"My father should know," she told me. "He knows how unhappy I am." But he didn't know, because she had never made it clear to him. And sure enough, when she told him, her dad changed his behavior. He had had no idea of the impact he'd been having.

I had been like that client, nursing great emotional turmoil and unhappiness without making it obvious to others. I looked as if I was in control, but I wasn't.

---

* Marsha M. Linehan, *Cognitive-Behavioral Treatment of Borderline Personality Disorder* (New York: Guilford Press, 1993), p. 80.

Compassion Is Not Enough

I have no memory of Dr. O'Brien saying mean or invalidating things to me. How he avoided that is beyond me. As a young therapist, still a resident, treating me must have been very stressful. I know he did his best, but it wasn't enough to really help me. Nobody could help me.

I would tell people how miserable I was, and they would listen—compassionate Dr. O'Brien would listen. The French novelist Georges Bernanos captured the situation beautifully. He said, "I know the compassion of others is a relief at first. I don't despise it. But it can't quench pain, it slips through your soul as through a sieve."* The Dalai Lama puts it succinctly: "It is not enough to be compassionate. You must act." Compassion without action is like going into that small white room that is a person's individual hell, feeling a person's pain, feeling a desire to get a person out of hell—but never finding the door to get the person out.

Dr. O'Brien didn't know what action he should take with me. No one did. The idea that psychological interventions should be based on a carefully collected body of evidence—on research—was not even on the radar screen at that time. It was simply not viewed as important for scientists to gather evidence through research with patients and then develop treatments based on that evidence.

I was given a huge number of psychoactive drugs. No wonder I was a zombie! It's possible that the drug treatment made me worse rather than better. The psychoanalytic treatment of the time didn't help, either, and may have made me worse, too.

Not long after I got out of the institute, I visited Dr. O'Brien and his wife in Florida. Much later, when I became a tenured professor at the University of Washington, I wrote to tell him the news, because I thought he'd be pleased for me. Later we talked by phone.

---

* Georges Bernanos, *Journal d'un curé de campagne* (1936). English translation, *The Diary of a Country Priest* (New York: Doubleday, 1954), chap. 8.

He told me about many of the difficulties in his own life, and how much he had loved me (and it seemed still did). He died not long after that. I have always regretted not going to see him again. It felt as if the tables had turned, and he would have appreciated my demonstration of care for him, as he had once cared for me.

Besides the matter of Dr. O'Brien leaving the institute, which would require me to have a new doctor, the second practical issue in the timing of my discharge from the IOL concerned my rather bleak future.

According to the clinical notes, when I began the three-month stretch in seclusion, I was given an ultimatum: *Improve your behavior or it's a state hospital for you.* They were evidently ready to give up on me, having tried everything they could think of. Some probably considered me a hopeless case.

I knew that if I went to a state hospital I would never get out. It would be the end of me. I also found out from Sebern, through her therapist, that the head doctor at the institute had little hope for me and had told my parents to put me into a state hospital in Oklahoma. And while I was at the institute, Mother had told me by phone that I had to get better or Dad was going to put me in a state hospital because this was costing too much. (I have a vague recollection of finding out after Dad died that his best friend, "Uncle Jerry" to us, had paid for a lot of my hospitalization.) Whatever the facts, I was indeed let loose from seclusion, and my behavior did indeed improve, but not for the reason that the staff believed.

"The turning point in her treatment came sometime during this three-month period of time" in seclusion, Dr. O'Brien wrote in my clinical notes. The implication is that the process of seclusion—an extended seclusion—had at last had its desired effect. I believe, instead, that it was something else. Dr. O'Brien did something that was not part of the treatment protocol, but in retrospect should have been. It is a process I thought about a lot, once I became a therapist of highly suicidal people. It involves actively not rewarding suicidal behaviors, and instead providing an aversive response following suicidal behaviors. It takes a lot of courage to do it, but it can be very effective when done well.

Breaking the Link with Suicidal Behaviors, and an Unexpected Turning Point

Here's what happened. Dr. O'Brien came to see me, sat down, and said, "We need to have a talk." His tone was completely different from what I had grown accustomed to, much sterner in a way. "Well, Marsha, I have finally accepted that you might kill yourself," he continued. "And if you do, I'm going to have one Mass said for you and I'm going to say one rosary for you."

I was aghast. "What, you mean you're not going to come to my funeral?" "No," he said. "I'm on my way out of town. I'm going to be gone for two weeks, and I hope you're alive when I get back. Okay?" Then he left.

I was immediately certain I was going to kill myself. I became completely hysterical. "I'm going to kill myself," I cried to the nurses after he had left. "You've got to stop me. You've got to stop me. I know I'm going to do it. I'll be dead when he gets back. I don't want to be dead; I don't want to die before he gets back. You've got to stop me." I had wanted to be dead, to escape the agony of that white room, but at the same time I didn't want to die. I cried uncontrollably and had to be restrained.

Dr. O'Brien's emotional withdrawal had a big impact on me. I had been in an environment where no one could effectively help me, so the only thing I could do was try to get them to try harder. Trying to kill myself, or obsessively dwelling on it as I did, had the effect of getting people to help me more.

It wasn't a conscious strategy on my part. (And I don't think it is a conscious strategy in most people who repeatedly threaten suicide.) But I now suspect that my suicidal behavior was likely being reinforced by increased efforts to help me. (This is such an important insight into patient–clinician interaction that it bears repeating several times, as I have.) The problem was that the staff did not have an effective intervention, so I was more and more out of control, not less. The staff at the institute simply didn't recognize the cycle of reinforcement that may have been promoting more out-of-control behavior.

Was it a mistake? Their efforts obviously kept me alive, and perhaps that was all they could do. Alas, more than drugs, more than periods of seclusion, more than cold packs and constant observation, and more than sessions with a compassionate psychiatrist, I needed *skills*. Skills to regulate my own emotions and behavior, skills to tolerate the pain I was living with, and the skills to effectively ask for and get what I needed. Today, after the development of DBT and the suite of skills it includes, I can give suicidal people behavioral skills that will help them, first, to accept their lives as they are so that they can then change their lives from being unbearable to being bearable. But in 1962 and 1963, the staff at the IOL, well-intentioned as they were, simply didn't have anything that could have helped me.

When Dr. O'Brien made his stand that day, I came to realize for the first time that I did not want to die. That was the turning point. I realized that killing myself was incompatible with my vow to get myself out of hell. I had to find a way to stop wanting to kill myself, and I did.

Dear Dr. O'Brien,
I admit I will miss you & all you have tried to give me. I'll miss the comparative safety & security of being here. But isn't it better that when you realize something is impossible, to stop trying & try another way around the obstacle. Please don't think I am trying to make you mad because—sincerely I'm not. Just can't see the point of being locked up & spending one hell of a lot of money, on what? Nothing.
I realize I will never come close to being happy, that I will always

be afraid of myself & of my effect on others & that maybe the rest of
my life will be a senseless mess. But again you must realize that
maybe that is the will of god. Maybe my road to heaven is through
unhappiness, fear & that senseless mess. Perhaps I should learn to
accept instead of trying to change it.

Dr. O'Brien, I hope you understand at last a little bit of what I
am trying to say.

Sincerely, Marsha

When I heard that the hospital was giving up on me, and that my
parents might really put me in a state hospital, I decided that I would
prove them all wrong if it was the last thing I did on earth. I also
decided that I was not going to let my parents or anyone else get any
credit for my recovery, which was going to have to include night
school in order to make up for my not having gone to college after
high school. And I was determined that I was going to walk out of
the institute on my own.

The idea of proving everyone wrong kept me going. Much later,
when I was in college at Loyola University in Chicago, one of my
professors told me that this kind of anger could be very helpful in
keeping a person from giving up.

On May 30, 1963, at the age of twenty, I walked out of the Institute of Living after two years and one month. I went to the airport
and got on a plane to Chicago, where I met up with my brother Earl,
who then got on a plane with me to Tulsa. I will never forget that
ride. I kept hearing frightening noises, and Earl keep reassuring me
that all was well. Earl ultimately took care of me when new troubles
came on the scene.

CHAPTER FOUR

A Traumatic Invalidating Environment

How did I go from the outgoing and popular girl described in my high school yearbook to the person I just described in the institute? Another mystery is this: How did I pull myself together to function so well on my own once I got out of the hospital?

Ever since my talk at the institute, when some aspects of my story appeared in *The New York Times* in June of 2011, just about everyone has assumed that I must have had borderline personality disorder (BPD). (More than once I have been introduced as a person with the disorder.) So the question is, is that true? Did I have borderline personality disorder before and during my time at the institute? How about now?

My family, and particularly my sister, Aline, are adamant that before going to the institute I did not come close to meeting the criteria for BPD. Aline has volunteered with an organization called Family Connections, which provides support for families in which someone has been diagnosed as borderline. "I listened to how people described borderline behavior, and their relationship with their loved ones with this diagnosis," Aline wrote to me. "I couldn't relate to what they were talking about. I had never seen you exhibit any of these behaviors—the anger, the erratic behavior, etc. etc. My feeling is: You did not have BPD before you went to the institute."

Diane Siegfried, a longtime friend from school, also describes a girl far away from BPD before I went to the institute.

It is true that I had headaches and serious depression before going to the IOL, and was perhaps sensitive to invalidation and disapproval, which is common for borderline individuals. And once I was put in the hospital, much of my behavior appeared to meet criteria for borderline personality disorder: behaving impulsively; having suicidal thoughts and deliberately injuring myself; volatile mood swings; constantly feeling "empty"; and what in the profession we call "severe dissociative symptoms," such as experiencing someone other than myself pursuing me and doing harm to me.

Five criteria are all that is required to label someone as borderline, and I met about five. The mystery is: How did I become a girl with these symptoms?

The Inspiration of Saint Agatha

My brother Earl says this of the young me: "She was fun-loving, bubbly; we used to play canasta all the time. She was a lot of fun, laughing a lot." On the other side of that bubbly young woman was (according to others) a very serious person, intellectually and spiritually, an accomplished musician, and a competent scholar. Actually, a bit of an intellectual rebel, always thinking out of the box, always questioning assumptions. I was a voracious reader. I could sit in the library for hours by myself, reading. Because I was growing up in a seriously Catholic family and being educated by nuns, my questioning mind was, shall we say, not always appreciated.

But the real core of me was a deep spirituality. One of my few clear memories of childhood is from fourth grade, reading a book on the lives of saints, martyrs who opted to suffer excruciating torture and death rather than deny their faith in God. Like the story of Saint Isaac Jogues, who had his nails pulled off because he wouldn't give up his faith in Jesus, and was later killed. And Saint Agnes of

Rome, who was sentenced to burn at the stake at the age of twelve but died by the sword when the bundles of wood refused to ignite. Saint Clement I was tied to an anchor and thrown into the sea on the orders of the emperor Trajan.

I cherished this book.

My all-time favorite martyrdom story, though, was of Saint Agatha of Sicily. She decided at a young age to devote her life and her body to God. Senator Quintianus proclaimed his passion for her, but when Agatha rebuffed him, he had her confined to a brothel for a month, hoping this would change her mind. It did not, and she refused him again. This time Quintianus had her thrown into prison, there to be subject to various cruel tortures, the most barbaric of which was having her breasts cut off. (Paintings of Saint Agatha typically show her holding a tray, upon which rest her two severed breasts.) Throughout all these horrors—she was a mere twenty years old—she steadfastly maintained her complete and unbreakable devotion to God.

I picked Saint Agatha's name as my confirmation name. I then had to figure out a way to avoid telling anyone why I had made that choice, because to me it was a very private matter. My brothers were relentless in trying to get it out of me. But they never did.

The stories of these saints, and of Saint Thérèse of Lisieux, whose autobiography, *Story of a Soul,* I read over and over, inspired me to try to be just like them. I would stand up for and fight for what I thought was right, and I would never let myself do what I thought was wrong, or go against God. I really did want to be a saint, but when I confided this to a friend many years later she said, "Marsha, you are no saint."

Sadly, she was right. I have fallen off the track many times, but that intensity of desire sustained me for many years. Even if I wasn't a saint, as a young child I had decided I would be prepared to have my nails pulled off, die at the stake, be thrown into the sea, and have my breasts cut off, rather than give up my faith in or break a promise made to God.

This was the beginning of my love affair with God, which would flood much of my life for many, many years. It gave me an important spiritual structure.

For most of my young life, I tried to hide this love affair. At one point I decided to sleep without a pillow, as a sacrifice to God. (How I came up with that idea is not clear, but it was probably from reading all those saints books.) My relationship with the church has been a source of difficulty, but I went to Catholic Mass just about every day in high school and in college, and for many years thereafter.

Having a love affair with God can sound pretty weird. I myself thought it was weird for many years. That changed when I read a book by Bruno Borchert called *Mysticism: Its History and Challenge*. He says that mystical experiences, which can be found in every religion, perhaps can be understood as the state of being in love. When I read that, I stopped thinking I was weird or crazy. It fit perfectly. I practically screamed hallelujah.

Teenage Pranks, Serious and Not So Serious

Cousin Nancy was two months younger than me, and also very spiritual. Our families visited often. Nancy's family lived just a couple of blocks from our first house, on Birmingham Place. I was about ten when we moved to the bigger house on Twenty-sixth Street, and Nancy and I saw much less of each other until junior high, when we went to the same school. Nancy has many stories to tell of those years, some of which stir latent emotions. I have no memory of our friendship, so when I tell those stories here, it really is "according to Nancy."

Besides doing a lot of normal things, like hiking and playing tennis, we apparently got up to some pranks, too. This is how Nancy describes one of them. "When we were fifteen, the summer before we had our licenses, we sometimes schemed to go to the drive-in late at night. Marsha would sleep downstairs, in the den. I would push the car out of the garage at my house, drive over to Marsha's house. She would leave the patio door open so I could go in and wake her up. I would park the car down the street and go get her. The twenty-four-hour drive-in was about five miles away. We'd pull in, get a Coke. This was one in the morning. We never did get caught."

Nancy and I spent hours playing duets on the piano together. At school, we were members of the Triple Trios: three altos, three second sopranos, and three sopranos. I was the group's leader and, according to my loyal friend Margie Pielsticker, I "sang beautifully."

My Parents

I have looked through family photographs while writing this memoir, hoping that the process might stir some memories. I did notice something surprising. In many of the pictures I am physically very close to my dad, sitting on his lap, his arm around my shoulders. This suggests he was emotionally close to me, too. I used to go to his office on weekends, helping the person on the switchboard while he was working. We seem to have had a close relationship before I went to the hospital. And I was named after him: Marsha, for Marston. Perhaps his inability to take my side, to support me, was more important than I have thought. Dad's position was that none of us should upset Mom. This wasn't good for me and my brother John, the two most likely to do something to upset her.

Dad was definitely a conservative Southern man of his times. He had no concept whatsoever of mental disorders. Like many people, even today, I think he believed that I could just "get over it" if I tried harder. He had no idea what to do with me. Both he and Mom, like almost everyone in Tulsa, Oklahoma, believed young women should be pretty and should eventually marry a nice man and become a good (that is, submissive) wife and mother, while men should do important work and make money. They thought boys should be treated as superior to girls. (I'm not sure Mom thought they actually *were* superior, but she acted that way.) Boys could express their opinions; girls should be compliant and sweet.

Mom didn't think of herself as being "above" others. She did a lot of volunteer work for the poor and needy. My image of her is that she was not above cleaning someone's bathroom in her mink coat if it was needed. In many ways, I greatly admired both of my parents as I grew up, and still do now. Dad was known for his integrity and trustworthiness. He had many friends. He was loyal to them and to his employees. They were pillars of the community. I loved it when Mother came to my school, so I could show her off. I was always so proud. I particularly admired Mother for her luminescent beauty, her compassion for the needy, for the fact that she went to Mass every morning. Sometimes I went with her, driving in the misty early mornings through the dark. Poor Mother, with six children. Mass was her only place to be alone.

I wanted to be like Mother, but in so many ways I was not like her. I didn't realize, until many years after she died, the ways we were alike. Like her, I cherish beauty, love flowers, work in my garden, and attend Mass in the mornings, and I have a similar sense of humor. I am quite uninhibited and am always willing to dance when we have parties at our home—just like she did.

Tough Standards to Meet

Mother was a very Southern woman, and that came with expectations about what her daughter should look like and be. Unfortunately, I met none of these expectations. Except, perhaps, that I became quite good at making lunches for my brothers and making breakfast after church on Sundays. Southern girls cooked, made lunches, and helped with the house. My older brothers worked in the oil fields in the summer. Girls didn't take jobs.

Both Mom and Dad were very conscious of image. You had to

dress up when going to church, for instance. My brother Earl tells a story about his own child that captures this:

> My son, Brendon, visited his grandparents once when he was ten. He said to me, "When I went to Tulsa, I went with this big bucket of love for Grandma and Grandpa. When they told me my jacket didn't look right and I needed to get a new jacket, I just put my head in the bucket and shook it, and said to myself, 'Okay, I love you, Grandma, I love you, Grandpa. We will get me a new jacket.'"
>
> Brendon was playing with some kid they didn't think was socially right for him, so they stopped him. He said to himself, "Okay, and I put my head in the bucket again and shook it. 'Okay, Grandma. Okay, Grandpa.'"
>
> It goes on and on like this for Brendon. "And on the last day," he told me, "I was looking forward so much to going skiing with a friend, and Grandpa wanted to take me to get a new suit instead. Dad, I put my head in the bucket, and there just wasn't anything left in the bucket." Brendon had seen it in a way that I had never quite seen it. My parents had sucked up all the love Brendon had for them, with their obsession that he should look right rather than listen to what he wanted, and they hadn't even noticed it.

Alas, this says a lot about the home environment we grew up in. Someone was always in trouble for not meeting their standards in some way. Earl describes our parents as "very judgmental people, never making positive comments, never praising us."

A House with Tension

Our house was often tense. Even Aline, Mother's perfect daughter, felt pressure. "I was Miss Goody Two-shoes," she now says, "but I was terrified I would get into trouble, and I lived in fear that I wouldn't get Mother's approval." There were often tears, Mother's usually, especially at holiday times, and especially at Christmas, when my father gave Mother a gift she didn't like.

We ate dinner together as a family every night. My siblings remember there being no genuine reaching out to one another, asking, "How was your day?" At dinner each night, we traded any positive things we had heard about others. The game went as follows: "I will tell you something nice I heard about you if you will tell me something nice you heard about me."

I have no doubt that my mother wanted all of us to be happy. The problem was the way she went about it. She grew up on a plantation in Louisiana. During the Great Depression, her dad lost almost everything he owned (to a neighbor who scammed them, they say). Mom went to college so that she could work as a teacher to help the family. While she was in school, her parents died. She worked as a teacher to support her brothers until they could be on their own. Then she moved to be with Tante Aline, "Grandma," in Dallas.

Tante Aline was a sophisticated, intellectual woman with a husband in the oil business. At this point, Mother had little education in how to present oneself well, how to dress attractively, how to speak well in social settings, and so forth. She showed up at Tante Aline's overweight and single. She was twenty-two, at a time when women were expected to be married by twenty-two.

Tante Aline was certain that it would be easier to find a husband if Mom lost weight, learned to dress better, learned sophisticated social skills, and looked cute. So Tante Aline went to work on the makeover, and Mom was very happy for her help. The next step was to send Mom to another aunt in Tulsa, to search for a husband. There she met Dad, a debonair guy in the oil business who was also Catholic and acceptable to the family. The entire plan had worked.

It is therefore not surprising that Mom tried to improve me just as Grandma Aline had improved her, hoping for a similar positive outcome. Given that she talked to Grandma almost every day, I suspect that Grandma supported her in her efforts. Mom tried to change me into a girl who conformed to their idea of a successful person. The problem was that, unlike Mother, I was just not able to make the changes they wanted.

The tension between us went from bad to worse. I just wasn't a malleable daughter. I couldn't have been a socialite if I wanted to. Nevertheless, she was determined and constantly badgered me to dress properly, do my hair, lose weight, speak only when appropriate. Alas, Mother's unceasing advice did not come across as caring, only demanding and invalidating.

As Aline said, to feel Mother's love, you had to fit a certain mold, and I didn't. I was constantly aware of her disapproval, the look in her eyes, her tone of voice. She just couldn't hide it. Aline has told me that there was nothing about me that my mother really approved of—that I just couldn't win. No matter my efforts, there would be something else the next day that she didn't like.

I don't know how many times Mother came home from parties and talked glowingly about some girl my age, praising her poise, her looks, the whole nine yards. It always seemed that Mother was really telling us that we didn't have any of these admirable qualities. Naturally, it made me think, "There must be something wrong with me." Mom had no idea of her negative impact on me, and how her constant efforts to improve me had the opposite effect.

The way I describe the situation is that Mother saw me as a tulip and desperately wanted to make me into a rose. She thought I'd be happier as a rose. But I did not have what it took to be a rose, not then and not now. This tulip/rose conflict eventually became part of the way I talk to my clients in DBT.

This is what I tell them:

If you're a tulip, don't try to be a rose. Go find a tulip garden.

All of my clients are tulips, and they're trying to be roses. It doesn't work. They drive themselves crazy trying. I recognize that some people don't have the skills to plant the garden they need. But everybody can learn how to garden.

An Invalidating Environment

This constant disapproval, this constant pressure to be someone else—this is an example of a concept I came up with as I developed DBT: an invalidating environment and, in the extreme, a traumatic invalidating environment.

Traumatic invalidation may occur only once, as when a mother refuses to believe that her daughter is telling the truth when she reports sexual abuse, or when a witness falsely testifies that a person committed a crime he did not commit. It can be an accumulation of pervasive misreading of emotions by others, such as when someone insists incorrectly that a person is angry, jealous, afraid, or lying or insists that the person has internal motives he or she doesn't have. Trauma is most likely when these actions make the individual feel like an outsider.

In the extreme, traumatic invalidation can lead an individual to thoughts of suicide and actual self-harm as a source of relief from the toxic environment they are in. Cutting oneself very often brings relief from extreme emotional pain and suffering, primarily because it stimulates release of the body's own opiates into the bloodstream. When hope of ever living a life experienced as worth living fades away, and no alternative can be found, thoughts of suicide can begin. The very thought of committing suicide can fill the mind with the belief that death can soon end pain. This belief can be so soothing that suicide becomes the only solution. (Of course, I tell clients that there is no evidence whatsoever that suicide will end their suffering.)

Love That Was Invisible

I realized much later in life that my father had the same desire for Mother's approval. He hardly ever got it. Like me, in many ways he failed to be the person Mother wanted him to be.

As a teenager, I very often felt unacceptable in my own home. My older brothers were away at college. My sister was protecting herself from Mother and staying away from me. My younger brothers had no idea what was going on. Aline recently said to me, "You had no one, Marsha, not even me, your own sister, to turn to for comfort. You were alone in a family of eight." This is not to say my brothers might not have helped me if I had asked. Instead, it is likely that no one knew anything was wrong.

I am sure that everyone in my family, my parents and my siblings, did love me, but no one showed it very well. Sadly, my ability to hide how I really felt, the pain within me, kept them from knowing how much I wanted approval. Recently my brother John emailed high school photographs of me to the family and wrote, "This is the most beautiful woman in the world." I wanted to scream. "Why didn't you say that all those years ago!" Of course, maybe he did and I just did not hear it.

In the same vein, I have to tell you what Mother's last words to me were. She whispered, "I want you to know I have loved you as much as Aline."

A Different Way of Thinking

My friend Diane was a year ahead of me at Monte Cassino. Diane said something to me recently that has been echoed by others from that time: that I had a different way of thinking, a quality that in later life helped me be a creative researcher. "I always came over to your house, Marsha, to play with you," Diane told me, "because you never thought like other people. You always had interesting new ways to think about things."

It's true: I didn't think like everybody else, and still don't. Many friends have told me the reason they like me is that I think out of the box. On the other hand, I view my thinking as ordinary and in the box, which is why I often argue for my point of view—sometimes to my detriment. From the beginning, I was a liberal in a very conservative city and state. I was surrounded by a lot of wealthy people, including some of the students at Monte Cassino.

Internally, I disparaged wealth because I saw all the unhappiness associated with it. When I was around eleven or twelve, when my parents went out of town, I would invite poor people to come to our house for dinner, setting the table with Mother's best silver. I am just about certain that I got Lulu, our maid, to help me with this. Where I found these people—or anything about them, really—completely escapes me. My memory!

In my senior year at Monte Cassino, I started having difficulties fitting in. So what happened? These are my best guesses. I didn't fit in with the nuns. There were some I got along with, like Sister Pauline, who taught English and religion. She encouraged my unorthodox way of thinking and questioning. I adored her. But for the most part, the nuns didn't appreciate my not accepting their words as the unquestionable truth. They didn't like me questioning authority. I was always in trouble over this.

As Aline said, "Marsha, your big problem was that you didn't fit in—anywhere!"

Not fitting in, seeing things differently and often outside the box—that became a pattern in my life. As a behaviorist through and through, I didn't fit in at the Buffalo crisis clinic I worked at right out of graduate school; I didn't fit in at my first faculty job, at Catholic University of America, in Washington, D.C.; and I didn't fit in with the clinical training at my next faculty job, at the University of Washington, in Seattle, which is where I am now. My strategy was always to keep to my values and beliefs and to cause as little trouble as possible. Unfortunately, with an automatic motor mouth, I frequently failed to recognize the impact of things I said. Just like Mother!

A Single Beacon of Validation: Aunt Julia

There was one family member with whom I fit in perfectly: my aunt Julia, my father's sister, who lived not far from our house. Aunt Julia was the one person who loved and approved of me, unconditionally.

Her house was a haven of safety and comfort. She taught me to type, and I would practice at her house for hours at a time. (This turned out to be a very important skill!) She also taught me to cook, which is to say, she let me cook. Her husband and her sons would say the sweetest things about my cooking. Aunt Julia loved me like the daughter she always wanted. I learned later that she and Uncle Jerry (not the Uncle Jerry who was my father's best friend) had tried to get my parents, my mother in particular, to back off from the never-ending criticism. Aunt Julia was a voice of validation, a voice saying, "We love you as you are and for who you are. You do *not* have to change to be valued."

Why didn't this love and validation save me? Aunt Julia was overweight and talked a lot, just like me, and so she wasn't perfect in my dad's eyes. Maybe that's why she felt a connection with me. Her husband, Uncle Jerry, had no social standing. My dad looked down on both of them. Aunt Julia told me, "We just could not get through to your mother and father what was happening to you at home." Quite simply, Aunt Julia's opinion had no value to my parents.

As close as I was with Aunt Julia, even she wasn't fully aware of what was happening to the internal me. I could not tell her, nor Aline, nor my cousin Nancy, nor my friend Diane. No one had the ability to see inside me, to *see* the real me. I couldn't even really articulate it myself. I did confide in and cry with one person, Jane Sherry, a classmate in senior year. I could call Jane and she would come pick me up and we would drive around, with me sobbing the whole time as I talked.

But by then the damage had been done.

I Wanted a Support Group, a Sorority

There was no sorority at Monte Cassino, my high school. I suppose sororities were deemed to be immoral by the nuns. I wanted to be a member of a sorority, so I joined the one at Central, the local public school. I had wanted to attend Central, but Mother insisted I go to a Catholic school. Had I gone to Central, the environment would have been much more supportive of the things I wanted to do, and perhaps my life would have turned out differently. Who knows? (Not long before she died, Mother said that the biggest mistake she made was not letting me go to the public school.)

I did have a few friends at Central, and I went to sorority parties. But I was anxious there; I worried about being attractive to the boys at the parties. I'm sure I never told anyone about this. I didn't seem to appreciate the popularity that I had at Monte Cassino, being nominated as Mardi Gras queen and so on. At the time, I was urgently looking for inclusion elsewhere.

The nuns strongly disapproved of my joining the sorority, but I refused to quit, because I didn't believe it was wrong. Nancy has told me that, as a result of my defiance, the nuns didn't treat me well. One teacher was so mean to me that other students went to the principal to complain about it. It did little good.

Some girls in my class disapproved of sororities, too. I think this single act of defiance, this act of standing up for what I thought was right, was the beginning of a downhill slide in my friendships. This accelerated in junior year, the beginning of feeling isolated.

I started going to the local health club with Diane and Brooke Calvert, an attempt to shed those unwanted pounds. Diane and Brooke were one year ahead of me in school and graduated at the end of my junior year. I was devastated to lose these friendships.

A few years back, I sat down and wrote as many lightbulb memories of my childhood as I could. One was about this moment of loss:

> Brooke graduating
> Diane graduating
> grief
> loss
> death
> nightmare
> "I'll be seeing you"
> unending tears

That song, "I'll Be Seeing You," was playing on the radio around the time I was grieving my loss of Brooke. It had seemed so poignant, it made me cry more. Even now I feel sad when I hear that music.

Senior year, I fell into a deep depression and refused to come out of my bedroom. I see now that this could have been expected. Mom was depressed when she was pregnant with Aline. Mom's brother had very severe depression. When I visited Mom's relatives in Louisiana, I found that many of them were extremely depressed, unable to leave their homes.

But even so, I looked the same on the outside, while my internal self was suffering a terrible, painful depression. I was part of a small clique of girls at school, about four or five of us, including Margie Pielsticker. Margie says that this group ran everything in the school, got the awards. She says that I "kept everybody together, kept everybody happy." Even in senior year, says Margie, I never talked about my issues, what was happening to the internal me.

"Marsha seemed happy in that group," Margie now says. "She covered up what I now know was her unhappiness with outgoing kindness to others. For instance, she often picked up everybody in our group after school and drove us to Pennington's, a drive-through, to get Cokes. She always made sure I was included."

Hearing this is like hearing about the actions of some other person.

Unintended Consequences of Good Intentions

During this period, I was still intent on being a saint. In her autobiography, Saint Thérèse wrote the following: "What matters in life is not great deeds, but great love." I knew those words had a deep truth, but I didn't fully understand how. And now, five decades on, here I am writing about my life as being the story of the power of love.

I find that to be quite amazing and humbling at the same time. Thérèse loved nature and saw the seasons as reflecting God's love affair with each one of us. She described herself as the "little flower of Jesus." She is often known simply as "the Little Flower."

Back when I was reading Saint Thérèse of Lisieux, I had decided I needed to do something more on the path of becoming a saint. I needed to sacrifice something that was very dear to me, something that would be hard for me to do. It had to mean a lot to me, otherwise it wouldn't count as a real sacrifice. I decided I should quit the sorority.

The sorority had been a rock in my life. It was something I could depend on both for having fun but also, more pertinently, for having supportive relationships, a sense of belonging. It was the one group where I felt accepted. "Yes," I said to myself, "to quit the sorority would be a big sacrifice. I need to do that."

I am somewhat ambivalent about talking about this sacrifice, because I promised God that I would never say anything to anyone about why I had quit the sorority. I must have come up with some fake, believable reason. Even now, I don't feel especially good talking about it, but I think it is necessary, because it is so important to my story.

By quitting the sorority, I cut myself off even more, became even more isolated. My internal self was in a state of increasing torment and shame. I thought I was fat and unlovable. Not that I was really a bad person, and not that there was nothing about me that was lovable, but that no one loved me. At least that was what I thought then.

My sacrifice accelerated my spiral descent toward depression. The headaches became even worse. According to my clinical notes from the Institute of Living, I started seeing Dr. Knox in August of 1960, the very beginning of senior year. The notes say that "no organic basis has been found [for the headaches]." My guess is that they were some form of tension headache. I also gained a lot of weight and fell into a major depression.

I withdrew socially and from my family. I wouldn't leave my room. I was so profoundly and desperately miserable, I wanted to be dead. I felt I was an unacceptable human being. I told Dr. Knox that I was suicidal and wanted to run away from home. I have no idea whether I told my parents, or whether Dr. Knox told them. Then, toward the end of April of 1961, I found myself in a state of constant weeping, for more than two weeks. I had no idea what was happening to me. It was just happening to me. I had no control over it. All I did know was that I wanted to be dead.

Hell had found me.

A Disappearing Act

It was a disappearing act, my going to the hospital. Aline recently told me that nobody knew what had happened. "My two older brothers were at college, so they weren't aware of anything, and my two younger brothers were too young to notice," she said. "I didn't know, either."

My friend Diane Siegfried, whom, admittedly, I had seen less of in my senior year, since she had graduated, says, "No one knew there was anything going on; only later. You just disappeared. You were there one day and not the next. I had no clue you had a problem."

Many of my friends knew that I was having trouble at home with

Mother, but they didn't know what was really happening. "They didn't even tell me where you were for two years," Nancy told me recently. "We knew you were gone. We figured out it was something problematic. But mum was the word." According to Margie Pielsticker, "All of a sudden she was gone. We were told that she was at home, sick. No one knew why. Those were the years when you didn't talk about mental illness."

What Happened to Me?

One of my closest colleagues and friends, Martin Bohus, a psychiatrist in Germany, has spent many hours with me trying to dissect what could have happened to me. Martin is an expert in Dialectical Behavior Therapy and head of one of the world's largest research laboratories, where he conducts research on borderline personality disorder and associated disorders. He is convinced I must have had some sort of damage to my brain, sometime before I fell apart in the institute.

Tante Aline believed that the entire problem was biological. My mother hoped it was. It is certainly possible that there was a genetic predisposition, given the long history of depression on Mother's side of the family.

I eventually came to suspect that there was indeed a biological component, an innate vulnerability. The combination of the biological predisposition and a toxic home environment proves to be a psychologically deadly mix. Had I grown up in a different family environment, one where I was accepted for who I was and what I valued (an environment such as Aunt Julia's, for example), my life might have been different.

But none of this fully explains my out-of-control behavior once I got to the hospital. Being hospitalized and overmedicated likely played an important part in my descent into hell. It sent the message that no one at home could help me. And who knows what effects such high doses of antipsychotic medications may have on a teenage brain?

Whatever the truth is, as soon as I got out of the hospital, I knew that I would never have a child of my own. The thought that anyone else in the universe might go through what I went through is beyond my ability to tolerate. It's not that a child of mine, with my genes, would inevitably have my problems. It's that I simply could not take that chance.

So Very Sad

Five decades after my two-plus years at the Institute of Living, during the summer of 2012, I was teaching a course on emotion dysregulation at the New England Educational Institute, on Cape Cod, Massachusetts. My cousin Nancy joined me for the week, as did Sebern and our annual group of colleagues and friends. I had the afternoons to relax and talk. Nancy brought the Monte Cassino 1961 yearbook and went through it with me.

Someone asked what I felt when I looked at my photograph, knowing what lay ahead for that young girl. "Sad. I feel sad," I said. "But it's not like being sad for myself so much as being sad for another person. I look at that young girl and think, 'What happened to her?'"

Could I feel love for the girl in the photograph? I thought for a minute and then said, "I don't know, because I don't know her." The girl in the photo—the eighteen-year-old me—looked like a stranger to me.

···

CHAPTER FIVE

A Stranger in a Strange Land

I DON'T REMEMBER HOW I felt about coming back home, in early
June of 1963, mainly because I don't remember coming home.
What I do remember is the distress of finding out how severe my
memory loss was.

At our house in Tulsa, I didn't remember where the silverware
was kept, where the pots and pans were, which cupboard had the
glasses for everyday use and which for more formal occasions. It
was like walking into a stranger's house. The multiple shock treatments I'd received at the IOL apparently had had a much greater
effect than I realized.

I dreaded going anywhere I might see someone I was supposed to
know. Not recognizing people you have known for years is humiliating. To make you feel better, people almost always say, "I forget
names also." It sometimes makes me want to scream: "You have no
idea what it is like to lose so much of your memory!"

"When Marsha went into the institute, she was from an upper-
class family" is how Aline describes that time. "When she came out,
it was like she was a pauper. She ate differently. She forgot her man-
ners. She forgot everything. It was as if she had lost all memory of
who she was. She said she couldn't be around people with money.
Was much more comfortable being around poor people. She was
different. Maybe it was the medications."

At home, I continued to be profoundly miserable, and I just wanted the pain to stop.

Moving Out

Heaven knows how Mother and Dad felt about the prospects of having me back. It wasn't a happy homecoming. Mother told Aline to keep her distance, because she thought I would corrupt her— first, with my craziness, but also because of my attitudes about the wealthy and concern for the poor. Ironically, within a couple of years, Aline left for Oklahoma City to live and work with the poor! Aline told me later that as she was preparing to drive away, Mother was on her knees, holding on to Aline's coat, crying, begging her not to go, begging her to stay home. I doubt that Mother would have gotten upset if I had done that, but Aline? Her pride and joy!

Within a couple of weeks of arriving home, I deliberately cut my arm quite badly, with a razor. Aline says she was with me in the bathroom at the time but wasn't able to stop me. "There was blood everywhere," she says. I recall watching the blood stream down my arm, splashing on the white tiled floor. I was taken to the hospital, where the nurses were pretty rough with me and threatened that if this happened again I would be arrested. Attempting suicide was illegal in Oklahoma at that time, a felony. And even though suicide hadn't been what I was doing, that was how they treated me.

It cannot have come as much of a surprise, and I'm sure it brought considerable relief to my parents, when I announced that I was leaving. This was about a month after I'd come home. I had gone to Southern Hills Country Club with Mother that afternoon. The visit finished with Mother getting mad at me, probably about something inappropriate I had done or said. I decided I would move out.

Adjusting to Life on My Own

My new home was the YWCA in downtown Tulsa, quite close to the offices of the Indiana Oil Purchasing Company, where my father had arranged for me to have a part-time job. I walked to work, where I was a receptionist, did filing, licked envelopes, all the menial jobs that girls did in offices in those days, but I loved it, as I have loved pretty much every job I've ever had. I especially loved figuring out the most efficient ways of organizing my workload.

Not long after I moved into the Y, I discovered that I could easily become an alcoholic. I liked having a glass of orange juice in the morning before work, but I didn't really like orange juice unless it had vodka in it. So I started putting vodka in my juice. I quickly saw where this might lead me. We had known quite a few people in Tulsa who were alcoholic. I could see what that did to their lives and to the people close to them.

If I thought I was miserable now, that would be nothing compared with the misery of becoming an alcoholic and then having to get off alcohol, which I figured I would have to do at some point. When I was in seclusion at the institute, getting off cigarettes had been painful, and I thought getting off alcohol would probably be even worse. So I decided to come up with a rule that I kept all the way until I was forty: No drinking alcohol when alone.

First Steps to Building a Life Experienced as Worth Living

Imposing this rule on myself, to prevent destructive behavior and stay in a place that was at least tolerable, is an example of what I later termed "building a life experienced as worth living." This is the overall goal of DBT. Even if you can't create an ideal life for yourself, you have sufficient control to live a life that has enough positive elements to it that it is indeed worth living.

Once I turned forty, I decided that I was safe and didn't need the drinking rule anymore. A month or two later, I realized that I could easily be in danger again, so I went back to my rule and have stayed with it ever since. (As you are no doubt beginning to realize, I can be a person of both no control and of immense control, seemingly at the same time.)

A Stranger in a Strange Land

I was very naïve when I first got back to Tulsa, thrust into a world where I had virtually no experience in handling practical, everyday matters. I was barely eighteen when I entered the institute, and I had lived a sheltered life. And now, just twenty years old, I was living on my own, earning very little money at my part-time job, with only my skewed experience to guide me. I had refused to allow my parents to subsidize me financially, because I was not going to let them have any credit for my getting out of hell.

I had no idea how to manage money. Mother always shopped at the best clothes stores, and I often went with her. So when I needed to buy a dress for work, it didn't occur to me to shop anywhere but at the best store. I bought the dress, expensive as it was, and paid for it with a credit card. When the credit card bill came due, it didn't occur to me that I didn't have to pay it off completely right away. So I paid the entire amount, which left me with precisely thirty cents to live on for the rest of the month. I thought about my situation quite a bit, and bought three of those round chocolate mints, the ones with white inside, wrapped in silver-and-blue foil. I must have scrounged around the office for food, because I know I wasn't able to buy any.

Occasionally I went to my parents' house for dinner, but it rarely worked out well. "Last night I went over to dinner but didn't eat because I was too nervous—just stayed up in my room and cried," I wrote to Dr. John O'Brien. "Then Mother wouldn't let me come back because she said I was in too bad of shape and she might kick me out for upsetting her so. PARENTS!!! Said a rosary and immediately felt better."

Taking Pills Doesn't Help

Happy though my moments at my job were, there was a constant background of episodic depression and frequent wishes to be dead. I was big into pills, and I had a handy supply of them thanks to Dr. Proctor, my new psychiatrist in Tulsa. "I have taken many overdoses," I wrote Dr. O'Brien. "The last was a week ago of thirty Stellizines and thirty Cojenton (however you spell it). All it did was make me a nervous, hysterical wreck for three days. Mother wouldn't let me stay at the Y as she said I would get kicked out if they saw me in that condition."

Mother had reason to be concerned, as I explained to Dr. O'Brien. "A mother of one of the girls at the Y came and said she doesn't think that they should let a girl who has been in a mental institution who burns herself (I have told no one but my roommate about the burns) stay at the Y. . . . What I have done to create trouble I don't know."

Then I got serious about pills. "Have some news that is good and bad. Mostly bad, I should say," I wrote Dr. O'Brien. "For the first time in my life I actually tried suicide. TWICE! Was never so shocked to awaken both times. The first time I took one full bottle of Thorazine, but was only out for about a day and a half. The second time I went out, got a motel room, and took two full bottles of the junk plus a bottle of Darvon compound. It was quite a shock. But, alas, from that too I awakened. Somewhere along the way I guess I called Dr. Proctor who called my mother, who came and got me. Naturally, she was worried."

My only memory of any of these suicide attempts is of lying in bed at home, able to think but unable to move any part of my body, feeling awful. The trauma of that episode was, I think, enough to keep me from trying again.

Writing this now, I am shocked that I did all this. I must have been more ambivalent than the letters to Dr. O'Brien tell. It seems I had lost myself, particularly my spiritual self. I had lost my vow to get out of hell. How could I not have realized that suicide was definitely not God's will for me? As with many people who are suicidal, perhaps the pain was so all-embracing that thoughts of others, including family and God, were simply lost to consciousness.

Not a Good Model

Mother had good reason to be concerned. The police came to the house after that final suicide attempt, and a detective told me I had committed a felony by attempting to kill myself, and I could be put in jail. I got rather upset and cried hysterically to my younger brother that I didn't want to go to jail. Not a very good role model for a younger brother.

When I wrote John O'Brien about the incident, my thinking had changed. "Of course, I will go to jail sooner or later, as the chances are a million to one that I will do it again," I said, showing myself to be not such a good statistician. "No matter how hard I try, how much I pray, or how many tears fall, I occasionally fail. Have been doing so much better, but seem unable to control the few setbacks all the time. So now I realize it is God's will that I go to jail. I did not realize at first what a tremendous opportunity it will be to help all the mixed up women there. What better place is there to do social work than in a jail? I am determined to be the kindest, most understanding and best behaved prisoner ever. Perhaps, if only by example, I can help some one person find the road back. Am really kind of excited about it, except that my family would be awfully hurt-mad-embarrassed."

I told Dr. O'Brien that there was a good side to this suicide episode, which was that I didn't want to commit suicide anymore. "I really didn't before but felt I had to," I wrote. "Although I thought I would die, I didn't want to die. Now I don't even want to try."

I was obsessed with the notion that I did nothing but hurt people who were close to me. "I say I want to help others but have never helped anyone," I wrote Dr. O'Brien. "Am so tired of the merry-go-round. Thank God, though, that everyone at work and all my friends think I am the happiest thing going." I was still good at hiding my inner reality. "It is amusing to think of their reaction if they knew the truth. The worst thing I have done is give Mike and Bill [my younger brothers] no one to look up to. It is so wonderful to be proud of your brothers and sisters. Placing them on a pedestal is a never-ending pastime. It is for sure that no one is proud of me for I have cut the pedestal to pieces and burned it to ashes. Older brothers and sisters are teachers, and I have taught them nothing but cruelty [in the pain I constantly inflicted on the family]. Am seriously considering moving to some big city and living alone. Then I could not hurt anyone in the family and I would know no one there to care whom I hurt. . . . What they should do is lock me up on an island."

I Get a Grip at Last

I had to move out of the Tulsa Y because of that last pill-taking episode. I got a small, dingy apartment at 1111 South Denver Avenue, a very seedy neighborhood at that time. I thought it was terrific. My parents, however, were appalled. Mother was in floods of tears and Dad wanted to pay the rent for a better apartment in a "good" part of town. But a better apartment would only show that I had money, and since I didn't, I saw no point in trying to show that I did. "As you can guess," I wrote Dr. O'Brien, "they have all but disowned me—they are acting as if I married a tramp and was doomed to a life in hell."

Despite all this, I was beginning to get a grip on my life, renewing my vow to get out of hell and help others get out, too. In order to help others, I would eventually need to go to college.

That would be my next step.

My First Paper on Suicide

I enrolled in night school at the University of Tulsa while I was working as a receptionist/mail girl. Three classes—sociology, English, and speech. Very soon I was scoring good grades in all three classes. I was determined to become a psychiatrist on the back ward of a state mental hospital and help people get out of hell.

The back ward is where the most disturbed patients go, like me in Thompson Two, at the institute. I imagined the pay in state hospitals would be pretty low, but making a lot of money was not a priority, so this wouldn't be a problem. I thought, "Fine, I'll be good at my work and they won't be able to hire someone as good as I am for such a low price."

But even with this plan to become a psychiatrist, the seeds of the nascent researcher began to sprout. I decided to write a paper on suicide for my sociology class.

How I came to this decision escapes me. It was the only area in psychology I found intrinsically interesting. (What could be more fascinating than life and death, when you get right down to it?) I wanted to work with the most miserable people in the world, and if you want to die, you must be very miserable indeed.

I somehow persuaded the county coroner's office and police department to give me past records of suicides and suicide attempts. Why they agreed, I have no idea. I must have made a good case and sounded like a genuine researcher.

That project in the coroner's office set a path for me. From then on, I wrote papers about suicide wherever I was—as an undergraduate and postgraduate, as a member of a university faculty. If there was a paper to be written, I'd find a way to make it a paper on suicide. But that Tulsa project came to a swift end when I found the records of someone my family had known. "Oh, my God," I exclaimed. "Nobody knows this person killed himself." I never told anybody, and I stopped the project. It was clear that this information should stay private.

Leaving Behind an Old Self, Finding a New Self

Within a year of leaving the Institute of Living and going back to Tulsa, I experienced a significant shift. It is hard to explain, but it was as if a new and happier me emerged from the cocoon of the anguished old me. And, remarkably, the metamorphosis just *happened*, unprompted by anything I said or did. This is how I explained it in a letter to Dr. O'Brien:

> *Fundamentally what has happened is that, as [Dr.] Proctor puts it, I have found myself. The only conclusion we can draw is that my 21st birthday [year] had a profound effect on me. May 6 I was at the office and all of a sudden it happened. It felt as if someone had taken the chains off my arms. As if all my life I have been running into a brick wall, trying to find the gate leading to mental health or, more truly, freedom. All of a sudden, the gate is in front of me. Dr. O'Brien, I can't tell you how wonderful it is. I have cut myself for years, yet never wanted to. Now, I don't have to unless I choose to. I have hurt others, not wanting to. No more do I have to unless I want to. I have been sick & not wanted to be sick. I don't have to be sick anymore. Dr. O'Brien, I don't have to do anything I don't want to. . . . It is happiness inside. Yes, I get depressed, I cry, I get mad, I decide the hell with it all, but underneath when it passes there is a happiness. Remember, though, I have but found the gate. I still have a long walk ahead of me.*

At that point, I had no idea just how long that walk would be. Or what I would discover along the way.

I've been told that what I wrote in my letters to Dr. O'Brien sounds similar to the way I talk now in therapy, as a behaviorist. So you might say that I was already thinking like a behaviorist before I actively became one. But it was all completely unconscious at the time.

CHAPTER SIX

I Had to Leave Tulsa

I T WAS AT night school, in English class, that I met Bob. He was a policeman, a few years older than me. We started dating, and it soon became quite serious, serious enough for Bob to tell me he loved me. The relationship was serious enough for me, a good Catholic girl, to give up my virginity. I had made him wait, because I wanted to be sure it was my decision, not an impulsive response in some romantic moment. We would meet pretty late in the evening, because his schedule as a cop was crazy, or so he told me. We went to parties, went to the movies; I met his friends and went with him to boxing fights, sitting way up in the stands while he was watching out for problems in the audience.

It was a very important relationship for me, my first serious sexual relationship. Bob was very kind, gave me things when he saw I needed them. I had never known a guy to be so considerate and sweet. When I left the Y, he moved me into my apartment, fixed my radio, painted a chest for me, brought me flowers late at night, and never, ever did anything I didn't want him to do.

Bob was very attentive and very sensitive. I had told him about my history, and he offered me comfort, not scorn. He had been married, he told me, but his wife—now ex-wife—had been committed to a mental institution. He understood me in a way I hadn't ever been understood, perhaps because of his history. I loved him, but I can't say if I was in love with him. I felt nurtured in a new way.

My parents knew about my relationship with Bob, as did Aline, and I *assumed* they approved. For their part, my family and friends and his friends *assumed* that I knew what they knew—namely, that Bob wasn't telling me the whole truth.

Bob had indeed been married. But he still was. His wife was still his wife and was not in a mental institution, but at home with their children. My sister finally told me. My parents knew also but had said nothing. I was completely shattered when I discovered this. Some time later, Bob put a statuette of the Virgin Mary (or a rosary—I can't remember which) in my car with a note saying how sorry he was for deceiving me.

I thought I had found what I had yearned for those past painful years: love. Not that Bob didn't love me; I believe he did, but not enough. I was now faced with a choice, between Bob, on the one hand, and the Catholic Church and God, on the other. Bob did not win that contest.

As it turned out, Bob was the first in a long line of married men who were attracted to me. I don't know why. And I also don't know why I considered myself unattractive to men, because, objectively, I obviously was. But I have never been able to accept that.

I had to leave Tulsa because I knew that, if I were to stay, I would continue to see Bob. I would not be able to prevent myself, so powerful had the relationship become. My brother Earl was in Chicago, working for Arthur Andersen. Earl had recently married, and he and Darielle had a house in Evanston, just north of Chicago, right on Lake Michigan. I had really wanted to live in Manhattan, but I thought it was too big and daunting for a first stop beyond Tulsa. I decided I would practice on Chicago and then move to Manhattan. This was in 1965, about eighteen months after I had left the institute and gone back to Tulsa.

Believe, Whether You Believe or Not

I should not have been surprised at my father's response. Almost before I had finished describing my plan, to move and find a job to support myself, he said sharply, "You won't be able to get a job in Chicago." He probably thought he was being honest, and, given my history, he had a point. But he didn't know me, or my determination.

This dynamic became something of a pattern in my life: people telling me what I couldn't do, and me thinking, "You just wait and see. I'll show you."

And eventually it became a good message for me, and also for my clients and their families: Believe, whether you believe or not. I tell them that it may be difficult to believe, but believe you must. You can do it.

Part Two

....

CHAPTER SEVEN

On My Way to Chicago

DAD SOMEWHAT GRUDGINGLY gave me money for the overnight train trip to Chicago, enough for coach. Without telling him, Mother slipped me extra so I could get a berth in a sleeping car. I've always considered this to be one of the nicer things she did for me.

I arrived in Chicago, got a room at the YWCA, and started looking for a job. Soon I was working as a clerk/typist for the Reserve Insurance Company, on Michigan Avenue a few blocks from the Y. (Thank you, Aunt Julia, for teaching me how to type.)

Even though I had triumphed over my father's challenge—I had a job!—the first few weeks were a little difficult. My greatest supporter during this time, ironically, was Bob, back in Tulsa. I talked with him almost every day. He was my rock, emotionally and practically. He helped me organize my new life and gave me practical advice for getting established in a new, big city.

My new life involved my job during the day; finding a nearby local church where I prayed practically every day; and making plans to attend night school at Loyola University, the beginning of the long path to becoming a psychiatrist.

Over time I came to really like my job—I liked my colleagues, and I had more and more responsibility—but it did not fit with my vow to get people out of hell. So I quit and got a job at a social work agency so that I could help people. After several weeks of typing, I went to my boss and asked, "When do I get to do social work?" She told me I had been hired to manage reports, not to do social work, which was crushing. I wound up returning to my previous job, where they actually valued my work.

I figured if I did well in night school and got the teachers to like me, it would be a lot easier to get in as a college student. I deliberately chose Loyola, a good Catholic institution, because I was afraid that if the teachers at a state school were a lot smarter than me, I might lose my faith. (Looking back, I should have known myself better than that.) I also taught catechism on Saturdays at Old Saint Mary's, where Ted Vierra, a priest and associate pastor, became a very important person in my life.

The Urge to Cut Returns

On the face of it, I was managing life quite adequately, in both the practical realm and the spiritual realm. On the other hand, I was still lonely, often racked with inchoate despair and pain, wanting the pain to stop—but not wanting to be dead. I had given up on that idea.

The cravings to cut still lurked. One night, about a month into my time in Chicago, they became overwhelming. But most of me didn't *want* to cut, so I was in a great struggle. I had the number of the crisis clinic on hand. "I need to talk with someone. Is there someone I can come and see tonight?" I pleaded to the person who answered. "Well, I'm sorry, but there's no one here until tomorrow," the person said. I was terrified, panicked. "But I need help tonight, now! Because I'm afraid I'm going to cut myself—*now!*" They apologized and said again that help wasn't available until the next day.

I put the phone down, found a sharp knife, and cut my inside forearm. I had become quite practiced at this, so I was able to make a cut that wasn't too big or messy. It had its desired effect: it completely calmed me. I applied a butterfly bandage and went to bed.

I'm not sure how long it was after I'd fallen asleep, but I was woken by loud banging on my door. Alarmed, I got up, opened the door, and found three Chicago cops standing there. "You have to come with us," one of them brusquely told me. Apparently the crisis clinic had traced my call and informed the police. They had obviously expected to find someone in a desperate state and a real physical danger to herself. "I'm fine," I insisted. "I have to go to work tomorrow. I can't go with you." I was getting quite scared. Couldn't they see I was just fine and didn't need to go anywhere? "Look, I have to go to work tomorrow," I protested. "You can't do this to me. I need to go back to bed."

Eventually I realized I had no option but to go with them. The noise had caught the attention of the person in charge at the Y. He confronted me as I was leaving. "Take your things with you," he demanded. "We can't have a person with your problems stay here." Turning to the cops, he said, "She can't come back here tonight."

In Bedlam, Again

The cops, who were friendly enough, told me they had no alternative because of the call I had made to the crisis center. Something about procedure. They were taking me to Cook County Insane Asylum. My heart sank, because that place had quite a reputation. I was headed back to bedlam, back to the world of Thompson Two.

Even if the cops were on my side, the nurses at the hospital were most definitely not. It was two in the morning, my head was splitting, and I just wanted to lie down. "No, you may not lie down," the head nurse barked at me. "You have to be evaluated."

And so began a Kafkaesque nightmare.

The more I protested that I was just fine, the more the nurses threatened to commit me. As soon as I could, I called my psychiatrist in Tulsa. It was very late by now, and I have always thought perhaps the doctor had had a little too much bourbon. He insisted that the hospital administrators had no right to keep me there against my wishes; that I should tell them I was leaving right now; and that if they tried to stop me I should tell them I would sue the hospital. Big mistake. I then called my brother Earl, who said much the same thing. He promised to help get me out. The next morning someone on the staff told me, "Oh, you'll be out tomorrow, don't worry."

I was terrified I would lose my job. That first morning, I called my sister-in-law Darielle and asked her to call my boss and say I was sick with flu or something, and that I would be back soon. She said she would. Earl did what he could to try to get me out. No effect. My father made some half-hearted attempts, including contacting the head of psychiatry at the medical school. He contacted the hospital. Again, no effect. And with each passing day, it was the same thing: the promise, the denial, for almost a week, a week of horrors that only those who have been in bedlam can begin to imagine.

The ward was spare and grim. Iron beds bolted to the floor in the middle of a large room. They were high and arranged in rows, as in a barracks. During the day, the bed area was marked off by colored tape. If you crossed that line, to get into bed or something, the nurses put you in seclusion. Around the walls of the room were benches, simple park benches where you were supposed to sit all day. But you weren't allowed to lie down. Aides sat around, reading magazines. It was all terrifyingly familiar to me.

Can We Ever Get Her Out of Here?

And the food. It was hard to recognize as actual food; I thought of it more as tasteless slop on a plate. When Earl found out how awful the food was, he came in with a hamburger for me. But I couldn't eat a decent hamburger if everybody else was eating slop, so he brought hamburgers for everyone every day after that. Earl recalls the place as being "dirty, frightening, full of crazy people." Initially he thought it would just take a signature from him to get me released. But when he experienced the bureaucracy, he now admits he was frightened, wondering, "Can we ever get her out of here?"

Very soon I slipped into my social worker mode. There was one young woman, anorexic most likely, lying on a bed, trying unsuccessfully to feed herself with a spoon. The slop just slipped off every time. ("No hamburgers for her," the staff insisted.) So I said to one of the aides, "Can I go over there and help her eat? She's having trouble getting the food into her mouth." They said, "Aw, she can get that food if she wants to; she just doesn't want to."

There was another woman who was schizophrenic. She was totally delusional, and probably about seventy-five. She thought her father was going to come pick her up and take her home. I tried to keep her calm by playing games with her, because the nurses kept threatening to put her into seclusion if she didn't shut up. She would leap up and yell, "Wait a minute, my father's coming, my father's coming!" As she was dragged off to seclusion, one of the aides said to her, in a voice dripping with sarcasm, "Aw, honey, your father's six feet under. He's *not* coming."

It was horrendous.

By now I was a complete puzzle to the staff, because I was in fully competent mode. I was calm and answered questions without obvious emotion. They officially diagnosed me as schizophrenic. The psychiatrist told me that for a person to be as smart as I was, and to be on that unit, I must be schizophrenic.

A nurse asked me, "Why did you do it? Why did you cut yourself like that?" I told her, "I don't know," and that was the truth. It was a compulsion that I sometimes couldn't override. My guess is that only people who have been down this path, other cutters, can understand it. The staff certainly didn't.

Brother Earl Comes to the Rescue

Toward the end, the psychiatrist my parents had hired (to try to get me out of there) sat down with me. "When you threatened to sue the hospital, you completely terrified them," he said. "The administration felt they were in a corner, so they felt they needed to prove that you are indeed mentally ill. If you want to get out of here, you are going to have to admit that you need help and accept being under the care and custody of a responsible adult. Can you do that, Marsha? Otherwise they can easily commit you to a state mental hospital, and you can't stop them. And you know what that means, don't you?" I took the threat seriously, and I did know what it would mean. It meant there was a fairly good chance I would never get out.

I bit my lip at the injustice of it and said I could accept that, even though it was just a ruse, and I knew I was just fine. My father refused to step forward as the "responsible adult." So dear brother Earl, who is two years my senior, agreed to take on that role. I was twenty-one, and Earl was twenty-three.

A time in court was set, and Earl said he would be there. The psychiatrist sat down with me and, very serious, said, "Marsha, I need to know. Can you count on your brother to be there? Because if he's not, you'll go to a state hospital." I was terrified, because as far as I knew, Earl had not been on time for *anything* in his life.

I arrived in court wearing paper slippers, paper gown, paper everything—the epitome of "the mental patient." My psychiatrist coached me to "just go in, sit down, don't say anything, and let your brother do the talking." The appointed hour arrived. No Earl. My heart moved into my throat. Then, just in the nick of time, he walked into the courtroom, entering through the side door, not the one he was supposed to have used! The judge went through the motions, Earl responded correctly, and a timetable for evaluation was agreed upon. And I was free, with a second erroneous diagnosis of schizophrenia.

When we got to Earl's car, instead of berating me for causing all this trouble and getting myself into this mess, as I'd gotten used to everyone doing, he said, "We'll get through this, Marsha. We all know you are just fine, and we are doing this for legal reasons. It'll soon be all over. As soon as we can, we will go in and see the judge and say you are fine and he will end the care-and-custody stuff. We know you don't need it."

I felt the profound touch of his love at that moment.

CHAPTER EIGHT

Intellectual and Spiritual Transformations

A FTER I HAD been back at work for several months, the Reserve Insurance Company offered to pay for me to go to night school, for which I was very grateful. With both my job and night school, there was a lot of work to be done. I had to get up early in the morning to go to the office, and at the end of the day go to school, then do homework when I got home, then get up the next morning and do it all over again.

My room at the YWCA was so small that getting homework done was really hard. I had to sit on the bed to study and write. So I devised a new strategy. The Y was near the high-end hotels up and down Michigan Avenue. The hotels had very nice lobbies where I would go to study, walking in as if I was staying at the hotel. I had my bags filled with textbooks and notebooks, and I could read and write in great comfort at the nice big desks or on the comfy couches. There were pay phones, so I could call people if I needed to. I rotated among three or four hotels. I found that if I acted as if I belonged, no one bothered me. It was, in its small way, an enormously wonderful life.

Adaptive Denial

I had barely enough money to get by, given the cost of college books and food and phone bills and riding the "L" train. I developed a strategy for managing my money so that I wouldn't run out. I had to close a door in my mind, to tell myself a fiction about how much money I had, and to believe what I said to myself.

The L cost twenty-five cents each way. I bought everything I needed for the month in one outing—food, cigarettes, tampons, everything. I divided the meat up (when I had meat) and froze enough for each day. But, with the way the L worked, I couldn't buy my tickets in advance. I therefore lined my quarters up on a shelf for the month, two for each day, and when I had just enough money for the L for the month, I told myself that I had no money left and treated the quarters as if they did not exist.

This sleight of mind, convincing yourself that something is true when in fact it is not, turned out to be a very helpful skill. It ultimately became an important DBT skill, particularly for people with addictions, a skill I named adaptive denial. Like many ideas in DBT, it is based on acceptance: accepting things as they are. In a later chapter I will tell you in detail how I used adaptive denial to help me stop smoking.

A Blessing out of the Blue

In the summer of 1967, two years after arriving in Chicago, I got news that changed my life. My father's best friend, Uncle Jerry, had set up a college trust fund for me, as he had for all the siblings. Jerry knew Dad well and arranged for a lawyer to manage the money for me instead of Dad.

With Uncle Jerry's money, I could enroll full-time as an undergraduate. The day I was accepted at Loyola as a full-time student, standing behind a high counter and receiving my papers, I nearly cried with joy. I just couldn't believe it. I was going to college.

I had enough money to get my own apartment, on West Albion, very close to the Loyola campus. There would be just enough money, I calculated, to take me through to graduation if I used it sparingly. I majored in psychology and took premed courses, the first step toward becoming a psychiatrist.

A Shocking Recognition of Lost Memories

When classes started, my sense of elation gave way to something of a psychological shock. My very first college class was a biology class. The other students seemed much younger than me. (They were, of course, because of those lost years locked up in a mental hospital.) The professor began asking very detailed questions about biological topics. To my surprise, the other students started answering the questions. "What?" I thought. "Nobody told me I was supposed to study these topics before I came to class."

But the professor was simply testing the students' high school knowledge of biology. Not only did I not have that high school knowledge, but I had no recollection of having *been* to a biology class in high school. I must have had the same biology classes as everybody else, but I had a complete memory blank of the experience. I had no memory at all, of any high school class, and I had to devote a lot of time to matching the heap of knowledge that everybody else had in their heads, as well as learning new course material.

Since my plan was to become a psychiatrist, I had to take all those very difficult courses required for acceptance into a medical program. When I failed one big exam, I asked the teacher to let me take the course again. He said yes, but that he was just doing this as a favor, because I was a woman and he did not expect me to succeed. Hearing that, as you can imagine, I was determined to prove him wrong, and I did.

I loved being a student at Loyola, but I was also lonely. The other students were much younger, I didn't have a past I could share with them, and living alone in an apartment was different from their experience. And they didn't seem to take school very seriously. This made it difficult to form friendships.

Miscalculations

What I hadn't put into my college financial equation was the possibility that Loyola's tuition fees might go up, and they did. As a result, I was going to run out of money in March of my senior year. I immediately went to the head of my department (psychology) and almost cried and asked if there was any work I could do in the department. He had been so supportive of me before that I thought there was a good chance he could help me. Sure enough, he gave me a small job to tide me over for the year.

Living alone in my apartment on Albion Avenue, I didn't even think to try to share a place with other students. That was partly because they were a lot younger and I didn't feel close to anyone. But it was also because I thought I should be able to manage living by myself before trying to live with others. This was a huge mistake, one that I perpetuated for far too many years before I discovered my error.

My Spiritual Director, Anselm

As at many Catholic universities, Loyola had a chaplain who was available for consultation and spiritual direction. Anselm Romb, a Franciscan priest, agreed to be my spiritual director. We met once or twice a month, sometimes more, and would talk about where God was, how to have a relationship with God, what God was calling me to do. Just like at the Institute of Living, I was still searching, searching to find God. Anselm could be warm, and he could be tough. Once, I cried because of some criticism he had made. He responded, "Marsha, I am just telling you the holes you have to fill." Somehow it was a very soothing response.

Anselm saw me—the spiritual Marsha—to a depth that no one else had reached. He validated and verified my spiritual experiences, and he helped me move to a mystical track. Sometimes he seemed to put me on a pedestal. At one point in our relationship, he disappeared for a long time. When he returned, he told me that he had left so he could consider whether he should leave the priesthood and ask me to marry him. He decided no—a good decision, in my opinion.

Anselm gave me my all-time best advice about prayer. "Marsha," he told me very early on, "when you pray, don't say anything." I was completely surprised, and probably protested, "How can I possibly pray without saying anything?" Anselm refused to explain. He merely said, "Marsha, just try it."

I was shocked by the experience. If you talk when you pray, it is a dialogue with someone *separate from you*. But if you don't talk, there is nothing separate from *you*. You are as one with God. If you keep it up, there is every chance that you will ultimately experience that oneness. It is hard to articulate what I mean, just as with love it is hard to articulate what we really, deeply mean. In this case, it means I am in the middle of God.

My practice was to lie on the floor of my apartment, palms turned up at my sides, saying the prayer "Thy will be done" at the start, and then the silent acceptance. A prayer without any expectation of a response from God. It was this practice that ultimately led to transformation, because it helped me form a relationship with God that led to a spiritual experience.

I have Anselm to thank for a second piece of advice, too. It was more of a statement. I had contemplated becoming a nun, which is not so very surprising for a Catholic girl. Mother would have been ecstatic; she often urged me to go down that path. When I told Anselm this, he said, "Marsha, if you enter a convent, the only serious question to be asked will be 'Will they kick you out first, or will you walk out first?' because you'll never make it in a convent." Anselm was likely right. I was not cut out to be a nun.

A Lay Religious

I spent many hours talking with Anselm about what was best for me in this spiritual realm. In the end, we decided that a good compromise was to become a "lay religious." It is like being a nun, but on your own, without the formalities of life in a convent. Anselm officiated at the ceremony, which we held at my apartment on Albion Avenue, a few blocks from Loyola. Earl, Darielle, and Aline came for the event. I took the usual vows of chastity, poverty, and obedience to the church, just as nuns do. And I was fully determined to lead a life that God intended me to lead. Friends occasionally said to me, "Marsha, why in the world would you do that?" My answer was as simple as it was sincere: "I am existentially unable to do otherwise." I had never felt so certain about anything in my life.

Ted Vierra: A Shoulder to Cry On

A second part of my spiritual life at Loyola was through Ted Vierra, the priest I introduced you to earlier who was a member of a community of priests at Old Saint Mary's church, a few blocks from the insurance company where I first worked. It was providential, because at times Ted literally kept me alive. Now it was a long ride on the L from my apartment, but I never stopped going there. I had found Old Saint Mary's soon after I arrived in Chicago.

Ted and I had an immediate connection. He treated me like the little sister he never had. He invited me to become one of the lay assistants at Old Saint Mary's for people who were inquiring about

Catholicism. Ted wanted laypeople to be part of these sessions, to talk about the practices of Catholic life. Soon I was teaching catechism more formally.

Over time I became closer with Ted. I turned to him in my many moments of torment. "I have to talk to someone," I would say, crying. "I am so miserable, I want to die." Ted was always there for me, always ready to listen, again and again, always giving comfort. He had a schizophrenic brother, so there was a point of empathy. But it was much more profound than that. He loved me, in the purest sense, and I loved him. This is how Ted kept me alive.

Three Lessons

I learned some important lessons from that relationship with Ted, which I apply to my work today. Although Ted was fully and freely giving me what I needed, which was unconditional love and support, I was unable to say "Thank you." I could say it later, but not as I was wrestling with such despair and loneliness. So, if you also are helping someone who is in hell, holding them physically and emotionally, don't interpret their absence of thanks as a sign that you are not giving them what they desperately need. You very probably are. That's the first lesson.

The second lesson is about what it is like to have to say goodbye to someone when you are still in hell. When you're in distress, and the meeting or phone call eventually ends, it is one of the worst moments of your life. The other person has hung up the phone, you cannot call back, and now you are alone again, alone with the hell that is your life. It's the same with a meeting in person. One of the worst moments is walking down the hall after a meeting or a session, and now you won't see the person who is helping you for a whole week and you're unbelievably alone.

The last lesson is about love, which comes both from Ted and from Anselm (and later from Willigis, who became my Zen teacher in Germany). If you are with someone who is in hell, *keep loving them*, because in the end it will be transformative. They are like someone walking in a mist. They don't see the mist, and you may not see it, either. They don't see that they are getting wet. But if they have a pail for water, you put it out in the mist. Each moment of love adds to the mist, adds to the water in the pail. By itself, each moment of love may not be enough. But ultimately the pail fills and the person who has been in hell will be able to drink that water of love and be transformed. I know. I have been there. I have drunk from that pail.

The Little Brothers

I almost always got depressed when left alone. One way to alleviate the depression, which I continued to experience for many years, was to get involved doing volunteer work. There was a special organization called Little Brothers of the Poor, or, simply, Little Brothers. It was founded in France shortly after the end of World War II, to help the elderly of Paris. There are now branches in half a dozen cities throughout the United States. I love the organization's motto: "Flowers before bread." People need the special pleasures in life, in addition to the necessities. "Love, dignity and beauty in life are as essential to life as physical needs," they assert. If I learned anything from my mother, I learned the value of beauty, and that the effort to bring beauty into any setting is worth the work it entails.

On Christmas, on Thanksgiving, and on Easter, I helped the Little Brothers serve celebration meals, and did whatever was needed for the people who came to the center. One time, I was given a whole half of a turkey breast to take home. Of all the wonderful things I've been given in my life, this felt like the best. I would have food for the whole week. Such joy.

I could count on the people at the Little Brothers, and that is wonderful when you are by yourself on Christmas, Easter, and Thanksgiving. The Little Brothers would always give you a flower on your birthday. Mother Teresa had a beautiful phrase that captures some of this: "Kind words can be short and easy to speak, but their echoes are truly endless."

CHAPTER NINE

The Path to Thinking Like a Scientist

I PLUNGED INTO MY undergraduate life at Loyola with energy and enthusiasm. I loved Freud and read everything he wrote. (Those of you who know me now are probably in shock at this, because later I became a scientist, and Freud was not scientific.) In those days, my plan was to become a psychiatrist working on a back ward. But, like a lot of students who enter college with definite ideas, I ended up changing my plans. The changes came from two small but powerful developments.

I Discover Circular Thinking

The first was in a class taught by Naomi Weisstein, a fabulous teacher. Early on, she asked me to defend some particular argument I was making. I stood up and launched into my argument, then she stopped me. "Your argument is circular," she said. "You don't have the information to prove your point."

I had never heard the phrase "circular thinking." Naomi explained what it was, and I realized that *much* of my thinking up until then was probably circular. Clearly, I had a lot to learn. This happened in the middle of class, so you would think I'd have been embarrassed, but I wasn't. I felt genuinely grateful.

So what is circular thinking? Essentially, it is when you attempt to prove something by beginning with an assumption that what you are trying to prove is already true. Here is an example:

PROFESSOR: You are not smart enough to get into grad school.
STUDENT: Why do you say that?
PROFESSOR: You are not ready to go.
STUDENT: How do you know that?
PROFESSOR: Because you are not very smart.
STUDENT: Why do you say that?
PROFESSOR: Because you are not ready for graduate school.

My very favorite example goes something like this:

JOHN: I definitely believe in God.
SUSAN: Why do you believe in God?
JOHN: I believe in God because the Bible says God exists.
SUSAN: Why do you believe in the Bible?
JOHN: Because God wrote the Bible.

When I learned about circular thinking, it jolted many of my thoughts about Freudian treatment. It was my first inkling that psychiatric treatments should be held to scientific standards, that their effectiveness should be evaluated using evidence collected through scientific research. Opinions, I now knew, were no substitute for hard evidence.

Naomi's essential lesson was the first step to my becoming a scientist. Not that I had any good idea of what science was.

My First Taste of Science

The second important event came in a social psychology class taught by Patrick Laughlin. He said something like "I want each of you working in small groups to conduct a research project that is sufficiently rigorous to be presented at a conference." I thought to myself, "What does he mean? We're just undergraduates. We can't do that." But then I thought, "Well, he is the professor, so I suppose he knows what he is talking about." And, in fact, our group wound up presenting our results at a conference. How exciting was that! Our little group presenting real research.

Some of the psychological literature I was reading as an undergraduate at Loyola was about how people often fail to make accurate correlations, whether in assessing risk or in judging others. Emotion, rather than cool calculation, plays a large part in assessments of probabilities. Most people believe they are more likely to die from a terrorist bomb in their plane than from a car accident, even though the odds say otherwise. Grim images of a shattered airplane and disintegrated bodies loom large in the emotional mind. Similarly, people overestimate the likelihood of winning big in the lottery. Pleasant thoughts of big houses, big cars, and Caribbean vacations overwhelm the fact of the known, vanishingly small chance that they will win.

In that social psychology class, I had the thought that if prior opinions control people's choices, the same must be true when people evaluate other things—like when a white person meets an African American. (This was in the sixties, when civil rights were a big topic. I was involved in that and other, similar issues.) So my idea (simple now, but exciting then) was that unconscious prejudices strongly influence our judgments. Are our neighbors good people and smart or bad people and unintelligent? Our answer is swayed by these prejudices: white is good, black is bad, or vice versa. Today this is referred to as implicit bias.

So in 1967 I embarked on my very first independent research

study, focused on biases in people's judgments about race. I got several high schools to let me come into their classes to collect data. After I wrote up the article, it got accepted for presentation at the Midwestern Psychological Association meeting in Chicago. I was twenty-three years old, and I got to present the research, titled "Intentional and Incidental Learning as a Function of the Racial Context of Incidental Stimuli."

Professor Laughlin's prompting me to do the research is less relevant than his *belief* that I could do it, that my research would be worthwhile. I found research to be a lot of fun. Quickly thereafter, I'm sure, I became a pain about it. I'd ask people, "Well, what data do you have to support what you are saying?" or "You can't say that, because you don't have the data."

When I look back at this time—this transformation in my thinking, to becoming a research scientist—I am in awe of the power of these small actions to change my life. One professor pointed out the flaw in my thinking; the other professor believed in me. I sometimes wonder where I would be now were it not for those two professors. If my work had not been based in scientific, logical thinking, would I ever have succeeded in getting anyone out of hell?

CHAPTER TEN

My Enlightenment Moment
in the Cenacle Chapel

IN MY EARLY years as an undergraduate at Loyola, I sometimes spent weekends at the Cenacle Retreat Center, on Fullerton Parkway about six blocks from Lake Michigan. Its buildings were red brick and convent-like, appropriate for a place of spiritual retreats.

The Cenacle Sisters describe their mission as working toward "the transformation of the world by awakening and deepening faith with and for the people of our times." The Cenacle Sisters are a congregation of Catholic women religious founded in 1826 in southern France. Sister Thérèse Couderc, one of the founders, was eventually canonized. Sister Thérèse had a vision, which she described in a letter in 1866: "I saw as in letters of gold this word *Goodness*, which I repeated for a long while with an indescribable sweetness. I saw it, I say, written on all creatures, animate and inanimate, rational or not, all bore this name of goodness." I thought this vision of goodness was beautiful.

The sisters at the center were very kind to me when I came for solitary retreats. They gave me a room and a blanket for free. Each morning, before breakfast at a long table, a nun silently put a piece of paper by my plate, on which she had written a psalm from the Bible, in red ink. I don't know how much she knew of my tortured soul, but in the midst of my perpetual hopelessness, this simple act touched me deeply.

I prayed a lot while I was there, and read a lot. I liked to sit in silence in the chapel, which had two beautiful stained glass windows, one at the north end, the other behind the altar. Both windows were abstract representations of the fundamentals of Christian doctrine, crafted by Adolfas Valeška, a Lithuanian artist who had established a famous studio in Chicago not long after World War II. If you ever find yourself in the Lincoln Park neighborhood of Chicago, you will thank yourself for making a diversion to the Cenacle Center to see them.

God Loves Me—I Love Myself

On one especially cold January evening at the center in 1967, while I was in my junior year at Loyola, I was in the small anteroom of the chapel. A wood fire was burning in the grate. I was sitting on one of those overstuffed sofas, deep in a trough of bleakness and misery as bad as I had ever experienced. A nun stopped, looked kindly at me, and said something like "Can I do anything to help you?" or "Do you need anything?" I felt that no one could do anything for me, that there was no help for me. I said something like "No, thanks. I'm fine." I was in despair, but I felt deeply that no one could help me.

Then I went into the chapel, knelt at a pew, and gazed at the cross behind the altar. I don't recall what I was saying to God at the time, if anything, but as I gazed at the large crucifix, all of a sudden the whole of the chapel became suffused with a bright golden light, shimmering all over.

And I immediately, joyfully knew with complete certainty that God loved me. That I was not alone. God was within me. I was within God.

I leapt up and ran out the chapel and up the stairs to my room on the second floor. When I was back in my room, I stood still for a moment. I said out loud, "I love myself." The minute the word "myself" came out, I knew I had been transformed. If anyone had asked me up to that point, "Do you love *yourself*?" I might have responded, "I love *her*."

After I descended into hell in the institute, I had always thought or spoken of myself in the third person, as if there were two of me, split somehow. I hadn't been split like this before I went to the institute, but during that experience, and until this moment in the chapel, I had been somehow split.

Then I said, again out loud, "I love myself." I ran downstairs—I was so elated—to call my psychiatrist to tell him. But he wasn't available. And then I *really* knew I'd been transformed, because I didn't give a damn. Normally, if I hadn't been able to talk with him, I would have been distressed. Not this time. I was me again. I had crossed a line, and I knew I would never go back.

After I hung up, the sister who placed a psalm by my breakfast plate happened to walk by. I told her what had just happened. She smiled, held me in her arms, and hugged me. I have no memory of what she said, if indeed she said anything at all. But I knew she understood.

Recently, after reading a description of my experience as reported in *The New York Times,* Sister Rosemary Duncan, one of the nuns at the Cenacle Center, wrote to a friend that she was "struck by the similarity of Marsha's experience to that of our foundress, Saint Therese Couderc, who had a vision of goodness," the one I quoted earlier. Sister Rosemary went on to say, "When Marsha said 'I love myself,' it was a recognition and acceptance of her own goodness. A miracle of grace! As Cenacle sisters, we are privileged to witness miracles of grace in our ministry, perhaps not as dramatic as Marsha's but, nonetheless, very real."* It's a flattering comparison, but all I know is that my enlightenment experience changed my life. I would never go back to being that crazy person again.

---

* Sister Rosemary Duncan to Roger Lewin, July 2013, private correspondence.

Gradually, my personal experience expanded to become a more universal understanding that God is in everyone and everything, loves everyone and everything. It was a recognition of a universal unity, a great oneness, and, as Sister Thérèse said, a universal goodness. Everywhere. Riding the bus in Chicago, I wanted to scream at each person, "Do you know you have God within you?" (I kept my mouth shut for once!)

I told very few people of my experience. Partly because it was a private experience, but also because I didn't know how to describe it. I knew most people would not be able to understand what had happened, and, to be honest, I did not understand it completely, either. What I understood was that something transformative had happened. I did tell Anselm, my spiritual director at the university, and I told Ted Vierra quite a while later.

Ted says that, after that experience in 1967, I told him, "I am going to dedicate my life to helping people who are driven to suicide." The idea thrilled him, he says. I don't remember this, but I suppose it affirmed and reinforced my vow to God.

For years following this experience, while I was still at Loyola, I used to love coming home to my apartment and just throwing myself down on the floor and sinking down into my center and experiencing the joy of God's presence. In those years, I would stack my bedside table with spiritual books and read them nightly for solace. You could always tell my mood by counting how many spiritual books I was reading.

One of the required books in my undergrad classes was *The Phenomenon of Man*, the work of the French paleontologist, philosopher, and Jesuit priest Pierre Teilhard de Chardin. I read the entire book in one night, from midnight to morning. In it, Teilhard de Chardin talks about consciousness and the universe and its inexorable evolution to a point of unity, of oneness that he called the Omega Point, a place of universal consciousness and a convergence with the divine. Echoing Saint Thérèse, Teilhard de Chardin sees in the Omega Point a universal goodness, too. I loved and felt connected to the thinking of these two wonderful minds, Saint Thérèse and Teilhard de Chardin.

The Meaning of Mystical Experiences

Many years later, as I told you in an earlier chapter, I read a book by Bruno Borchert, *Mysticism: Its History and Challenge*. I recognized in his description of mystical experiences exactly what had been my experience that January day in 1967, especially the sense of unity, "a reality that has always been there, though it has been unperceived," as he put it. "It is a reality that is hidden, so to speak, in the ego and in the surrounding real world. It emerges out of the depths of the ego."*

Borchert described mystics as having love affairs with God, just as I had felt I had had a love affair with God. I had always thought that that part of me might be a little bit weird. Who ever heard of a love affair with God? Borchert's statement was very validating.

Mystical experiences are more common than most people suppose. I've learned this through many years of listening to the stories of clients, Zen students, and attendees of the Zen retreats I lead. They may be transformative, as mine was, or more modest, such as experiencing your oneness with nature, with the mountains above, with the ground you are walking on, with the trees above, with the person you love.

Where's the Band?

My psychiatrist at this time, Dr. Victor Zielinski, was associated with the Chicago Institute for Psychoanalysis and was quite famous.

* Bruno Borchert, *Mysticism: Its History and Challenge* (York Beach, Maine: Samuel Weiser, 1994), p. 7.

Because he was an analyst, sessions would normally take place with me lying on a couch and with him sitting out of my line of sight. Not this time. This time, shortly after my enlightenment experience, I told him I wanted to sit facing him. He listened patiently as I told him the whole story. Finally he said, slowly and deliberately, "Marsha, I'm an atheist, so I have no idea what happened to you. But I can tell you this: you don't need therapy anymore." What is amazing is, first, that he was perceptive enough to see this and, second, that he would say it out loud, and not say, "We have to keep going in case you lose this." At the end of our time, I said goodbye and left.

Now, you have to understand how remarkable that simple action of walking out of his office was. I said earlier that the worst moment in a patient's life is when he or she leaves the therapist at the end of a session. Even when a decision has been made that it is time for therapy to come to an end, it is normally done through a long, slow transition period, a tapering-off period. I can spend months going through this process with my clients. That day, leaving Dr. Zielinski for the last time, I felt nothing but joy.

I was standing on Michigan Avenue. I looked up the avenue, then down the avenue, and said to myself, "Where's the band?" It was as if I had truly expected there to be a grand recognition and celebration of my final emergence from hell.

Not really, but that's how profound it felt.

CHAPTER ELEVEN

I Have Proved My Point!

IN MY SENIOR year at Loyola, I slammed into an unfortunate reality that changed my long-held plan of becoming a psychiatrist.

The reality was that psychiatry did not seem to have effective treatments for serious mental disorders, in particular for suicidal individuals. I don't remember how I came to realize this, but I do know that I was completely shocked. I was planning on going to medical school and becoming a psychiatrist. I had already completed all the required courses and had submitted my applications to medical schools.

Looking back, this revelation should not have come as such a surprise. After all, I had been like the people I planned to help. And I had been in a premium institution, not on a back ward in a state hospital where resources were much scarcer. And yet the people at the institute had had no idea what to do to help me. Somewhere in my mind, I knew that fact, and it seems it should have registered sooner.

I Will Become a Researcher Instead

I have a lightbulb memory from this time. I was sitting in philosophy class at Loyola, not long after I had realized psychiatry's inadequacies. My gaze idly shifted between the professor, at the front of class, and the hardwood floor beside me. Out of nowhere, the following thought came to my mind: "If psychiatry has no effective treatments to help the people I want to help, and if I continue along my path and become a psychiatrist, as planned, I will be ineffective my whole life."

This realization appalled me. It was the last thing I could tolerate. I decided, at that instant, that I would become a researcher instead. I would go into clinical research and develop treatments that would be effective with the people I wanted to help.

So, with plan B before me, I would still be going to medical school, but instead of getting an M.D. followed by a specialty in psychiatry, I would focus on research training. I applied to medical schools with this new orientation firmly in mind.

Soon after I had decided on that plan, however, I was having a conversation with Professor Patrick Laughlin, who had first turned me on to the idea of my doing research. Pat said something to the effect of "You know, Marsha, research training in medical school just isn't rigorous enough, not scientific enough. You would be better off doing a doctorate in experimental psych and doing a clinical postdoc internship someplace after that."

This was the more scientific research path: a doctorate in a psychological science, which studies human (and animal) behaviors, brain and mental activities and processes, and mental disorders but does not provide training in hands-on clinical treatments, as medical school would. But I could then step into the treatment milieu by doing an internship in clinical psychology, after I had gotten my doctorate. Okay, I said, plan C it is.

Electing to follow plan C was the easy part. Implementing it was not.

First, as I noted earlier, it looked at one point as if I might not even finish senior year at Loyola, because of an increase in tuition fees. Ron Walker, the department chair of psychology at Loyola, said to me, "Don't worry, Marsha, we'll figure something out." He found me part-time work in the department that paid enough to sustain me until my graduation in 1968. Ron's help was an important lesson: you can make an unbelievable difference in a person's life with simple kindness. I have often been blessed with people being kind to me, helping me when I needed help. I'm not exactly sure why—perhaps because I have always been open to receiving help. I have always tried to live up to the kindness of the professors in my program at Loyola. I am still working on that.

Did My Past Stalk Me?

Because I was one of the top undergraduate students in my year, Loyola had selected me as a nominee for a graduate program at the University of Illinois. No one who had been a nominee at Loyola had ever been rejected by U of I. Friends and faculty told me not to worry about getting in. My friends told me not to bother applying anywhere else. But my top choice for graduate school in social psych was Yale. So I applied to both. What worries did I have? I was finally on my way.

I had very strong references from the faculty who knew me at Loyola. My advisers had read my application letters and believed that if I didn't get into Yale, I would surely get into the University of Illinois. And since U of I was my second choice, there was really no point in spending a lot of money applying to other schools. I had to wait an almost unbearable amount of time to learn my fate, but I wasn't worried.

Perhaps you can imagine how I felt when I got two rejection letters. Okay, maybe Yale. But U of I? When I was a nominee from Loyola? Patrick Laughlin called U of I to find out what had happened. They told him it was my Graduate Record Examination (GRE) scores. I don't remember my scores, but I would think they were solid enough, since none of my advisers thought there would be a problem. Their explanation of weak GREs may have been the truth, or it may have been an excuse. In my applications, I had to explain my missing years and thus my years in a psychiatric institution, followed by a certain period of work and night school. My best guess is that this affected their decision. Being explicit about my history before I had been accepted was a mistake, one that later I would not let one of my students make.

"We'll Take You Here at Loyola"

I was shocked, hysterical. My life's plan appeared to lie in ruins. In Ron Walker's office, I collapsed in a chair, crying, while I told him the news. He was shocked, too. Everyone was shocked. But Ron came to my rescue again. "Stop crying, Marsha. We'll take you here at Loyola."

Patrick Laughlin arranged for me to receive a three-year National Defense Education Act fellowship, which was available because the government was trying to get more women into science. Pat gave me two days to decide. I was also advised to talk to the University of Chicago, on the city's South Side, to see if they had a spot for me.

I had a fabulous interview at the University of Chicago. The professor said he would accept me as a student but did not have the funds to pay for my studies. He said I should stay at Loyola, because they had a scholarship for me. And he said the only thing important in grad school was how good the library was.

I took Pat's offer and stayed at Loyola. I was on my way to becoming a research scientist after all.

My goal was what it had always been: I would get people out of hell. But first I had to learn how to be a researcher. I had a good teacher in Pat. Now that I had enthusiastically embraced being a scientist, I felt sure that I could learn what I needed to know and figure out how to do it.

In Trouble Again

According to my friend Gus Crivolio, who was also in my graduate program, the great majority of students in the psychology graduate programs at that time were male, conservative, and strongly opinionated about how female students should look and behave. Girls were supposed to be demure, sweetly charming, quietly spoken, and not given to expressing strong opinions, especially around men. They should defer to men at all times and in all things. (Sounds like Mother speaking, doesn't it?) I did not fit that mold any better at graduate school than I had at home. Good old Million-Ton Motor Mouth had not been shut down.

I had a number of friends in graduate school, but Gus is the only one I have stayed in touch with. Gus was in clinical psychology, and I was in social psychology. He reminds me about how we quickly became close friends—not dating, but more like colleagues. We talked on the phone a lot and spent a lot of time together, often studying together at my apartment on Albion.

Prior to our preliminary exams to qualify for the PhD, studying at my apartment was a real bonding experience for our whole class. I coached everyone on social psychology, Gus on clinical, another student on learning theory, and so on. There were two days of testing, during which I wore green clothes. (I always dressed in colors that I thought would increase my belief that I would do well on tests, but why green, I'm not sure.) I took tests in social psych, human motivation, learning theory, and statistics, among others.

"Marsha was a very intense person," Gus said recently, stating the obvious to anyone who has met me. "Marsha either didn't know of Loyola men's expectations of how she should behave as a girl, or did know and didn't care. Probably didn't care. She was very vocal. Extremely smart, very quick, and not reluctant to give her opinion and to say when things didn't make sense or weren't supported by logic or data. No matter who it was, she would point out that there was no proof of what they were saying or no logic in it, if that was what she believed. She would go at them in an unrelenting way. She was perceived as being abrasive."

Many faculty were very supportive throughout my time as a graduate student. When I asked the chair if they had been as good to others as they were to me, he said they tried to be, but others did not always accept the help, as I did. At the same time, I did not get along very well with other students. I was a lot older, and according to Gus I was considered odd because I was so strident in my opinions, particularly that data was essential for supporting research outcomes.

I was in the social psychology program, an approach that focused primarily on research on human behavior, with no contact with patients. Just about everyone else was in the clinical program, which focused on mental disorders, and this involved a lot of contact with patients. On one occasion I asked a professor, "Why don't clinical people focus on the importance of research?" (I doubt that question went over very well.) A few of us students were working to coach other students in research and data analysis. We had a rule: we would not help clinical students unless we could see their research plan before they did the research. We did not have a lot of faith in them.

According to Gus, I talked a lot in every class, and the guys in the classes wanted me to shut up (not that I noticed that). I would go on and on, having a dialogue with the professor when I didn't agree. The professors never seemed to mind, and I wanted to make my points. I suspect that my passion interfered with my awareness of anyone else in the room.

I was lonely during most of my time as an undergraduate, and I was lonely again as a graduate student. I had a few friends at school, other students, and faculty who cared for me and looked out for my welfare. But I lived alone and was still lonely, even among friends.

I knew people in my building, including a kind, elderly woman. One time I had a big exam coming, and I was so afraid I would not hear my alarm clock that I asked this kind woman if I could sleep in her closet so she could wake me up on time. I had good reason to worry. Often I wouldn't hear my alarm clocks, and even when I put them on metal plates to make them louder, I still slept right through them. I finally hired a call service to wake me up each morning. But I would pick up the phone while still asleep, so the women with the service would call me back again and again. I felt very close to these women; they were so kind that it was like having another parent.

My Need to Belong

More than anything, at this time in my life I wanted to belong somewhere. I wanted to be important to someone, to count on someone when sadness came my way. I was in contact with my brother Earl, but he had his own family. With the exceptions of Anselm and Ted, my two priest friends, I did not have the experience of being loved. Even though I knew both of those priests loved me, it was a love with boundaries.

The loneliness got to me. I was afraid I would never belong anywhere, I would never be important to someone, I would always be alone. At times I wanted to die. My friend Gus picked up on this. "I had a sense she was often in desperate straits, struggling to keep things contained," he recalls. "But below the surface was a depression, trying to work with it and not let it intrude on her life. She told me something about her time at the institute, but she never told me she had been suicidal during the time I knew her at Loyola."

What happened? What about the spiritual experience that had transformed me? It is true that I had been transformed, but knowing that I would never walk back over the line to the seeming insanity of my previous life didn't mean that I wouldn't still suffer moments of depression. Still, the experience wouldn't destroy me, not anymore. No matter what, I managed to stay functional through whatever came my way. I also continued my relationship with God, praying, "Thy will be done."

The Vietnam War and My Generation's Response

I was in graduate school at Loyola from the years 1968 to 1971. Students of my generation were strongly against the war in Vietnam. Men were in danger of being drafted, but college students with grades of C or above were excluded. My biology teacher gave us weekly exams in which, if you had a C grade, he gave you the questions ahead of time. He didn't want to see his students sent off to war. For guys, just answer all the C questions and you would not be drafted.

In those days, most of us wore anti-war pins on our clothes. After school, I rode my bike across the park nearby. Once I stopped near a group of hippies sitting in the back of a big black truck. Out of the blue, suddenly coming over the hill, the police came racing right at us. I hid behind trees and then rode away as fast as I could to avoid being picked up.

Many times, I found myself marching against all those young men who had not gone to Canada to avoid the draft and who were about to be sent to Vietnam. Yes, we did yell at them! I regret that now.

Dad very much disapproved of my activism. He called me a "Communist," and Loyola a "pinko" school. He wasn't exactly wrong about this, of course. I was for liberation theology and civil rights (as were many of the Jesuits at Loyola, a Jesuit-run university). I used to tell him, "It's your fault, Dad. You shouldn't have given me the Bible to read in the first place. It's all in the Bible." He called the hippies "disgusting," because they had long hair and sideburns, for one thing. I kept showing him that Jesus had long hair, but I never got anywhere with these arguments. Dad thought that if the pope said something, he was right, because he was the pope and we should believe it. He had the same opinion about the president of the United States (who at that time was Richard Nixon). I, of course, disagreed.

From a Freudian Approach to a Behaviorist Point of View

As an undergraduate at Loyola, I was solidly attached to Freudian theory, and I had read everything Freud had written. Freudians often do free association exams with their patients. In fact, I had been given two such exams while at the institute. In graduate school, I asked other students to let me practice free association tests on them. I had a great time with this. I would sit down one-on-one with a student and say, "I am going to do a free association experiment with you. I will say a word and you say immediately what word comes to your mind. For instance, I might say 'Dark,' and you might say 'Night.'" We would do this several times, a classic Freudian procedure.

At the end of the test, I would tell the person something about himself or herself, and typically the person would say something like "You are so right! You are *good*. How do you do that?" It was a riot.

Going into my graduate years, though, I became more and more uncomfortable with Freudian theory, for two reasons: first, from the point of view of science, and second, from my own experience.

At that time, the importance of research data for psychological treatments was not as strong as it is now. I made a number of enemies by constantly asking people for data to back up claims. Before long I thought, "What is the research data for the psychoanalytic model, which is an outgrowth of Freud's theory and treatment methods?"

The psychoanalytic model involves meeting several times a week, the conversation focused on understanding and working with the individual's unconscious. This intervention cannot be tested or proven, because it is based on constructs of the unconscious that are invisible to everyone, and data-free.

Learning Theory: Behaviors Can Be Learned from Others

My area was social psychology, not clinical psychology, so no one in my area paid much attention to different types of psychotherapy. But around the time I entered graduate school, two books were published that transformed my thinking about psychotherapy—and transformed the field of psychology itself.

The first was Walter Mischel's *Personality and Assessment*. Never in my life have I felt so validated in my own thinking. When I read it, I went from being doubtful about psychoanalysis to becoming a behaviorist in no time.

This book swept away the theoretical foundations of the psychodynamic approach. It replaced that approach with a behaviorist outlook. A behaviorist outlook is based on social learning theory, which is what its name implies: that much of an individual's behavior is learned, through observing and mimicking others, rather than being driven by elusive inner forces or as mechanical responses to punishments or rewards.

I memorized almost everything Mischel said. Alas, my memory did not help me when I had to take my prelim exam. The main problem on the exam was to describe Mischel's theory. This was a gift from my professors—they knew how much I loved his ideas. The problem was, it never occurred to me that Mischel had a theory. I saw it as a set of facts—facts after facts. To this day, I am not sure how I passed that exam.

The second book, *Principles of Behavior Modification*, by Albert Bandura, also played a huge role in my becoming a behaviorist. A famous experiment that Bandura ran in the early sixties illustrates social learning very well. It is widely known as the Bobo doll experiment.

Bandura and his colleagues worked with thirty-six girls and thirty-six boys, aged between three and six, from Stanford University's nursery school. (This was, incidentally, the same source population that Mischel drew on in his famous marshmallow experiment a decade later.) The children were divided into three groups, twenty-four in each, half girls and half boys. The children in the first group saw an adult being aggressive to a five-foot-tall inflatable Bobo doll. The adult beat the doll with a mallet, tossed it into the air, jumped on it, and beat it with his fists—all manner of aggressive acts, often accompanied by derisory taunts, such as "Huh, keep coming back for more, do you? Well, take that," followed by another whack. (Bobo dolls keep popping right back up because they have a rounded base and a very low center of gravity.)

I must say, I have felt like a Bobo doll more than once in my life, popping right back up after having been pushed down. That's what happens to girls who have older brothers. It's a very good lesson in life, and this is what I tell my clients: "It doesn't matter how many times you fall; what's important is that you get up."

Anyway, back to the experiment. The kids in the second group saw an adult in the company of a Bobo doll, but no aggressive acts. The last group, a control, saw an adult, with no Bobo dolls in the room.

The goal of the experiment was to monitor the level of aggression in the children when they were later in a room with the same Bobo doll, plus other toys, some aggressive (such as toy guns) and some nonaggressive (such as crayons).

The outcome was exactly what Bandura had predicted. The children who had witnessed an adult being aggressive toward the Bobo doll were themselves aggressive toward it, both in ways they had seen the adult behave and in inventive new ways, such as using the gun on the doll. Children in groups two and three were much less aggressive. Unlike the children in the first group, those in groups two and three had not witnessed any aggressive behavior toward the Bobo doll by the adults; they hadn't learned that aggression was an expected and accepted behavior. Instead, they had seen the adults behave in a peaceful or neutral manner, and this is how the children subsequently behaved. This is the essence of social learning theory.

The children in the first group behaved aggressively based on the behavior of a "model" in their environment. They didn't have to be encouraged or rewarded to do those things; they just did them based on their experience. This is social learning. "Learning would be exceedingly laborious, not to mention hazardous, if people had to rely solely on the effects of their own actions to inform them what to do," Bandura wrote in a later book.

Graduation Day

Up to this point in my studies, I had never written on anything that did not relate to suicide in some way. So it was no great surprise that my PhD dissertation would be on some aspect of suicide, namely on why males are more likely to attempt and succeed at suicide than females are. Unfortunately, no one in the department had done research on suicide, so I was pretty much on my own. But I liked it that way, and they approved all of my work so I could graduate with a doctorate in social psychology. But this absence of review would later come back to hurt me, when the fatal errors in my dissertation (unknown to me at the time) interfered with my getting jobs.

Graduation day finally arrived. Mother, Father, and Aline came up to Chicago. Aline was due to be married in a couple of months, and Mother was consumed with the preparations for the five-hundred-guest gala. Mother had made a dress for me for Aline's wedding, and on the morning of graduation she was more focused on fitting my dress than she was on my getting a doctorate. Oh, Mom, if only you had known me better.

Like many other students in our long train of newly minted doctorates, crimson-and-black gowns flowing behind us, I had on my anti-Vietnam armband. "Pomp and Circumstance" was playing as we entered the arena, and I almost cried with joy. Our group walked in last. I always cry when the same music is played at my own students' graduations.

As I walked to the podium when my name was called, I was ecstatically aware that I had made it. It was like walking in slow motion. I was awash with the realization that I had done it on my own, had kept the promise I'd made to myself when I left the institute almost a decade before. I will never forget the moment when the dean put the beautiful velvet hood of the doctorate over my head. I said to myself, "I have proved my point, showing everyone to have been wrong about me."

CHAPTER TWELVE

Love That Came and Went, Came and Went

ONE OF THE very brightest of all my lightbulb memories comes from my first year of grad school in Chicago. It was a warm evening in the early summer of 1969. I was wearing a short-sleeved blue dress with a ribbed texture. There were about a dozen of us in a dimly lit room, moving slowly about, eyes closed. We had been instructed to hug whomever we might encounter, not just perfunctorily but genuinely, to communicate our state of being. Or something like that.

Anyone who knows anything about the sixties will instantly recognize that I was attending a T-group, sometimes called a sensitivity group or encounter group, led by one of our professors. ("T" stands for "training.") The idea was to raise self-awareness and heighten sensitivity to others. T-group-like gatherings were so popular at the time. Passing fads aside, I would say that there is great value in the spirit of these exercises. One of my heroes, the psychologist Carl Rogers, reportedly described the T-group as "the most significant social invention of the century."

At some point in the proceedings, the leader stopped us and told us all to sit down and then asked each of us to share our experience. When my turn came, I said something like "I don't know who I was with, but it was *wonderful*!" The depth of connection of the heart and the soul left me astonished.

A man in the group was looking at me. He nodded, and I knew it was him. The profound resonance I had experienced had been mutual. As soon as the gathering dispersed, this man—his name was Ed—and I walked down to the lakeshore and talked until the stars were out. When the evening got cooler, we went to my apartment. We talked and talked. I don't remember what we talked about. Doesn't matter, really. It was the *intensity* of our conversation that mattered. Maybe you will know exactly what I mean.

Late in the evening, before he left, Ed said to me, "Marsha, I'm in love with you." We sat there for a few minutes, quietly, and then I responded, "Well, Ed, I'm not in love with you right now, but I'm sure I'm going to be."

I quickly fell deeply, deeply in love with Ed. But there were many complications.

Love Had Found Us Both

Ed was a brother in a Catholic religious order in New York, which meant that, like me, he had taken vows of celibacy, as well as of poverty and obedience to the church. The vows were important to me, as they were to Ed. We talked very seriously about all this and eventually agreed that we would honor our vows, which we did for a long time.

Ed was also studying at Loyola when we met. When his studies were over, he drove back to his order in New York. Missing him already, I followed his trip on a map all the way as we talked off and on by phone.

After he left, he would call me once a day, sometimes more often. Ed was not happy as a brother. It became clear over time that he wanted to be a Catholic priest, which meant he could not get married. But he also wanted me, and I wanted him. My desire to be with him never changed, but Ed's pulled one way and then the other, a torturous process that went on for a long time.

Later, I went to New York to visit Aline. Ed picked me up at the airport. I literally fell into the cab, I was so eager to be with him. In New York, I introduced him to my sister, but I think Ed was somewhat anxious about my being with him in New York, so near his monastery. Once I got home, we continued talking, and later he came to visit me in Chicago. He took an overnight trip with me and my mother, and he and Mother got along fabulously. I told Mother that if Ed asked me to marry him I would say yes—but I also thought that at some point he might want a divorce from me. I loved him, but we were very different. He held to his opinions much more rigidly. He also was much less flexible than me, and he would likely have difficulties with my work schedules, work that I loved. I worked late often, and was also out of town a fair amount. Ed was a more simple guy, wanting to be home at five for dinner.

And Ed wanted to be a priest. The problem was that the Catholic Church forced him to decide between the priesthood and me. I can love God, but it doesn't mean I have to love the way the Catholic Church runs itself, which, by the way, seems to me very sexist.

I finally encouraged Ed to become a priest. It was clear he needed my permission to do so. He did, but he was still torn, and he did not stop calling me. He couldn't stop. Whenever he felt troubled or suffering, he would call me. This was too painful for me. I must have asked him a hundred times to please stop calling me. Every time he called, I could not stay off the phone with him, and it was always painful hanging up.

I Find Love Again, but Different This Time

A few years later, after I took a job in Buffalo, New York, a friend set me up on a blind date. Once again, I fell into a relationship that was immediate and in many ways wonderful—not quite the same as with Ed, but very warm and loving. He was a terrific man, whom I will call Peter. He was older and more mature. I loved him, and he loved me, and we had a wonderful year together. It would be hard to describe how good he was to me. But this time, the relationship was complicated for me.

Peter was an atheist. Where Ed and I had a relationship grounded mainly in the spiritual realm, with Peter, spirituality wasn't an important part of our bond. The bliss we experienced was more of the conventional kind, of each loving the other.

It was very sad, but I knew what I had to do. "We have to talk," I said to Peter toward the end of that wonderful year. "I'm sorry, but our relationship can't go anywhere, because my spirituality is too deep and I can't imagine being married and sharing life with someone who didn't share that." Now that I'm older, I realize that I could in fact make a relationship like this work. But back then it was beyond my imagination.

However, our relationship continued, while I was living in Buffalo, until Ed showed up in my life. Peter knew the whole story, and he was furious that I would see Ed again.

CHAPTER THIRTEEN

A Suicide Clinic in Buffalo

THE SUMMER OF 1971, after I received my doctorate at Loyola, there was a national meeting on suicide in Chicago. One afternoon at the meeting, I wound up with a group of people drinking cocktails and chatting. They were talking shop, the usual scene at such gatherings. I overheard Gene Brockopp, who was head of the Suicide Prevention and Crisis Service in Buffalo, saying he was looking to hire a secretary.

At the time, I needed a job in which I could work with patients. I started talking to Gene and asked him to hire me instead of a secretary. I told him I was better than any secretary he could find, that I needed a clinical internship, and that I would work very hard. "I'm sorry," he said, "I'm not looking for an intern. I'm looking for a secretary." I told him about all the work I had done on suicide. "Look," I said, "every single paper I've ever written has been about suicide. I'll be very good," I persisted. "All you have to do is call it an internship. I'll come for the secretary's salary. I will do whatever you ask me to do." Poor Gene. Eventually he relented and agreed to hire me.

Persistence has pretty much defined me throughout my life: I doggedly pursue my goals, never giving up. Fulfilling my vow to God is an overarching theme, of course. With Gene, I couldn't take no for an answer. It's something I try to inculcate in my clients:

Never give up. It doesn't matter how many times you fall; what's important is that you always get up and try again.

Clinical Outreach

It was Easter of 1972, and I was in church for midnight Mass. Someone from the clinic came to get me, telling me a man was threatening to kill himself. At Gene's crisis center, we did clinical outreach to help people like this. One person was allocated to talk with the family, the other with the suicidal individual—that was usually me.

I found the man in the bathroom of his house, lying on the floor. Apparently his wife had been very emotionally and physically abusive to him; his children had, too. They had drenched him with a hose, or some such crazy thing. He told me he was so miserable he wanted to die, that he was going to kill himself. My goal, as it was in every such situation, was pretty basic. I had to get him to agree, first, that he wasn't going to kill himself just yet and, second, that he would meet me in the office the next morning.

People who are so miserable that they want to die nevertheless often feel constrained *not* to kill themselves, for many reasons. In Buffalo, I did a research study with the goal of compiling a list of such reasons. One way we approached the study was to ask people, over drinks, "If the thought of suicide came into your head right now, why wouldn't you do it?" Not your usual cocktail chatter, but we got all kinds of interesting answers. This study eventually led to the development of what I called the "Reasons for Staying Alive When You Are Thinking of Killing Yourself" measure. We found forty-seven reasons that could fit into at least one of six sets: survival and coping beliefs, responsibility to family, child-related concerns, fear of suicide, fear of social disapproval, and moral objections. (See Appendix, page 341.)

That Easter day, however, the man I was trying to help was in no mood to think of any reason to live. I just kept on proposing ideas. Finally I said, "You know, just because your marriage is a disaster doesn't mean that your life has to be a disaster, too." For some reason, that got through to him. He looked at me and said, almost quizzically, "It doesn't? I hadn't thought of that." "No, it doesn't," I said. That was the turning point for him. We talked for quite a while about finding a path to new possibilities.

He came the next day to his appointment. This is the process known as suicide intervention and constitutes what is known as clinical outreach. If someone is threatening to kill themselves, you go talk with them and find a way for them to see that perhaps they don't want to die after all.

The lesson from that day was very simple but powerful: Never give up when you are trying to help your client. Never give up. I tell this story to my students to this day. It's my mantra.

Working to Change a Person's Behavior

In graduate school, while doing my doctorate, I had switched from a psychoanalytical perspective of dysfunctional behavior to a behaviorist perspective of dysfunctional behavior. These dysfunctional behaviors include, but are not confined to, conditions such as obsessive compulsive disorder, post-traumatic stress disorder, social phobia, personality disorders, eating disorders, self-harm, and so on. Traditional psychoanalysis, then, is a treatment of these disorders based on thoughts—delving into the unconscious to uncover injuries to our inner, unconscious selves that are causing these unwanted behaviors. It is a form of talk therapy.

This contrasts with psychiatry, which has a disease model of dysfunctional behavior. In other words, psychiatry sees an underlying biological (that is, chemical) imbalance as causing the unwanted behaviors. Changing the biology is what counts in psychiatry, and this is achieved through psychoactive medicines. Psychoanalysis and psychiatry are therefore quite different.

The behaviorist approach is yet another approach, also very different from psychiatry and psychoanalysis. It focuses on behavior, on what people do. And rather than change a disturbed person's biology (psychiatry) or change his thoughts (psychoanalysis), the behavior therapist seeks to directly change what the person does, their behavior. In graduate school, as I've noted, I had fully embraced the ideas of Walter Mischel and Albert Bandura on social learning theory. Their idea is that much of behavior is learned from observation of other people's behavior. This implies that behavior can be changed. (If behavior were innate, it would be much more difficult to change.) The work of behavior therapists, then, is to figure out which behaviors are causing problems in their clients' lives, and then work to change them. Behavior therapy is therefore a form of psychotherapy that is based on a behaviorist approach.

Behavior therapy is the behaviorist's tool to help people extinguish unwanted behaviors and ignite wanted behaviors. Behavior therapy may be thought of as a technology of behavioral change, in which assessment and treatment are soundly based on evidence collected in scientific observation. The focus of the treatment is to help clients replace negative behaviors, such as anger and aggression toward others, with positive behaviors, including acceptance and the understanding that there is no good or bad. It is about letting go of the negative in your life and embracing the positive.

Obviously, the therapist cannot go back and change whatever it was that caused the client's negative behavior in the first place. Instead, the therapist needs to understand what is going on in her client's life *now* that is maintaining those unwanted behaviors. Once the therapist identifies the causal factors, there is a possibility of changing them. The most important thing in determining whether therapy is successful or not is whether the client really does want to change his or her behavior.

What I Had Wasn't Enough

I was an avid behaviorist when I arrived at the suicide center in Buffalo. I had the earnest intent of using behavior therapy to work with suicidal people. Up to that point, I had had no clinical training in the *practice* of behavior therapy. I had taught some abnormal psychology at Loyola as a graduate student, because the faculty trusted me. But that was no substitute for clinical training as preparation for working with severely troubled patients.

Very soon I recognized that if I was going to do behavior therapy with these troubled people, I would need to learn the practice of behavior therapy.

I went to the local state university, found a professor who knew something about behavior therapy, and made a deal with him. I would consult with him on suicide cases and give talks on suicide to the faculty at his university. In return, he would supervise me in behavior therapy, teach me the basic approach.

This was a clear improvement, but I was going to need more than just someone to supervise and teach me week by week. I needed some sort of clinical education just as soon as I could. Despite my shortcomings in clinical experience, my claim to fame at the end of my year in Buffalo was that none of the patients had quit therapy and, happier still, none of them had killed themselves.

I Thrive as a Little Fish in a Big Pond—but Not the Other Way Round

The behavioral approach was still novel at the time—this was in the very early seventies—and most of the staff at the Buffalo clinic were suspicious of my zeal for it. I was not shy about saying that behaviorism was the one true way, and I was likely still as socially insensitive as I had been at Loyola.

I thrive in intellectually stimulating environments. I am good at being a little fish in a big pond, but not at being a big fish in a little pond. And at the clinic in Buffalo, I definitely felt like a big fish in a little bowl. I couldn't keep my judgments to myself and, not surprisingly, I was not very popular. My time there was something of a semi-disaster.

Being forthright about my opinions has persisted throughout my career, sometimes causing the same kinds of political and interpersonal storms as at Buffalo. I am grateful for my relationship with Peter, my warm and loving atheist boyfriend in Buffalo, because it helped me weather the friction at the center. It would take me decades to learn to be more politically savvy.

CHAPTER FOURTEEN
....

The Development
of Behaviorism and
Behavior Therapy

BEHAVIOR THERAPY WAS a minority pursuit in the larger realm of
psychotherapy in the late sixties and early seventies. Interest in
the new behavioral approach among clinical psychologists was ris-
ing, but those who wanted to pursue it seriously—that is, embark
on a custom postdoctoral program in behavior therapy—faced a
challenge. Because it was new in the field, no such programs existed
until the mid-sixties.

Leonard Krasner, a psychologist at the State University of New
York at Stony Brook, established the very first such program in the
United States in 1966. This was the same year the Association for
Advancement of Behavior Therapy was founded. (Later, in 2005, it
came to be called the Association for Behavioral and Cognitive
Therapies.)

When behavior therapy programs started to pop up all over the
country, following in the pioneering footsteps of Stony Brook, there
was a difference of opinion among practitioners. On one side, people insisted that psychotherapy should be taught in medical institutions, and certainly not in the ivory towers of academia. Behavior
therapy was a clinical procedure, after all, treating mentally ill pa-

tients. A medically oriented facility was the appropriate venue, this side argued.*

On the other side were those people whose reasoning was as follows. Behavior therapy was a new *approach* to helping people change dysfunctional patterns of behavior. It was not simply a *toolbox* of fully developed techniques and procedures that could be taught in a program and applied in a clinic. Because of the novel approach, the tools of behavior therapy were still being developed and were likely to evolve over time. Therefore, behavior therapy programs should be located in academic environments, this side argued, where research and new approaches were encouraged.

The postdoctoral program in behavior modification that Krasner established at Stony Brook was a model for this second philosophy, solidly based in science and new research. Jerry Davison directed the program from 1967 to 1974, with his close colleague Marvin Goldfried. Jerry had done his doctorate in 1965 at Stanford, with Bandura as his mentor, and had taken coursework with Walter Mischel and Arnold Lazarus. The whole approach at Stanford was firmly based in critical scientific thinking. "At the time," Jerry now says, "that was of overriding importance to me."

Although Marv didn't have the good fortune of being mentored by Lazarus, Bandura, and Mischel, he was equally avid about hewing to a rigorous approach, one backed by experimental test and observation, as he and Jerry developed the tools of behavior modification. Jerry and Marv played a big part in nurturing the development of behavior therapy at a critical time. Together they wrote a book, *Clinical Behavior Therapy*, published in 1976, which became a classic in the field.

In the book they described how behavior therapy was actually

---

* See, for example, Gerald C. Davison, Marvin R. Goldfried, and Leonard Krasner, "A Postdoctoral Program in Behavior Modification: Theory and Practice," *American Psychologist* 25, no. 8 (August 1970): 767–72.

done in practice and the complexities of applying experimental principles in the clinical domain. The book contained every practical detail, not some mechanical or abstract presentation, as was so common in manuals at the time. This would be something of a model for me later on.

Earlier, in 1970, Jerry and Marv had published a paper, together with Leonard Krasner, that described the Stony Brook program: "A Postdoctoral Program in Behavior Modification: Theory and Practice." It very clearly lays out their program's philosophical orientation, namely that behavior therapists recognize that their tools are a work in progress, always under refinement. Critical thinking and the collecting of data were the core of their philosophy. Given my epiphanies during graduate school, when I became passionate about critical thinking and reliance on data, Jerry Davison and Marvin Goldfried's approach resonated with me completely.

CHAPTER FIFTEEN

Fitting In at Last:
Small Fish in a Big Pond

THE PROGRAM AT Stony Brook was designed to give its fellows formal instruction (lectures, seminars, and so on) while also letting them have hands-on experience doing behavior therapy with patients.

The program was meant for people who had obtained their doctorates in some form of clinical psychology, or who at least had done a postdoctoral internship in clinical psychology, but had no behavioral orientation yet. I had obtained my doctorate in social, not clinical, psychology; I hadn't had a clinical internship worth speaking of; and I did have a behavioral orientation. On paper, I did not fit in.

But not fitting in was something of a fact of life for me.

So, in the spring of 1972, I wrote to Jerry and said I very much wanted to work with suicidal people, and I needed to do his program. Was I confident I would get in? I don't remember. But, given my record of applications followed by rejections, it was, I should think, somewhat doubtful.

Nevertheless, I got a letter from Jerry, inviting me to meet him in Stony Brook, in the café at the railway station. Much later, Jerry told me that it was a plus for him that I had come from a scientific rather than a clinical background. It was a distinct minus for his colleagues. He told me recently, "I had to cajole and pressure them. I said to them, 'This woman is very special. She has unusual clinical acumen. She is intellectually exciting. Her solid background in social psychology could be a real plus. I think she'd be great for the program. We could really make a difference in our field by bringing her here. We should take a chance on her.'"

Jerry's intuition was my entry ticket to the premier postdoctoral behavior therapy program in the country, in September 1972. This was absolutely what I needed to go forward with energy, enthusiasm, and confidence and fulfill my vow to God to help other people get out of hell.

An Intuitive Choice, and a Good One

It wasn't until I had been out of the program for quite some time that I realized how special it was. I had been completely ignorant that Stony Brook was the number one program in the country. I had stumbled into exactly what I needed without recognizing my good fortune. Even more bizarre and lucky was that this was the only postdoc program I applied to. As though I somehow knew where I should be, knew what suited my needs best, but without *really* knowing it.

What would have happened had Jerry not seen something special in me, or not acted on it, or not persisted in twisting arms until he prevailed? Would I have been able to achieve what I have? I don't know. It would have been much more difficult, I know that. But happily, for once, I applied for something important and was not rejected.

And, for once, I was going to fit in. Little fish in a big pond.

Learning the New Language of Behaviorism

On the first formal day of the program, in September 1972, that year's fellows gathered in a conference room. There was Steve Lisman, David Kipper, Peter Hoon, and me. Steve had graduated from one of the country's top clinical training programs, at Rutgers, and subsequently worked with the Veterans Administration. David had been director of clinical training at Bar-Ilan University, in Israel, and was developing programs using psychodrama in therapy. Peter had begun a collaborative research program on female sexuality. And then there was me. I was the only one with limited clinical experience.

Steve and I arrived a little early, and we chatted. Steve remembers that I thought I was getting in over my head. "Marsha said to me, 'Here are all these smart postdoctoral guys, and I'm going to have to struggle to keep up with all of you,' " he said recently. "But I told her I was a little nervous, too." We were both right to be.

Jerry outlined what lay ahead for the four of us. It would include at least twelve hours a week of one-on-one sessions with undergraduate clients who had a variety of behavioral problems, such as refusal to eat, deficits in social skills, relationship problems, obesity, depression, post-traumatic stress, drug addiction, and so forth. There would be occasional emergency cases, too, such as suicide threats or psychotic episodes.

The aim of the various clinical sessions, Jerry explained, was to provide us with, in the words of his and Marv's 1970 paper, "a working and living laboratory to try out a variety of behavioral approaches and techniques." We would learn about these approaches and techniques through supervision and more formal instruction. We each would have an hour a week with a mentor during which we could bring up whatever issues we might be struggling with or were curious about. There would be a weekly seminar with Jerry, sometimes supplemented by visits from leading researchers in our field. We would have opportunities to sit in therapy sessions with clinical faculty and observe sessions through a one-way mirror. And much, much more. I would also take the clinical courses I had never had, along with Stony Brook graduate students.

The goal of all this, Jerry explained, was for us to be an active part of the practice and development of behavior therapy that defined the Stony Brook program. And he finished by saying, "We just want you at first to keep doing what you're doing, because you're already good, and we know you're good. As the year progresses, your clinical work will change from what you are already familiar with to the cognitive behavioral therapy that you're going to be learning."

After the meeting, I said to Steve, "I'm really terrified now, Steve." He said, "I am, too." I knew we would be friends for life.

Teaching About Suicide

We were also encouraged to break out projects of our own. One thing I did was co-teach a course on suicide for graduate students. Another was to become a suicide intervention counselor in the community. I established a relationship with the Stony Brook police, just as I had in Buffalo. Steve remembers one particular incident:

> Marsha asked me if I would be interested in learning more about suicide. I said yes. One night she called me and said, "Steve, there's a fellow who is holed up with a gun in his bedroom in town, says he's going to kill himself. I'm going to help him. Do you want to come with me?" I said, "Sure, I'd love to."
>
> Marsha picked me up in her car and we drove to the house. The wife let us in. We went to the bedroom where the man was. Marsha walked calmly over toward him and sat next to him. She then said, in a very reassuring, comforting voice, "Do you want to give me your gun?" She used his name, but I don't recall what it was. The man simply said, "Yes." And handed the gun to Marsha.

Marsha turned round and gave the gun to me and said, "Can you unload this please, Steve." I took it from her. She turned back to the man and began talking with him, doing her suicide intervention thing, getting him to come to a point where he didn't want to kill himself, apparently completely at ease.

I, meanwhile, was horror-struck. I had never held a gun in my life and had no idea what to do. In the movies, you pull something and a bullet pops out. That's about all I knew about it. I was in a total sweat. I had no notion of what I was supposed to do. I was afraid I would shoot myself in the foot. I think Marsha was completely oblivious to my predicament. Eventually I thought, "I know this isn't protocol, but I've got to interrupt and ask how to unload the damn gun." All I remember is somehow shooting it into the wastebasket, putting a bullet hole in the wastebasket.

That's not protocol, either.

Those Scars Again

I had long since learned to be discreet about my history, my time at the Institute of Living, particularly in professional environments. And I tried to keep the scars on my arms and legs out of sight as best I could. There were many months of the year when seasonal clothing made that easy, but it didn't work all the time, of course. I'm sure some people must have noticed, but no one said anything to me.

Steve Lisman recalls, "One day I saw her arms, and something told me, 'Don't pursue this.' I knew that something had happened. I could see they were cuts or cigarette burns. It was the first time I had seen arms like that. I thought it wasn't my business to ask about it. So I kept quiet." Sweet Steve.

And despite the close relationship I had with Jerry, his love for me, mine for him, I kept quiet. I thought it wise not to.

A couple of years after I had finished at Stony Brook, I felt I had to tell Jerry. I had become good friends with Jerry's then-wife and was visiting them in Port Jefferson, staying over at their house. As Jerry remembers it:

> We were sitting together talking, after dinner, and at some point Marsha said to us, "There's something I'd like to tell you. But I need to ask you to keep it confidential." And I said, "Marsha, you can tell us anything." My ex said, "Yes, Marsha, anything." I had no idea what she was going to say. And then she told us this story: the Institute of Living and the jumping off of chairs and cutting and hitting her head. I mean, it was just incredible. I was completely surprised. Now, I had indeed noticed some scarring on her arms, but not a lot. But I hadn't attributed any significance to it. I just was overlooking it. So when she told us the story, I was amazed, because she had seemed so fit psychologically. She was a rock in the best sense of the word, strong. So, yes, I was surprised. But then it began to make sense: her interest in suicide, her subsequent interest in borderline personality disorder. There's that old saying, "We study what pains us."

Dreaming Dreams

On a professional and personal level, and aside from the brief interlude when Ed reappeared and then disappeared from my life, I was entirely happy. My friendships sustained me, and I greatly enjoyed the many, many times Steve and I would find time to chat. Here's Steve's recollection of one such occasion.

> We often sat together and talked about everything, Marsha and I. We talked about the experience of being in this amazing program, of how intellectually stimulating it was to be in this cauldron of new thinking. We talked about the leading figures in the field we were privileged to meet. We talked about our aspirations. One day Marsha looked at me, in that intense way she has, and said, "I don't know what it is going to be, Steve, but somehow I have to

develop a grand theory about clinical work that will help us think about things differently." My attitude was "Yeah, right, like all the rest of us." A bit cynical, you could say.

I mean, I didn't know she was going to go on and develop something as big and important as DBT.

A Parting Gift to Jerry

At the end of our one-year fellowship, our group decided to give Jerry a gift. A few months earlier, Jerry had read a quote from *Letters to a Young Poet,* by the Bohemian-Austrian poet Rainer Maria Rilke, and he had given copies to us. We thought the sentiment expressed was so pertinent to our work as therapists:

> Do not believe that he who seeks to comfort you lives untroubled among the simple and quiet words that sometimes do you good. His life has much difficulty and sadness. . . . Were it otherwise he would never have been able to find those words.*

We gave Jerry a framed calligraphic rendition of the quote (I was the designated calligrapher), which he found very moving. We also made copies for each of us postdocs. Mine is still in my therapy office. Each year at commencement, I give framed copies to my graduating students and fellows.

---

* Rainer Maria Rilke, *Letters to a Young Poet,* trans. M. D. Herter Norton (New York: Norton, paperback, 1993).

CHAPTER SIXTEEN

What Have I Done?

ABOUT HALFWAY THROUGH the postdoctoral program at Stony Brook, I began to apply for jobs. I applied to every position I might have a chance at that was also in a city, anywhere across the country.

I was not overwhelmed with offers, let me put it that way.

By April I still hadn't gotten a job, and it was getting late for receiving an offer for the next academic year. Jerry was very kind and reassuring. "Don't you worry, Marsha," he said gently. "You are going to get a job."

Not the Best Environment for Me

I was asked to interview at the Catholic University of America, in the northeast section of Washington, D.C., an edgy neighborhood at the time. The campus is dominated by the Basilica of the National Shrine of the Immaculate Conception, the largest Catholic church in the country.

For my interview process, I elected to give a talk on suicide. Very few people know anything at all about suicide, and many find it fascinating, so that was an advantage for me. By this point I had become extremely good at lecturing about suicide.

I believe that my deep compassion for these unhappy people comes across, and it makes people want to work with me. I am much more likely to be hired by a prospective employer if I am seen as a good clinician, someone who works effectively with patients, rather than as a good researcher, someone who is able to get solid, evidence-based results through research. I find that a little odd, because I think I am both. Anyway, I was offered the job, mainly on the strength of that presentation.

But I wasn't aware of what I was stepping into. When I went for the interview, the director of clinical training had been away and had left instructions for the faculty: *Hire someone, but do not hire a behaviorist.* The department was deeply entrenched in the psychodynamic worldview. Behaviorism was, if not anathema, then at least a foreign language to them. I think it must have been the power of my suicide lecture that swept these considerations aside, because they did hire me.

Right away, I was expected to teach a course on psychodynamic therapy. I simply could not do it, and I told them so. They then said, "Well, how about a course that integrates psychodynamic therapy and behavior therapy?" I told them I just could not do that, either.

I was shocked to realize just how deeply the department was focused on traditional psychodynamic thinking. To me, a behaviorist, it seemed so old-school. But for once, and uncharacteristically, I kept my mouth shut about this. Unfortunately, I did not keep my mouth shut about how wonderful Stony Brook had been. I would often talk about the terrific things Stony Brook did to train students, with the clear implication that Catholic should do the same. Did I say that outright? No. Did I imply it? Yes. Did that help my cause? No. I must have been a good teacher, though, because I got excellent student evaluations.

I started to get grants for research projects, which was the beginning of a wonderful, long-term relationship with staff at the National Institute of Mental Health, beginning with Stephanie Stolz, who ran a special program on applied behavior analysis. Pretty soon I was bringing in more grant money than anyone else in the department and publishing more than anyone else.

One of the research projects was on assertiveness. I had a model that understood suicide as a cry for help—that suicidal people can't get the help they need. Learning assertiveness is learning to be effective in the world, to be able to get what you need through effective behavior, while at the same time maintaining good relationships and maintaining your self-respect. If I could teach suicidal individuals how to be assertive, how to be effective, they would then be able to get the help they need.

Assertiveness: A DBT Skill That Helps Interpersonal Effectiveness

Assertiveness became one of a suite of DBT skills that enable people to be effective in their interactions with others. These skills equip individuals with the ability to achieve their goals while at the same time not alienating the other person or losing their self-respect. Assertiveness skills are change skills. (You will see later that DBT skills fall into one of two major categories: acceptance skills and change skills.)

Assertiveness skills are also the social skills you need to make new friends, maintain existing friendships, and recognize when a relationship is toxic and act on that. These skills come naturally to us, some more so than others. It is part of being the social creatures we are. But, no matter how good we are, practice always makes for greater effectiveness, and being effective in our relationships is the goal of interpersonal effectiveness skills.

Being assertive, for instance, helps you make clear to others what your immediate goals are. It is about being effective, doing what works. For instance, with a boss you might say, "I would like a raise. Can you give it to me?" Or with a spouse: "We simply do not have the money for the vacation we planned this year." It is about being unambiguous in what you say and in your relationships with others.

One of my favorite interpersonal effectiveness skill sets, which I developed later, at the University of Washington, and one that clients appreciate a lot, is DEAR MAN. (I love acronyms.) The goal of this set of skills is to be as effective as possible in achieving a desired objective. You will see what I mean when you read the following:

DEAR MAN stands for "describe, express, assert, reinforce, (stay) mindful, appear confident, negotiate."

Describe the Situation:

Begin by briefly describing the situation you are reacting to. This ensures that the other person is oriented to the events that led to the request.

> *Example:* "I've been working here for two years and have not gotten a raise, even though my performance reviews have been very positive."
>
> *Example:* "I have gone over our budget and our outstanding debt very carefully to see whether we do or do not have enough money for a vacation."

Express Clearly:

Express clearly how you feel or what you believe about the situation. Don't expect the other person to read your mind or know how you feel.

> *Example:* "I believe that I deserve a raise."
>
> *Example:* "I am very worried about our current finances."

Assert Wishes:

Don't beat around the bush, never really asking or saying no. Be clear, concise, and assertive. Bite the bullet and ask or say no.

Example: "I would like a raise. Can you give it to me?"
Example: "We simply do not have the money for the vacation we planned."

Reinforce:

Explain to the other person that they, too, will benefit if they agree with what you are asking or saying. At a minimum, express appreciation after anyone does something related to what you are asking or saying.

Example: "I will be a lot happier and probably a lot more productive if I get a salary that reflects my value to the company."
Example: "I think we will both sleep better if we stay within our budget."

(Stay) Mindful:

Be persistent in what it is you are asking for, saying, or expressing your opinion about. Do not be distracted or diverted into discussions about other topics. Keep going down the same path, in a mellow tone of voice.

Appear Confident:

Use a confident tone of voice, and display a confident physical manner and posture, with appropriate eye contact. No stammering, whispering, staring at the floor, retreating, saying you're not sure, or the like. It is perfectly normal to be nervous or scared in a difficult situation; however, acting nervous or scared will interfere with effectiveness.

Negotiate:

Be willing to give to get. Offer and ask for alternatives.

> *Example:* "What do you think we should do? What can we do here? How can we solve this problem?"

Can you imagine yourself going through these steps, with a specific objective in mind? I'm sure you can.

Check the Facts

During this time at Catholic University, as I was thinking about teaching assertiveness to suicidal individuals, I experienced a shift in my worldview. At Stony Brook, I readily absorbed the notion that people's behaviors are quite heavily influenced by their cognition, their thinking. This implies that people's problems might be in their *thinking* rather than in their *behaviors*. At Catholic, I came across the work of Arthur Staats, specifically his social behaviorism theory, which argues that cognition is just another form of behavior. Everything is behavior, and if you change one thing, you change everything—thinking, acting, everything. Everything is connected to everything else. Everything is one, which is very Zen-like, really. It had a big influence on me.

So what shifted in me? First, I did not give up the notion that changing some thoughts can be helpful. If you are too afraid to go outside because you think a tornado is coming, and then you hear on the radio that the tornado is three states away, you will likely change your thinking, your fear will go down, and you will be willing to walk outside to get in your car. How did that happen? You got new information that changed your behavior. In DBT, getting information is the skill we call "check the facts." In the example I just gave, if you check the weather information and discover the tornado is safely far away, you then change your behavior, and you'll be willing to go outside.

Opposite Action

But sometimes the emotion (fear) doesn't go away, even when the facts objectively indicate that there is no danger. We have all had this experience. Children have a fear of a monster in their room. We have a fear of being assertive and asking for what we want. We fall off a horse and we're too afraid to get back on. A nurse fears that a dead person might rise up in bed if she sits in the room with the corpse. Sometimes all the facts in the world have no effect. Our fear is still there.

Staats's theory says: Change your behavior and you will change your emotions. (Fear is an emotion.) When the facts say that what you are afraid of is not actually dangerous, the trick is to do just the opposite of your fear. Parents walk their child into the room; we get up our courage and assert ourselves with a person who is likely to respond well; you get back on the horse that is unlikely to throw you again. Sit in the room with the corpse to absorb the information that dead people don't spontaneously rise up and your fear will go down.

Much later, I called this process "opposite action," an emotion regulation skill for dealing with fear. (Opposite action is a change skill.) In opposite action, you force yourself to do the very thing you don't want to do. Saying to yourself, "People do like me" or "I'm not fat" doesn't really change how you feel. You have to *act*. I had a client whose problems mostly involved hating her own body. Telling her that her body was just fine didn't help. I had to get her to act differently, to act as if she had a beautiful body. When she did, she carried herself in public with assumed poise and confidence, and she felt beautiful. It worked. It is like that mantra "Fake it till you make it." It is also the equivalent of Aristotle's notion that acting virtuous will make you virtuous.

Maybe you are afraid to go to parties because you think people will disapprove of you or even be hostile to you. So you don't go. With opposite action, you force yourself to go to the party and be as present as you can. You don't skulk in the corner and look no one in the eye or talk with no one. Nor do you have to try to be the heart and soul of the party. You do what you can. There is usually some-one at a party who is happy to have small talk with you. You will discover that, although people might not love you to death, they will not be openly hostile to you. If you keep going to parties, you will gradually become less afraid as you discover that what you feared doesn't actually happen. Opposite action takes practice.

Repeat opposite action as often as you can, over and over, every chance you get. Some of the time, opposite action works immedi-ately. But most of the time you have to practice a lot before the emo-tion you are trying to control (fear, for example) abates.

I developed a line that encapsulates this new worldview:

You can't think yourself into new ways of acting; you can only act yourself into new ways of thinking.

CHAPTER SEVENTEEN

Finding a Nurturing Community

AT CATHOLIC, I really had nothing in common with the faculty, and I felt like the outsider again. Before long I felt myself slipping back into the muck of self-doubt and feelings of inadequacy. It was painful, especially after the year of personal and professional joy at Stony Brook. I was back to living alone, Ed was still gone, and God was often missing.

I had a rather elegant apartment close to Dupont Circle. Each day, I went to a church nearby for contemplative prayer. I often noticed another group there, which in retrospect must have been Zen. I thought it was weird: they were sitting there with their eyes open. In contemplative prayer, you always have your eyes closed.

My prayer at that time was to slowly breathe in and out, and in my mind I would walk down a staircase to the center inside of myself, which was God. Much of the time, although I was so earnestly searching, searching, searching for God, simultaneously I had enormous contact with God. Off and on, it was as if God was talking to me. It wasn't me *thinking* about God talking to me. It was so real. I read recently that people who spend a lot of time in prayer change the way they use their minds. "The prayer warriors said that as they became immersed in prayer, their senses became more acute," writes Tanya Marie Luhrmann, an anthropologist at Stanford who has studied people in prayer. "Smells seemed richer, colors more vibrant. Their inner sensory worlds grew more vivid and more detailed, and their thoughts and images sometimes seemed as if they were external to the mind."*

Sounds plausible to me. In any case, I knew that God was speaking to me at that time, even as I was seeking God.

A Search Rewarded

One of the first things I did after getting to D.C. was search for a Catholic community that would be congenial to my own liberal views. The Newman Catholic Student Center was beyond perfect for me, and it was just a mile south of my apartment, an easy walk.

The George Washington University (GWU) Newman Center is one of numerous Catholic ministry centers at non-Catholic universities around the world. Members of the center were mostly Catholic, but students of other denominations went there, too, as did people from the local community, producing a rich diversity of views and backgrounds.

In the early seventies, the Newman Center had a reputation for being super-liberal. "The university itself was the center for a lot of social movements of the time," recalls Jack Windermyer, who was appointed chaplain in 1968. "The anti-war movement, the peace movement, the people's movement, the poor people's campaign, and so on. The center reflected this prevailing mood of liberalism and compassion."

One of the things I loved most about the center was the dialogue homilies, where Jack or his assistant chaplain, Allanah Cleary, would talk with a religious slant on an issue of the day, such as the peace movement, Vietnam, the environment, or, more generally, the meaning of love and what we mean by God. Then, anyone could go up to the dais and add to the conversation. Very participatory.

* T. M. Luhrmann, "Is That God Talking?," op-ed, *New York Times*, May 2, 2013, p. A23.

For a woman, used to being muzzled in the church, it was quite extraordinary. It is hardly the Catholic Church most people would recognize today. But those were special times, and I loved it all.

I also deeply appreciated the people who were the center's community, including many women who quickly became fast friends, some of whom still are. Allanah, Mary Harrington, and others whose names have long since slipped from this fragile memory of mine. I have these women to thank for helping me weather the emotional turbulence that had reentered my life.

"I don't ever remember being with Marsha in the community where we worshipped without a smile on her face," Allanah now says. "She was always smiling." Allanah tells me I was ever present at the dialogue homilies, offering my point of view. Of course I was. "Marsha would always have something to say, a question—she always asked the question that nobody else asked," Allanah says. But she saw the other side of me, too. "Marsha always saw the light, the brighter part of things. But also she was always weighted down by this total blackness that she knew."

I was close enough with Allanah that I let her into my history. She was the only person, at that time, whom I told about my past. "Marsha couldn't say anything to her colleagues at Catholic; she'd be out of there so fast had they known," Allanah says. "And she really knew she could trust me. My heart just broke for her so many times. And I would just hold her. What else can you do? Marsha provided a friendship that protected both of our privacies."

Allanah is a most wonderful human being. Before joining the center as assistant chaplain—the first female chaplain in the place— she had spent some years in Africa, a member of the Missionary Sisters of Our Lady of Africa, more popularly known as the White Sisters, for obvious reasons. "I worked in villages in Malawi, planting and harvesting groundnuts, teaching Bible, if you could," she says. "I was trying to learn the language. Fixing motorbikes. Mudding huts. Anything that needed to be done. I had a Canadian passport and could drive a car, so being a driver was another thing I did."

The two of us would often spend time in my apartment, which was something of a sanctuary for Allanah, because she was always in demand at the center by someone needing her help or advice. She told me stories about Malawi, the terrible drought and terrible suffering she saw and experienced. It often tested her faith. "I would go out and just scream at the sky," she says. "I mean, 'If anybody can send us a drop of rain, if you're up there, we're here. We need rain. We're in droughts for three years. People are dying all around us.' We felt like we were dying ourselves. And no relief."

We found time to play, too. I had a secondhand convertible, and Allanah has happy memories of trips we took. "We would go zipping along the Blue Ridge Mountains of Virginia," she says. "Or go to the beach. One year, at Christmastime, Marsha and I decided to go down to Rehoboth Beach, in Delaware, for a couple of days. There was a hotel there that had an ice-skating rink. I'm from Nova Scotia, so I was dying to ice-skate. Marsha put on the skates, and I don't think she had ever skated in her life. She could hardly move. It was hysterical, but I was so afraid she would fall and hurt herself. All I have of that time is a picture she took of me skating. I don't have a picture of her, because I didn't have a camera; I never had anything. Marsha had everything. She was very into sports cars."

Seeking Support Is a Positive Skill

My active decision to find a community where I would feel supported emotionally and spiritually was exactly what DBT encourages clients to do. Some people believe that "needing" friends is a sign of weakness or emotional dependence, and that people should be able to be happy alone. Well, finding happiness and emotional support in solitude might work for some. But for most human beings, being part of a group of "friendly others" is vital to their emotional and spiritual health. Achieving that state can require effort and social skills. And it's important not just for those who struggle with behavioral problems. It is important for all of us.

I Follow My Vow of Poverty

After a few years in my elegant Dupont Circle apartment, I decided it was too grand for me, given my faith and my vow of poverty. "Elegant high ceilings, white walls, with well-placed art" is how Allanah remembers it. "Her house was always perfect. She had somebody who would come in and clean for her, which I thought was the ultimate thing in the world." But I decided I should live in something more modest. I moved to a small row apartment near American University, still in D.C. but no longer downtown. It was a small one-bedroom with a tiny kitchen, teensy porch, tiny backyard.

The Newman Center was more like a four-mile bike ride now, but I kept going. It was my community of support and love. It was my community of giving. For much of my time in D.C., I helped street people, women mostly, a lot of whom had mental health problems. I talked with them—therapy, really—tried to get them oriented, helped them find a place in a shelter. It was also my community of searching for God. The homilies almost always involved God, how we see God in the events around us, how he/she manifests in our lives and the lives of others. I was back to my relentless search. "God, where are you?" I would ask, like a terrier dog, never wanting to let go. I think Allanah found this a little irksome. Like "Okay, let's talk about something else, shall we?"

Mary Harrington was more patient with me. She was a seeker, too, though more relaxed about it. "My notion of God was a sea of light, and that was it," she said recently. "I always had the sense of the immanence of God—here, now, very concrete, very ordinary, in the ordinary moment. Marsha and I talked about that kind of thing." We were both seeking the same thing, but we were coming from different places.

Distress Tolerance Skills

As part of the community at the Newman Center, I had also become very close friends with Ann Wake and her husband. When, on one memorable occasion, my apartment erupted into flames, they took me in for the night. In my tiny new apartment, my neighbors had come banging on my door, yelling that I had set their apartment on fire by not turning off the electricity on my back porch that night. Wrong! Later, I won the battle when I proved that the fire had started in their apartment.

I learned two important things from this fire. First, when they tell you to keep important papers low, not high, do it. Everything more than ten inches high in my apartment was covered with black soot.

Second, when you are overwhelmed by what is happening in your life, it can be very hard to do what you need to do, even though you *know* what you need to do, even though you have the ability to do it. When Aline called me the next morning to see how I was doing, I said, "I'm fine." What I was actually doing was sitting on my couch, reading *Time* magazine. I had done nothing to cope with the soot, burns, and mess of my apartment. I was too overwhelmed by the fire to think straight. This happens to people often. This is what being overwhelmed means. What I needed was a skill to calm down my mind. I needed certain skills that I later developed for DBT to help people tolerate distress, often when facing some kind of crisis. (These are what I call TIP skills, which I will describe shortly.)

In the mental health arena, the focus is on changing distressing events and circumstances. That seems like the natural thing to do, doesn't it? But to approach problems more from a religious or spiritual perspective by learning to *tolerate* distress can be just as effective, and more readily achieved. This is my approach. An important distinguishing factor of DBT is its emphasis on learning how to tolerate and accept distress.

Why take this path? Two reasons. First, pain and distress are part of life; they cannot be entirely avoided or removed. A person who cannot accept this will find herself in more pain and more suffering in the long run. Second, in the larger context of life and how you might want to improve yourself, learning how to tolerate and accept distress is part of that general change toward self-improvement.

Tolerance and acceptance of reality are not the same as approval of that reality. They are about accepting life as it is in the moment. You will see, later in this book, that *acceptance* is a very important theme in DBT, one that distinguishes it from standard behavior therapy, which, as I said earlier, is a technology of *change*.

Four TIP (Distress Tolerance) Skills

When we become highly emotional because of what is happening in our environment, we often feel overwhelmed and are unable to take the actions we should in order to deal with the situation—like me when I had that fire in my apartment. I developed four TIP skills that help people damp down their emotions when facing a crisis. These are physical actions designed to reduce the level of arousal in the nervous system. They are: temperature manipulation, intense exercise, paced breathing, and paired muscle relaxation. (Okay, so there are two P skills, which doesn't quite fit the acronym.) The goal of TIP skills is to change body chemistry in a way that reduces emotional arousal, among other things, which is the goal of tolerating distress. It works very quickly. I will describe just two of the skills here.

The intense exercise skill is simply engaging in an aerobic activity of your choice—running around the block or jumping on a trampoline, pedaling an exercise bike, using a StairMaster, anything that gets your heart rate up to around 70 percent of the maximum for your age—for about twenty minutes. Research shows that doing this increases positive emotions. You feel better about yourself and your circumstances, and you are better able to do whatever is necessary to start fixing your challenging circumstances.

Paced breathing involves finding a spot to sit comfortably and then very deliberately breathing slowly and deeply, counting the breaths as you go: breathe in (one), breathe out (two), breathe in (three), breathe out (four), and so on up to ten, and then start over. Aim for about five in/out breaths a minute. Breathing in activates your sympathetic nervous system and increases arousal, while breathing out activates your parasympathetic nervous system, decreases arousal, and calms you. The key is to take longer to breathe out than to breathe in: five seconds for the inhale, seven seconds for the exhale. Done for ten minutes, it produces a significant calming effect that can help you cope with hard-to-control emotions and do the things you need to do in the moment. For me, it was to start cleaning up the mess caused by the fire in my apartment, rather than just sitting inertly in the midst of it all. It could be getting your life together after a painful loss of some kind, such as a job or a girlfriend or boyfriend.

I will tell you about more DBT skills as they arise in my story.

CHAPTER EIGHTEEN

Like a Fish on a Hook

Not long after I moved to Washington, Ed called me out of the blue. "I have to see you, Marsha," he pleaded over the phone. "I can't be away from you." (Remember Ed? Love of my life, elusive Ed?)

I'd had other calls like this from Ed in the previous few years, but I had managed to resist, wanting to protect myself from more emotional hurt. Not this time. I was still in love with him, even though I didn't want to be. I wasn't talking to anyone about Ed except Aline, and she constantly assured me that Ed and I would be back together one day. There was no one to persuade me to say "*No!* Don't do this!" I told Ed he could come. He seemed so relieved, so happy. And I think I must have been happy, too, and let myself look forward to seeing him. He was going to drive down from New York to D.C. the next week.

On an Intermittent Reinforcement Schedule

By now I was firmly in what psychologists call an intermittent reinforcement schedule, like a fish on a hook. It is the same psychological force that keeps people sitting in front of slot machines for hours on end, essentially addicted. If the machines paid out little reasonable sums of money fairly regularly, players would quickly get bored, but the possibility of a jackpot at any given moment keeps them hooked. It is also why people often stay in abusive relationships. "Maybe it will be different this time." And it is why I relented with Ed and said, "Okay, come down." Maybe it would be different this time. Maybe I'd hit the jackpot.

I was waiting for him to arrive, sitting in my apartment on Dupont Circle, in something of a state of tension, I'm sure—nervous yet excited, too. The phone rang. It was Ed. He was just the other side of Baltimore, less than an hour away. "I can't do this," he almost cried. "I'm going back." "Devastated" doesn't begin to describe how I felt.

Somehow, I got myself to my brother Earl's house; he lived in Baltimore. I remember standing at the door, crying, telling him what had happened. Earl hugged me, calmed me down until I stopped crying. Then he said something to me that I have never forgotten—so wise, and so soothing. He looked intently at me and said, "Marsha, you are really lucky, because you know that you are capable of loving someone else. You know you are capable of great love. And many people don't know that about themselves." That was so profound that I was able to let go of the agony that had gripped me. It is still one of the best things anyone has ever said to me.

The First Tragedy

Ed would call me again not long after I moved to Seattle in 1977. (You will read about that journey in the following section.) This time Ed's story was different. "I never told you this," he began, "but when I moved to New York twelve years ago, I met someone there. I would have told you earlier, but friends advised me against doing that, because it would hurt you too much." He paused.

What was "I can't live without you" and "I need to see you" all about? I didn't actually say that, but that was what I felt. Finally he said, "And I'm thinking of marrying her, but I want to come see you." He was leaving the priesthood so he could marry her, whereas with me, it had been that he had to leave me so he could stay in the priesthood.

I was in shock at the call. My immediate response was to tell him he could come only if there was a possibility that he would still choose me. "If you're just coming to get my permission to marry her, then no, don't come. Is there a chance you will want to stay with me?" He told me there was, so I said okay.

When he arrived, he fell into me and then me into him, as if we were still in love. He whispered how much he loved me; I'm sure that was true. He stayed a week at my house. It was hell, again, because as the days passed it became ever clearer what my rational self probably knew but my emotional self wanted to deny: that he simply needed my permission to marry her. Alas, that was exactly what he needed.

I finally said, "Ed, you have to marry her." He said, "You think so?" I said, "Yes, you were not born to be a celibate Catholic priest. This is a mistake. And you can do as much good for the world married as not. You need to be married. Clearly, you've been involved with her and you've not been involved with me in any serious way for a long time. She is a nun and you are a priest. You have so much in common, you are in the same church; I am sure many people love you both. You simply should do this. It is time to leave the priesthood and marry her." The last thing he said to me was "Marsha, I love you, and I will always love you." I'm sure he meant it. I let him off at the airport and never saw or talked with him again. He wrote me, but I never responded. I just could not do it.

Ed, the love of my life, now out of my life. Forever.

The Second Tragedy

Every summer for the past twenty years or so, I've flown to Cape Cod, Massachusetts. My principal reason for being there is to teach a weeklong or longer workshop on DBT for the New England Educational Institute, to an audience consisting mainly of therapists but also anyone who happens to be interested in what I am teaching. We stay in a very large house with many bedrooms and outside patios, always right on the water. Enough for all my friends and relatives. Over time, the number of people who come has expanded greatly. The workshops are in the morning, which leaves the rest of the day free to sit in the sun, read books, enjoy one another's company, and go into town.

Aline sometimes comes. Cousin Nancy (our fabulous sandwich maker) comes every year. We usually finish the day with a dinner for ten to a couple dozen—simple food collectively cooked, and wine, of course, and good conversation. It's like a salon, really. I always look forward to this week on the Cape. It's my annual vacation.

The topic for the 2010 workshop was "Mindfulness, Radical Acceptance, and Willingness: Teaching DBT Acceptance Skills in Clinical Practice." Mindfulness and radical acceptance are the core DBT skills. You will learn a lot more about them as we continue on my journey.

This year, Aline was coming. I always love spending time with her. It was early evening on Saturday and I was in my bedroom, getting ready to go downstairs to have a glass of wine with Nancy and everyone else who was getting ready for dinner. Aline should have been there by now, but she wasn't. I wasn't too concerned, because she's not always on time. My cellphone rang. It was Aline. I asked if she was on her way. She immediately said, "Marsha, I have to tell you something." "What?" I asked. "Ed has died. He had an unexpected heart attack."

I think I must have dropped the phone, I don't know. I was completely stunned and immediately staggered to the dresser, holding myself up. At the same time, I began to involuntarily scream at the top of my lungs, greatly alarming people downstairs. My cousin Nancy ran up the stairs and burst into the room, not knowing what had happened to me. "Stay away, leave me alone, do not come in," I said. "I'll be okay, I'll be okay."

I stood at the dresser, holding on and bending over, all the time talking to myself. And then I started a mantra to myself, one that I would likely give to a patient if one were in my boat: "Marsha, you must grieve, you must not avoid this, do not suppress this. You must cry. Do not stop it." I was talking to myself as though there was me, who was grieving, and at the same time I was the therapist talking to me. "Don't worry about this. Just cry as much as you need to—you will be okay," and on and on.

Ed had died on July 17, 2010. About a month earlier, I had received a letter from him. I had not replied to it—I had not even read it.

One of the lessons I learned in all this time with Ed is that you can live a life based on hope. You really can. But now he was gone, so there wasn't any hope anymore.

The overpowering surge of my response to hearing that Ed was dead was, I think, very complex. It was the final, undeniable loss of the love of my life, obviously. But I think it also tapped in to the bottomless abyss of grief I felt—feel at times—about my past as a whole. So the screaming, the sobbing, the crying may have also been for the loss of my life, so long ago, so to speak, as well as the loss of the love of my life.

It did not take long for me to recover and also to remind myself of the gift of such a love in my life, to realize how lucky I had been to find someone to take me to the top of the world, even if at some point I had to come back down to earth.

CHAPTER NINETEEN

Finding a Therapist, and an Ironic Twist

ALLANAH SAID THAT she never saw me at the center without a smile on my face, and I think that most of the time I was indeed happy there. Sometimes I experienced happiness in the purest way, while at other times I fell into bouts of self-doubt and misery. I finally decided I needed a therapist, for the first time since leaving Chicago, four years earlier. My mentors Jerry Davison and Marv Goldfried put me in touch with someone they knew and respected very much as a behavior therapist. It was Allan Leventhal.

According to Allan, two years earlier I had interviewed with him for a job in a department he was assembling at American University. Allan had been an early adopter of behaviorism and was one of the mere hundred or so attendees at the first real gathering of the Association for Advancement of Behavior Therapy in 1967, in a small basement room of the One Washington Circle Hotel, in Washington, D.C. (These days these meetings attract as many as eight thousand.)

"As soon as I could, I started recruiting faculty for my department," Allan recalls, "looking for bright young people who would help establish a core of behaviorism at AU and develop the clinical side—that is, behavior therapy in practice. In the spring of 1973, I got an application in the mail from a young woman who completed the renowned postdoctoral program in behavior therapy at Stony

Brook. (Renowned to behaviorists, that is.) 'Perfect,' I thought, 'just the type of person I'm looking for.' I invited her for an interview and was extremely impressed by her presence, her knowledge, and her enthusiasm. I thought she would be a good addition to our program, so I recommended her highly for our position and, as far as I recall, I believed the department chair was going to offer her a job. That young woman was Marsha."

This is where the mystery, and more than a little irony, comes into this story. I have no recollection of receiving an offer from American University.

Allan now believes that, although he strongly recommended that I be offered a job, the department chair just didn't get around to sending out the offer. Had he done so, I definitely would have accepted it; I probably would not have sunk into misery; and I wouldn't have needed therapy. It would have been a perfect fit for me. Sometimes I use this phrase in my diaries, "Ah so," meaning that's just the way it is.

Allan had opened a private practice only a short while before my search for a therapist. "The office was just north of Georgetown, on Wisconsin Avenue," he recalls. "I saw Marsha mostly there at first but, as time went on, more often at my house. She was a psychologist, so we could talk about things with a language not possible with others."

Allan describes me at the time as being depressed, unhappy in my personal life, feeling poorly supported at Catholic, feeling isolated, alone, uncertain about what to do with my life, having a toxic self-image, having had terrible relationships with my parents, and having suffered a lot of damage from my time at the institute. The whole nine yards. "When you go through what Marsha went through, your definition of yourself becomes damaged," Allan says. "You begin to see yourself as defective, unworthy, a whole lot of negative things. So a lot of the work is to improve the sense of who the person is, to get rid of all that negative self-definition, to recognize the good qualities, and that is what you build on. This is what a behavior therapist does: to look at dysfunctional behaviors and look at functional behaviors, to reduce one and increase the other."

Poor Allan. He was so patient with me. I called him at all hours of the night, often crying. "I am so miserable. I want to die but not to kill myself. What can I do?" On and on and on. I don't know how he survived me. "Marsha feels more badly about it than I did at the time," Allan recalls.

Allan finally figured that he should stop trying to have a logical conversation with me, that my issues were on an emotional level. Emotions were where my real problem lay. We spent a lot of time talking about that, trying to understand that.

Why was I so unhappy? I think in many ways I was carrying with me the Million-Ton Motor Mouth, the girl who thought alone outside the box and had no road back in without sacrificing her identity. I had friends, and a lot of people had loved me. But what I needed was a loving family. I lived alone and I needed *family*. The happiness of Stony Brook had evaporated. I was no longer the insider who enjoyed a camaraderie that gave me a sense of family. I was alone again.

Allan helped me enormously, and I am so grateful for that. "Marsha became much less volatile, better at knowing what it was she wanted to do and planning on what to do, make better decisions," he says. "She came to know what she wanted. How to get out of a bad situation, believe in herself, respect herself more. She came to recognize that a lot of the negative views she had of herself weren't true, that there were things in herself that were valuable, special, to be built upon. I saw her as someone with very special abilities, very creative, brilliant intellectually. It was easy for me to talk to her in a way to help her respect herself more." That was progress.

The Lure of the West

Part of the progress was my decision to take a job at the University of Washington, in Seattle.

Out of the blue, in 1977, I got a phone call asking if I would be interested in applying for a faculty job. It was probably Jerry Davison who had told them to call me, but I am not sure. I wasn't looking for a new job, but I had never been to the West Coast in my life, so I said yes.

When I was picked up at the airport and driven to a hotel in the University District, I was in awe of the physical beauty of the place. Puget Sound, Lake Washington, the snowcapped mountains—I don't think I had ever seen anything as beautiful as the sun setting on the water and the beautiful lights in the early evening.

My interviews were the next day, and I was taken around from building to building to interviews, my hair and dress just so—in the *rain*! With no offer of an umbrella. At that time, I did not know that Seattleites don't notice rain, they are so used to it.

By the end of the second day I had met the faculty and students, had given my talk on my research, talked about future research on suicide, and had a long talk with the director of the clinical program. Going to bed that night, I knew that they were going to offer me the job, and that I would take it. (There has never been any doubt in my mind that the University of Washington is the place for me.) Then I cried myself to sleep every single night for two weeks, because I wasn't ready to leave D.C. I had to get out of Catholic University, because it was corrosive for me. But leaving my friends, leaving Allanah, leaving Allan—that was very hard. But I knew I had to do it.

On my way out of town, my car loaded up for the road trip from D.C. to Seattle with Aline, I gave Allan's wife, Carol, a gift. It was to say thank you for the time Allan had so willingly bestowed on me during those anguished late-night phone calls. It was time that had been taken away from her.

I say it again: Thank you, Carol.

Part Three

CHAPTER TWENTY

A Thumbnail Sketch of DBT

I ARRIVED AT THE University of Washington in the summer of 1977, firmly convinced that I was at last going to develop an effective treatment for highly suicidal people. A behavioral treatment. That much I knew. What I didn't know was just how complex the treatment—Dialectical Behavior Therapy—would turn out to be.

Before I tell the story of how DBT eventually emerged, in almost complete form, in the mid-1980s, I'd like to step back and describe in some detail what exactly the therapy is and how it works.

What Is Dialectical Behavior Therapy?

At the core of DBT is the dynamic balance between opposing therapeutic goals: acceptance of oneself and one's situation in life, on the one hand, and embracing change toward a better life, on the other. That is what "dialectics" means: the balance of opposites and the coming to a synthesis of two opposites. This focus on pursuing change strategies balanced by acceptance strategies is unique to DBT.

I will reiterate what I said in the opening chapter, because it is so relevant here. Namely, DBT is a behavioral treatment program, not so much an individual psychotherapy approach. It is a combination of individual psychotherapy sessions (about an hour, once a week), group training for skills, telephone coaching, a therapist consultation team, and the opportunity to help change the client's social or family situation as well (for example, with family interventions). Learning skills is central to the effectiveness of DBT: skills help a client find a way to make her life bearable.

Other forms of behavior therapy include some components of DBT, but not all. That's another way in which DBT is special.

More pertinent to DBT's specialness, however, are two other attributes.

The first is the emphasis I place on establishing a very real, egalitarian relationship between therapist and client, embracing the fact that both people are equal human beings outside of the specific roles of therapist and client, and should view each other as such. Things such as the therapists being open to talking about themselves to some degree and being willing to take phone calls at any time from a client when she desperately needs to talk make a big difference to clients and their willingness to stay in therapy and learn what they need to learn. With a highly suicidal client, the relationship with the therapist is sometimes what keeps her alive when all else fails.

The second is the central role of learning a set of DBT skills that help clients more effectively navigate their unbelievably stressful lives.

Clients' lives are typically roiled by unremitting emotional crises—such as painful criticism at work, an argument with a spouse over finances, getting drunk after swearing off alcohol, profoundly low self-esteem, an inability to form good relationships or break off bad relationships, an inability to achieve simple goals (such as getting your neighbor to loan you his lawn mower). Borderline individuals typically have a limited ability to control their emotions, which, as a result, are volatile in the extreme—volcanic, even. (This is described as "emotion dysregulation," which leads to "behavioral dysregulation," or out-of-control behavior.) My clients are constantly racked with feelings of self-loathing and shame, fear of abandonment, anger. Imagine navigating life when the most innocent of remarks can provoke paroxysms of despair, crushing shame, or perhaps hyper-exuberant joy. These people are the very definition of severely behaviorally dysfunctional individuals.

The role of DBT skills is to give clients practical ways of, first, accepting the problems they have and then, second, solving the problems they have. Each person will likely have a different set of problems, so each will need a different set of skills to solve them. All of this makes any idea of a neat, planned course of therapy quite unrealistic.

Four Categories of DBT Skills

DBT skills fall into four categories, each of which is designed to solve a different set of problems. The first two offer the path to *acceptance* of reality as it is, while the last two, taken together, are *change* skills that help clients embrace the changes they need to make in their lives.

1. Mindfulness skills, which help reduce pain and increase happiness.
2. Distress tolerance skills, which teach you how to tolerate crisis situations so that you can effectively find a solution to whatever is causing the stress.
3. Emotion regulation skills, which, as the name implies, teach you how to control your emotions so that you don't react to what's happening around you without reflection and don't say things or do things that make the situation worse.
4. Interpersonal effectiveness skills, which help you to be effective in relationships with others—relationships with people close to you and with people you interact with day to day, at work, for instance.

You have already seen some examples of DBT skills in earlier chapters: assertiveness, the DEAR MAN skills, and the TIP skills, for example. I will give further examples of these four categories of skills as we move through the book. You will remember that I developed these skills (mindfulness, distress tolerance, emotion regulation, and interpersonal effectiveness) in the context of treatment for severely dysfunctional people. But, as I have said, these are also life skills that can help every one of us live more fulfilled and emotionally stable lives. They are the stuff of everyday life.

It is not uncommon in other treatments that the therapist will decide he or she can no longer work with the client—too many problems, too emotionally exhausting a task, and so on. That's understandable. But DBT puts a huge emphasis on not terminating therapy because of a client's problems. In other words, if someone was attacking me (verbally and sometimes physically), that would be a reason why she needs to be in therapy, not a reason for me to decide I can no longer keep doing it. That is a principle of the treatment. It is against the idea of kicking people out.

When asked to describe the difference between conventional behavior therapy and Dialectical Behavior Therapy, people who have been through both typically say something like the following:

> Doing DBT was very different from my previous experience, a very different feeling. I had had a lot of cognitive therapy, talk therapy. With cognitive therapy, you are talking and discovering things about yourself, which is great. It can be very powerful. But I had done that for so long, I needed something more practical. With DBT, I learned the skills to redirect myself, especially about being effective in what I do.

You Have to Go Through the Fire

The goal of DBT is to help people find the path to getting out of hell. I know it works, because I've seen it happen for clients countless times. More important, that's what research studies—mine and other people's—demonstrate. But it is not an easy journey, going on that path. This is what I tell my clients:

> If you want to get out of hell, you have to get through the fire to the other side. It's like you are in a house, and it's on fire. There are flames all around, especially at the front of the house, surrounding the door that is the only way out. Your impulse is to retreat into the house, try to find someplace safe. But, of course, you will just die there. You've got to find the courage to go through the flames at the front of the house, the flames around the door. Then you can get to the other side. You have to go through your anger, open up to your therapist, keep going through the pain. It isn't overnight that you are going to feel better. But you will.

The Challenge for the Therapist

The therapist working with a BPD individual must ride the turbulence of her client's moods, pushing and pulling where it is appropriate. We developed a phrase to describe this dynamic dance: "movement, speed, and flow." It is often a wild ride. The therapist's task of trying to give clients skills that will help them navigate their turbulent lives is like trying to teach an individual how to build a house that will not fall down in a tornado—just as the tornado hits.

Traditional (psychodynamic) therapists believe that these people's problems are internal and that you have to get inside the person's head to treat their problems. This therapy is past-oriented, based on the premise that delving into some areas of the unconscious is the pathway to understanding what makes you the way you are. This approach can sometimes be helpful; I don't deny that. Back when I was developing DBT, there were virtually no data in support of the effectiveness of psychodynamic therapy. In any case, it doesn't help you change much of anything, especially with borderline people.

As a behaviorist, I figure out ways to replace negative (unwanted) behavior with positive or effective behavior by focusing on the context of the behavior, both what caused it and its consequences. DBT is a very pragmatic therapy, helping people to be effective in all aspects of their lives. DBT is a very problem-solving, focused, action-oriented treatment.

Source of DBT Skills

I arrived at some of the skills through drawing on my own life experiences. But I came to most of them by combing through all the very best behavior therapy manuals I could lay my hands on. I then asked, "Okay, what does the therapist ask the client to do in this therapy?" I'd then reframe it as a DBT skill, until I had a long list of them—dozens and dozens, in fact. No one had done that before DBT.

This should give you a sense of the overall picture of DBT. To repeat, DBT is a very pragmatic, down-to-earth therapy, quite unlike traditional psychotherapy. It is, literally, a program of self-improvement.

I'll finish this chapter with a typical observation about the power of DBT that I often hear from people who have experienced it:

Doing DBT, learning the skills and so on, it took me from being a victim of my depression to being more of a choice maker. Before I had DBT, if something bad happened at work, I would feel horrible, more horrible than the average person, emotionally flogging myself: "You are a bad, bad person." I would react to all of that and make myself depressed, blaming myself for not being good enough somehow, getting engaged in all of that, which can be draining. That would make me panic and blow it out of proportion. Now, when something bad happens to me—at work, with friends, anything—I can slow down and decide whether I need to react like that. Now I just exist with the anxiety and it goes away. Now I know I am a good person, I do have good qualities, and I do have control over what my mind can do. I am not as much of a victim.

*   *   *

You will learn in the following few chapters how I arrived at DBT. It was not a single eureka moment, with the therapy emerging fully formed in one step, as storybook versions of science research would often have us believe. Rather, the development process was more a gradual evolution. You will see that this involved much trial and error, false starts, unexpected insights, and lucky breaks as the many different components of the treatment steadily coalesced into a coherent therapy. Ultimately, I was able to conduct a strictly controlled clinical trial that demonstrated that DBT is effective in helping highly suicidal people live lives experienced as worth living, the results of which I published in 1991. Until this point there had been no effective therapy for this population; now there was.

CHAPTER TWENTY-ONE

Finding My Feet in Seattle and Learning to Live an Anti-Depressant Life

MY ROAD TRIP to Seattle wasn't my first such venture, but it would be by far the longest. Until my trip to Seattle for interviews, I had never been west of Oklahoma, so I thought, "Here's an opportunity to see a whole lot of North America that will be completely new to me." Aline was going to accompany me for the first part of the trip, so we would experience that part together.

I threw the few possessions I had into the car and tied my bike to the roof, and off we went. The journey would have been almost three thousand miles had I opted for the shortest route. But I didn't. We first went north through Canada and then drove west and south. We wended our way slowly, often on small back roads. I wanted to see everything: towns, villages, anything that might be interesting. On a road trip, there is just about nothing too unimportant for me to turn off and go see it.

It was four thousand miles and a month later that I got to Seattle, on August 16, 1977, the day Elvis Presley died. I thought that was so poignant, because he was a hero of mine at the time. Still is. I played his music all the time. But now I can't, because it makes me sad.

Two Lessons Learned

I learned two things about myself on this road trip. First, I discovered, completely unexpectedly, that a lover of nature lurked deep within me.

Growing up in Tulsa, I was surrounded by beauty—Mother saw to that. But it was all carefully manicured. You make your clothes look beautiful. You make your house look beautiful. You make your yard look beautiful. It was all for the looks, nothing about the inherent quality of beauty itself, and certainly not natural beauty. My parents planned our picnics at oil refineries. My father was an oilman, remember. I had absorbed this worldview.

My position had been "Why would you want to go see the Grand Canyon for real when you can look at a picture of it in a book?"

Even before we got anywhere near the Grand Canyon, the slumbering nature girl in me had already begun to stir, roused by the views of God's beautiful creations all around. That was the aesthetic reason for leisurely taking back roads: having the time to see our surroundings. But it also had the practical benefit of being easier on the car and closer to mechanical help if we needed it.

Aline was with me as far as Denver, and for one breakdown. The car lost the catalytic converter in the mountains. I then headed southwest, almost seven hundred miles to the Grand Canyon. Two more breakdowns.

It is hard to talk about the Grand Canyon without sounding clichéd. All I will say is that, for the girl who had picnicked in oil refineries and thought photographs of nature were enough, thank you very much, seeing the real thing was transformative. Like an enlightenment experience, because it really was for me.

So that was my first lesson: there is a big difference between pictures of natural beauty and *being* in natural beauty. For the first time, I experienced a sense of being and oneness when I was in nature. It's a sense that is now part of my core being.

The roadside breakdowns provided the context for the second

lesson. The assurance I'd been given about the car's reliability was, shall we say, a little overstated. I had three more breakdowns between the Grand Canyon and Seattle. I was exasperated and found myself in tears over them. But I discovered that good looks, a few tears, a sweet voice, and a healthy dose of helplessness were extremely effective in getting men to help me with the car. So I would cry at every car repair shop, and the mechanics would fix it right away. I planned to visit my cousin Ed in San Francisco, and just as I got there, the brakes went out. Ed offered to go with me to get it fixed. I said, "Absolutely not! If you go with me, they might not fix it for a long time. If I go by myself, they will do it right away."

So I went to this huge garage. I was standing there, wearing shorts, and thinking, "I should be crying." The guy was already coming toward me, across this huge space. By the time he got to me, I was sobbing so much I could barely talk. I gasped, "I've got to get this fixed, because I've got to get to Seattle." He said, "Why don't you go to that restaurant over there, have some breakfast."

But I thought, "If I leave, they may not get the car done quickly. I'd better pace." So that's what I did. I paced up and down in the garage, looking forlorn. The car was fixed just like that, by noon.

These days I tell people not to act helpless unless they really are helpless. The more helpless you act, the more incompetent you will feel. I put this piece of advice in my DBT skills book, in the section on interpersonal effectiveness skills. On the other hand, occasional strategic helplessness can be effective. That was my second lesson from the road trip.

Becoming a Seattleite—Up to a Point

I quickly fell in love with the city of Seattle, mostly for the majestic beauty of the Olympic Mountains, Lake Washington, Puget Sound, and the islands. You don't have to be rich to have a view of the mountains, because you can see them from almost every hill.

And the people. I loved the people. Seattleites are passionate about the outdoors, including hiking and camping. "Okay," I resolved, "I'm going to learn how to do that." I knew nothing about camping—zero, zip.

At the big REI store in downtown Seattle, I bought myself a tent, a sleeping bag, a camp light, and a small cookstove. I thought it wise to practice setting up the tent in my backyard before heading for the wilds. I was immediately baffled. I had no idea which end was the top and which was the bottom. Fortunately, a neighbor witnessed my plight and showed me what to do.

When I got to my first campsite, I thought, "Where do I park the car? How do I make coffee? Where is the bathroom?" I had to ask guys—it was mostly guys at these campsites—how to do absolutely everything. They were so sweet and kind and helpful, and they didn't laugh at my ineptitude.

Very soon, I became a devoted camper. Sometimes with friends, but mostly alone, which was both exhilarating—being by myself in the magnificent scenery—and occasionally a little scary, sometimes because of shady fellow campers but more often because of bear sightings. Still, I came to consider myself a true Seattleite through practice.

I had come from Washington, D.C., where I didn't give a second thought to seeing African American men and women every day. When I first got to Seattle, I thought, "My God, everyone is white." I was extremely uncomfortable in an all-white environment. When, later on, I told a realtor I was looking to buy a house in an integrated neighborhood, she looked at me as if I were from Mars and said, "There aren't any integrated neighborhoods in Seattle."

After a few years, I bought a house in the Central District, which in the 1970s was famous for being the heart of Seattle's civil rights movement and birthplace of Jimi Hendrix. On one side of the hill, it was white and wealthy. On the other side, it was black and impoverished. I was on the top, which was mostly African American. People would say to me in the street, "Hi, whitey." The area was in decline at the time, slipping deeper into poverty and crime. Eventually drug dealers (we think) torched my house. On the plus side, I got about $35,000 in replacement insurance, fixed up the house, and promptly sold it.

Early on, I was like a gypsy, moving from one apartment to another, for about three years. Eventually I thought it was about time to buy a house of my own again. Aline was visiting me at the time I was about to sign the papers. "You can't do that, Marsha," she scolded. "Remember your vows." She meant the vow of poverty I had taken years earlier in Chicago.

I'd had several such bursts of conscience before, and there would be more over the next decade or so. Ed, the love of my life, had been somewhat bemused by these gestures of piety. He once said to me, "Marsha, the idea is not that everybody should be poor. You are acting like you should be poor, like a saint. Our duty is to relieve the suffering of the poor, not for us to give everything away."

He was right that I was trying too hard to be like a saint.

After Aline's intervention in Seattle, I rented a one-room apartment on 17th Avenue, a distinctly undesirable and dangerous neighborhood. I had felt compelled to make the move, in order to align my physical surroundings with my spiritual commitment. The new apartment, if you could call it that, had one of those fold-into-the-wall Murphy beds, a couple of chairs, a small table, and a stove with no thermostat, so I never knew how hot the oven was.

I had half expected to walk into the apartment and find Jesus sitting on the bed, waiting to welcome me, because I had done the right thing. He wasn't. The only thing that greeted me that first night was police sirens. And every night thereafter, too. I thought to myself, "What have you done, Marsha? You are a professor at the university, and look at you. Look where you're living." But I stuck with it, just as I thought Saint Thérèse would have.

I occasionally had my students come to the apartment for meetings. But before long they pleaded, "Can we have meetings somewhere else, Marsha? Please!" It didn't help that I also invited some of the homeless people I worked with into my house, including to my famous Christmas party. At one of those parties, while I was getting something in the kitchen, one of my students asked one of the homeless women where she came from. As I came back into the room, I heard the woman say, "I'm out on parole for murder." I, of course, had known this, but the students were so shocked they did not know what to say.

The students were right, of course, and this jolted me into action. What I learned from living there was that I didn't need to have money to be happy. On the other hand, I found that my students weren't comfortable sitting on hard wooden floors, with the constant sound of police sirens. Not long after, I saved up enough money for a down payment on a house.

So much for Saint Thérèse.

A Place for Contemplation and Reflection

I needed a place for quiet contemplation, and I found it at the Kairos House of Prayer, a retreat center in Spokane, half a day's drive from Seattle. It is truly a most magical place, situated on twenty-seven acres of alpine desert, and there are deer, wild turkeys, and many species of smaller birds for company, as well as the occasional coyote.

My first time there, I asked whether it would be acceptable for me to stay in silence in my room instead of going to talks when there were talks. I wasn't going there to meet others or engage in activities. I wanted to fall into contemplative prayer, alone, but not be lonely. In silence. It was really wonderful. I took a blanket, laid it out on the grass, lay down in the sun, and let go completely of thoughts until it was time for dinner. So fabulous. It was the first of many visits.

Kairos House of Prayer was the spiritual inspiration of Sister Florence Leone, who established the place in the mid-1970s and runs it still, helped by her friend Rita Beaulieu. They are both wonderful. Sister Florence's goal was to "provide a place for all who wish to avail themselves of a contemplative experience for a period of time." And that was just what I needed from time to time. Plus Sister Florence's home cooking!

My friends might be surprised by the notion of my spending days in silent retreats. "What happened to Motor Mouth?" they might be asking. My spiritual life is the only arena where I am silent.

Here are a few things Sister Florence says about silence:

Only silence is deep enough to hold everything.

Silence is the language of God. Listen.

Entering the Cloud of Unknowing

In 1980, on maybe the second or third such retreat at the Kairos House, I was looking out toward the desert when a thought came urgently. I needed to make a decision: "You can hold on to the security of a concept of God as a person, a kindly old man in the sky who loves you, and you will get through your life just fine. You will feel loved all your life, and you will love God. And you will be safe. But there will be no more spiritual growth. Or you can take the risk of letting go of all of that and go on a mystical path, not knowing where it will lead." Where that thought came from, I have no idea. It just emerged from my soul.

I knew I would have to choose the latter and take the risk. I was spiritually quite content, but I felt compelled to go further. I wasn't giving up God. I was giving up the notion of God as a person—even if she was now female to me—to allow the possibility for spiritual growth. It was one of the most important decisions of my spiritual life, perhaps *the* most important.

There was the very real risk that there might be nothing after I let go of my long-held security. "The first time you practice contemplation, you'll only experience a darkness, like a cloud of unknowing," writes the anonymous author of the book by that name, *The Cloud of Unknowing*. The book was published in the latter half of the fourteenth century, as a spiritual guide to contemplative prayer. It was a how-to book: how to unite your soul with God. This is the path. Saint John of the Cross, the sixteenth-century Spanish mystic and poet, talks about it, too, in *Dark Night of the Soul*. It is going into the path and not experiencing anything, but not worrying, because this is the spiritual path.

It was very soothing to find that. It wasn't that there was something wrong. The path is the cloud of unknowing. The cloud of no words, of no experience, of nothing. You have to go through that to get to the other side. And on the other side, you hope, is God, Jesus. But it would take me a very long time to get to the other side.

In *The Cloud of Unknowing*, the author writes, "We can't think our way to God. . . . He can be loved, but not thought." It is all about *being*, not saying. That's where I was, casting myself upon the oceans in a boat without a rudder, being willing to go wherever I would be taken. "Beat on that thick cloud of unknowing with the sharp arrow of longing and never stop loving, no matter what comes your way," the author writes. That's exactly it. It's all about love. Life is all about love.

Loving and being loved.

Coming to My Senses: An Insight into Depression

I recognized that living by myself wasn't good for me, that it was a source of depression. In 1981, Kelly Egan, my first graduate student when I arrived in Seattle, and I bought a house together on the 5200 block of Brooklyn Avenue. Kelly was getting divorced at the time and needed somewhere to live with her seven-year-old twin boys, James and Joel. My only requirement was that the house have a basement so we could provide housing for the poor. Kelly was not really happy about this idea, but she went along, as long as I agreed that I would manage those living in the basement.

The architecture of the Brooklyn Avenue house was very typical for the U District. Two stories, three bedrooms, front porch, complete with rocking chairs. My students were very happy to have meetings there. "It was an older house, decorated with lovely antiques and art, and family photos on the walls," says Amy Wagner, another graduate student. "Marsha always had a big Christmas party, loads of people, candles everywhere, a buffet dinner. She was known for her homemade mustard, sweet and spicy. As you left the party, you'd get your mustard." I still do that. I used a recipe of one of Mother's friends. The house was always packed for these events, about sixty people. There was always a roomful of little kids, too, in one of the bedrooms upstairs, with toys and games. Some of them got to be "coat girls" (and boys).

An important motive for having these annual parties was so that kids could grow up going to the same house and the same party every year. I think tradition of that kind is good for people. One year, for some reason, I decided I wouldn't have the party. People were calling me, saying, "Marsha, we haven't received our invitations yet!" They were crushed. I didn't make that mistake again.

Kelly moved out after a couple of years, and I bought her share. I stayed in that house for almost twenty years, almost always sharing it with at least one other person. I had learned that particular lesson well—that I was happier living with people, not being alone.

Learning to Live an Anti-Depressant Life

My recognition that living alone was bad for me had been very slow in coming. But when it did come, my active decision never to live alone again encapsulates another eventual DBT skill: namely, living an anti-depressant life. This simply means taking steps to include things in your life that make you smile, make you feel happy, and also taking steps to avoid, where possible, those things that cause you unhappiness and depression. I see it working with clients all the time.

People who are depressed often say, "Oh, there's something wrong with me." They act as if depression is something over which they have no control. Mostly, that is not true. Mostly people get depressed because they are doing something that is causing the depression. Saying to them, "Buck up and stop being depressed" does not help. But identifying what is causing them to be depressed, and getting them to stop doing that, does help. It is an entirely different mentality.

Accumulating Positive Emotions

It is one of the best pieces of advice I am able to give my clients. Things that make you happy can be as simple as putting flowers on the kitchen table, stopping to really look and appreciate a sunset, taking your dogs for a walk. It can be being with people you like, doing things that give you a sense of competence. I call this "accumulating positive emotions." At the same time, avoid, where possible, those things that cause you unhappiness and depression. As you know, for me it was making sure I don't live alone. It's a useful exercise for anyone—make a mental list of those things that make you happy and those things that make you sad or depressed. Then act on it. I urge you to try it.

Mother

Among all of these adjustments to my new life in Seattle, there was a constant. Mother.

From time to time, I visited her and Father in Tulsa. It wasn't something I especially looked forward to or enjoyed. It was always the same. Nothing had changed. Pretty much everything I did or said when I was there was a target of her criticism, sometimes direct, often passive. Eventually I decided that there was no percentage in putting myself in that position. "Mother is critical about everything I do, everything about me, and she is not going to change," I said to myself. "I am always depressed when I go back. I am not going to do it anymore."

That was it. There were going to be no more visits to Tulsa for me. I didn't say anything to Mother about my decision. I was simply going to stop seeing her.

It took Mother three years to register that things were not as they had been, that I wasn't visiting every six months or so. When she said, "What's wrong, Marsha? Why aren't you coming home?" I said, "Well, Mother, I have decided I am never going to see you again." She was completely taken aback, clearly distressed and puzzled.

I wrote an eight-page letter, which included many examples of things she had said to me. I can't remember what I said in the letter, but it all had to do with how many times she had said things that were invalidating of me. For example, frequently talking about how pretty others were, how successful they were, how they did things in such a wonderful way. It always came across as "Why aren't you like that?"

After Mother got the letter, she called me, sobbing, saying, "This must be why all my children left me. All six of them." I said, "Yes, Mother, it is." She pleaded that she wanted to change, wanted to be better as a mother with me. I said, "If you want to change, I will see you, but I am going to ask you, 'Can you do this?' Because I don't want to see you if you can't." She assured me that she could.

I suspended my disbelief.

Not long after that exchange, she visited me in Seattle. She seemed genuinely happy to see me. As we were driving along the highway, she said, "Oh, guess what. Remember Mary Jones? Remember how fat she was, so overweight, remember that? Well, she lost so much weight and she met this wonderful guy. They just got married."

I about hit the roof.

I pulled off the road, brought the car to a stop, turned to her, and said, "Mother, let's go through this line by line. How do you think I could possibly feel when you say something like that, given what you know about me?" So I went through the whole thing, the constant criticism, direct and indirect. And here she was doing it again, after having promised she would change.

She cried. She said, "Oh, please tell me when I say things like that—please. I do want to be better."

I gave her a lot of feedback over time. And, remarkably, she really did change. Then, a few years later, she learned that she had cancer and knew that she was dying. She reverted to her previous self. She didn't want the extra stress of being on good behavior. She didn't want to put any effort into me. She became the center of her own universe again. I don't blame her for that. And I don't blame her for what she did to me as a young girl. She did her best, thinking she was helping me.

As a true behaviorist, I understand that her behavior was caused by her experience of being with Tante Aline. It was also caused by the norms of the society in which she lived, and thrived. For me to feel judgment and blame are useless. The sad fact is that Mother and I are alike in this respect. We are both sometimes insensitive to the effect our words have on others.

So she wasn't to be blamed. But the pain she inflicted will never go away.

Adaptive Denial Again

I used to be a heavy smoker. But not long after I arrived in Seattle, in the late seventies, I developed some respiratory problems. Unless I quit, the doctors could do nothing to help me. Like most smokers,

I had wanted to quit before, because I knew that in the long run it was bad for my health, even though I loved it so. But that never got me very far. This time had to be for real.

Going down the New Year's resolution path was usually ineffective. People mostly don't keep their resolutions. So I decided I would quit February 1 instead. The challenge then was "How am I going to do it?" (This was before they had all the medications that help people stop smoking.) I decided I would reward myself for not smoking. In a way, this led to one of the ideas in DBT.

Eating as a substitute wasn't an option; that would be just another problem behavior I'd have to quit later. And chewing gum didn't work. I needed an activity to focus on when the urge to smoke hit me.

I got two small jars, leaving one empty and filling the other with dimes. I put the two jars in my pocketbook. When I craved a cigarette, it was very intense. Sometimes I thought I would go crazy. (I know that you former smokers understand what I'm saying.) But when the urge welled up, I would deny I wanted a cigarette and instead say, "I have to have a dime! *I have to have a dime!*"

I would then move a dime from the full jar to the empty jar. I did that for quite a while, and eventually it worked.

Why? Reaching for a dime in my pocketbook was almost identical to reaching into my pocketbook for a cigarette. Instead, I reached into my pocketbook for a dime, got it, and transferred it. It somewhat replicated the physical motions involved in "I am going to have a cigarette."

I described this technique of adaptive denial earlier, where I used it to help me manage my limited finances in Chicago. It's a skill for people with addictive behaviors. It is not denying that the addictive urge is upon you. Instead it is about adamantly convincing yourself that you want something other than the addictive behavior you are trying to quit. A dime instead of a cigarette. Do something that is a similar action. Convince yourself that you want something other than the urge you are experiencing.

Adaptive denial is appropriate for any addiction—eating too

much chocolate, for instance, or overdoing alcoholic drinks; I'm sure you can think of more examples. It can be very effective, as long as you don't give up.

Cope Ahead: A Skill for Prevailing in Difficult Situations

Research has demonstrated that it is possible to learn new skills by imagining being in a difficult and challenging situation and figuring out a strategy for prevailing. I incorporated this mental ability in DBT, with a skill I call "Cope ahead." This one came from my own experience.

Some years ago, out of the blue, I started being afraid of driving through tunnels. In Seattle, there are *a lot* of tunnels. What was I afraid of? My fear was that there would be an earthquake while I was in the tunnel, and it would collapse on me. So when I approached a tunnel, I would look around and . . . *Okay, no earthquake.* But my fear didn't go away.

There is a thing that psychologists call a safety cue. If you are afraid of elevators, but you need to use them, you say to yourself, "Okay, if I have a cellphone with me, I will be safe." The phone is the safety cue, like a child's comfort blanket. With safety cues, you are able to do what you need to do and keep fear from holding you back. My safety cue was saying, "There isn't going to be an earthquake." But we are in Seattle, and there are earthquakes all the time. So it is ridiculous to say there isn't going to be an earthquake. Not such a good safety cue.

Then I thought, "What am I *really* afraid of?" I was afraid that the roof was going to come down and crush me. There have been terrible accidents in tunnels, and people died. But not everyone. So I imagined myself going into a tunnel, and the roof comes down. I fling open the car door, and I am wearing a Wonder Woman outfit. I start saving all the people around me. This worked pretty well, but not completely.

Psychologists measure someone's degree of unhappiness with something called the Subjective Units of Distress Scale (SUDS), which goes from zero (no stress) to 10 (extreme stress). Before I did my little stress-reducing exercise about tunnels, I was at 8; afterward, it was 3. So a definite improvement, but I was still stressed. I thought I must be afraid of something else. When you are trying to figure out what you're afraid of, you don't always get the right thing immediately.

So what I am really afraid of is that the roof is going to come down, and a piece of metal is going to go through my wrist, pinning me down. No one will know I'm there. There will be a fire, and I am going to die. When I told this story to my clients, I asked them, "What skill am I going to turn to now?" They all got it: acceptance. So in my mind I start going into the tunnel, practicing being buried in pain, dying. And it worked—SUDS down to zero.

The "cope ahead" skill, then, involves figuring out which situations are likely to cause you trouble, cause you anxiety, and then planning ahead how to cope with the expected difficulties—but also imagining being in the situation and coping effectively.

At this point, I'd like to stress the following observation: *A common element of all the DBT skills—indeed, the key to DBT as a whole—is the determination to be effective in whatever it is you are doing. Being effective is the key to success, in all walks of life.*

A Path to Understanding Death and Suicide

At some point during my time at Catholic University, I had seriously contemplated giving up my work on suicide. I often found myself tangling with psychiatrists, who made my life difficult. When I went out of town for the weekend and one of my clients had some kind of suicide crisis, the first response of psychiatrists was to admit them to a hospital. There are no data that show that hospitalization saves lives or is useful in any way with suicidal people. I believed then, and still do, that in the majority of cases, suicidal clients do just fine in outpatient treatment. Indeed, a study by one of my students showed that hospitalization is not effective in the way the profession has long assumed it to be.

As frustrating as it had been in D.C., it is not in my genes to quit. As far as I was aware, no one else was doing any good, serious work on suicide. Suicide remained my focus when I arrived at the University of Washington.

I eventually developed a graduate course on assessment and intervention with suicidal individuals. It runs a full weekend and is open to clinical psychology graduate students and residents in psychiatry. Friday evening we begin with wine and pizza, and the students have to answer three questions. First, "What is death?" Second, "Do individuals have a right to commit suicide; do you have that right?" And third, "Does anyone have the right to stop another person from committing suicide; do you have that right?" I ask everyone to write their thoughts on these questions for ten minutes or so. After each question, students share their thoughts. They can ask questions for clarification but cannot start a conversation or say they disagree with someone.

For many years, most students have said that adults with no mental illness have a right to suicide, while individuals with mental disorders do not have that right. Lately, more students have entertained the idea that those with mental disorders also should have the right to suicide. At the same time, all of them believe that, as mental health therapists, they have the right to stop a person from suicide.

André Ivanoff, who worked with me early on, describes the workshop experience as valuable prep for therapists. "If you aren't clear about where you stand on these issues when you are confronted with a suicidal client, you can't sort out these things in the moment," she says. "You have to be clear about that." Kelly Koerner agrees. "If you think there is a quality of life so desperate that suicide is justifiable, then you need to know that," she said recently. "I believe people do have that right, but my job as a therapist is to be an advocate for staying alive. You find your bottom line with this exercise, and you can therefore operate more clearly."

"It was an experience for me" is how Michael Addis, a graduate student, recently described the workshop. "You discover how you really feel about someone thinking about taking their own life, and you discover where your blind spots are. There are all kinds of things that come up when you contemplate this topic—not just intellectual puzzles, but strong feelings that can catch you off guard when working with really miserable people."

This is a good description of my goals for this workshop. I always tell students my opinions after they have given theirs. I believe that I do not have a moral right to suicide. I am too well known, and too many people would be hurt if I did kill myself. I also believe that adults with the capacity to think clearly have a right to suicide. This excludes individuals who are in psychotic episodes. I believe I have a right to do everything I can, short of taking away someone's freedom, to keep a person from suicide. This includes pounding on their door, calling their relatives, telling them I will tell others to not take care of their cats if they commit suicide, and so on.

As I tell my students, I believe that, just as I have a right to try to talk people into voting as I want them to, to march for various causes and stop traffic, to join protest groups outside the mayor's house, I have a right to try to talk someone out of killing himself. This does not mean that I have never hospitalized someone who is acutely suicidal, because I have. The tension here is that, even though I might be against something in principle, I accept that it might at times be necessary anyway.

Only the suicidal individual can really understand what it is like to be in that state. I have been there, of course, but it is still hard to put into words that fully communicate what it *feels* like. When you are faced with someone who is suicidal, you cannot help but be moved to compassion. But, as a former client said recently at a national conference, "Love may have kept me alive, but it didn't treat my suffering." Dr. John O'Brien, my therapist at the Institute of Living, came to mind when I heard her say that.

According to figures from the American Foundation for Suicide Prevention, in 2017 (the most recent year for which full figures are available) more than 47,000 people killed themselves in the United States, and as of 2015 more than half a million visited a hospital for self-harm behavior.

That is a lot of pain in the world, a lot of people suffering agonies in that metaphorical small, stark room.

CHAPTER TWENTY-TWO

My First Research Grant for Behavior Therapy and Suicide

WHEN I ARRIVED in Seattle, I was the truest believer in behavior therapy ever to walk the earth. I figured that all I had to do was hold a clinical trial to prove my point. Behavior therapy was going to be my tool for eliminating people's pain.

This was going to require a couple of years of preparation, getting myself set up in a new space, working out details of the treatment, getting the UW Human Subjects Division to approve my research, getting a research grant, and so on.

But before I was able to go ahead with the program, John Clarkin, of Weill Cornell Medical College, asked me to write a chapter on suicide for a book on depression. It was a gift, in a way, because I spent a full year going through everything that had been written about suicide.

And in doing so, I discovered that there were many unanswered questions. I developed a model of suicidal behavior that was an extension of Arthur Staats's social behaviorist model, which I had found so appealing when I was at Catholic University. Essentially, it says that suicidal people feel a sense of shame, hopelessness, and loneliness. Life is not worth living, and being dead seems the only real option. Writing that chapter gave a coherence to my thinking. It might be the best thing I have ever written. The chapter was, in effect, the culmination of a first, naïve foray into researching the topic two decades earlier, at night school in Tulsa.

By the time the chapter came out, in 1981, I was already embarked on a pilot study of the efficacy of behavior therapy for suicide prevention. The project was titled "Assessment and Treatment of Parasuicide Patients."

There had long been confusion over the terms that describe suicide and suicide attempts. When someone injures herself to the point of killing herself, you can justifiably call her behavior a suicide. But when intentional self-injury lands that person in the hospital, the situation is ambiguous. Therapists are often quick to describe this as "attempted suicide," a failed effort to kill oneself. But we have to remember that where therapists see suicide and intentional self-injury without death as the problem, the people doing it regard it as a solution. Research shows that self-injury can be very calming. I preferred to use the term "parasuicide," a term that encompasses suicide and non-suicidal intentional self-injury.

For our study population, I called local hospitals and said, "Send me your worst cases. Send me the most suicidal people you have, the most difficult to treat." They were more than happy to do that. They sent me people who had had multiple recent suicide attempts and episodes of self-injury. My rationale was very practical: If I did a study using people who did not have a severe disorder and a high risk of suicide, they might get better on their own. In that case the study would not be able to unambiguously evaluate my treatment.

I had applied for a research grant from the National Institute of Mental Health (NIMH) a year earlier, laying out my twelve-week behavior therapy program, which was going to help these most miserable of people. I had been supremely confident in the outcome.

I had been more than a little naïve, too, it turned out.

A Site Visit from an NIMH Panel—
and a Dropped Coffeepot

"My initial reaction," Barry Wolfe recalls, was 'A twelve-week behavior therapy program for seriously disturbed individuals?'" Barry was in the NIMH's division of clinical research programs at the time. "I didn't think Marsha's program was going to go anywhere in that short period of time. I mean, these were women who were attempting suicide on a fairly regular basis."

But the NIMH team apparently liked what I was attempting to do, and had a degree of freedom to offer guidance, something that later bureaucratic rules would make very difficult. "So, despite the conclusion that this application wasn't going to fly, we thought Marsha had a lot of talent," says Barry, "and we decided to work with her." A colleague of Barry's, who was not directly involved in my grant proposal, recalls, "We thought Marsha was very courageous working with this population, because most therapists wanted to avoid them if at all possible."

Over the next few months, the NIMH team patiently spent time with me on the telephone, gradually reformulating a more practical protocol, one more grounded in the realities of the terrain. Even with their help, I would discover that I still had a lot to learn about these populations. I found myself going from problem to solution to problem to solution, over and over, in creative ways.

At some point, a review committee from NIMH paid me a site visit in Seattle. Barry remembers the visit. "The committee were Hans Strupp, from Vanderbilt, who was one of the premier researchers from the psychoanalytic point of view, and Maria Kovacs, a child behavior therapist at University of Pittsburgh, very prominent." These visitations can be quite intimidating, especially with scholars of that caliber. And for me, this was a big one. I was so nervous that I dropped a pot of coffee in my office. It went everywhere, a terrible mess. Did they want me to make another pot? I asked sheepishly. No, they did not! It was "Let's get on with business here."

They discussed whether my research-and-treatment plan was promising or not, then discussed whether the treatment I was planning was identical to other treatments that had already been studied. One of the reviewers said that she thought I was treating individuals with borderline personality disorder. At the time, I had barely heard of BPD. Fortunately, one member of our team was a psychiatrist, and he knew about BPD. He agreed with the reviewer. BPD individuals have a high risk of suicidal behavior, so it was a good fit for my goals.

In order to be awarded an NIMH grant, I had to be studying people with a formal diagnosis. Borderline personality disorder was one such condition, whereas suicidal behavior by itself was not. So a BPD study it was going to be. Despite the coffeepot incident, I got funded.

Many years later, one of the original site visitors told me that the actual reason for the funding was that I was so passionate about my work. The committee believed that if anyone could develop an effective behavior therapy intervention for suicidal people, it would be me.

CHAPTER TWENTY-THREE

Science and Spirituality

IN 1978, ABOUT a year after I arrived in Seattle, I attended a summer program at the Shalem Institute for Spiritual Formation, in Washington, D.C., to learn how to be a spiritual director.

I had heard about the Shalem Institute shortly after I joined the faculty at Catholic University, back in 1973. It is an ecumenical Christian organization, with a mission to foster spiritual growth in communities and individuals. I signed up for a two-year course that would involve a lot of required reading, writing papers, and meeting as a group one evening a week, culminating in a more intense retreat. Other than Anselm's advice in Chicago that I should say nothing when I prayed, I had never had any formal teaching.

My experience at the Shalem Institute was mixed. It was both deeply rewarding, in terms of growth in my understanding of how to be in the world, and equally deeply disturbing, in terms of my completely surprising—and to this day still inexplicable—reaction to part of the process.

Tilden Edwards was the institute's director. Tilden was an Episcopalian priest at the National Cathedral. His co-director, also an Episcopalian priest, was Gerald May, brother of the existential psychologist Rollo May. Tilden and Gerald were both wonderful teachers. Gerald taught me the concept of "willingness," which he later wrote about in his book *Will and Spirit*.

The institute taught and practiced Christian contemplative prayer, which has deep roots in the early centuries of Christianity. It is beautifully outlined in *The Cloud of Unknowing,* which I mentioned earlier. One of my favorite pieces of advice from the book is this: "Go into the cloud of unknowing with a cloud of forgetting at your feet." I also love the direction to "pick a word of one syllable and fasten this word to your heart so that it never goes away from you. This word will be your shield and your spear. With this word, beat on this cloud and this darkness and strike down all thought under the cloud of forgetting."* Being truly present and spiritually open requires both perseverance and letting go.

In the mid-1970s, a Trappist monk came across a copy of *Cloud* and saw its potential as the basis for a teachable spiritual practice for uniting with God. That was the birth of contemporary Christian contemplative prayer, or centering prayer.

A Break with the Church—a Big Loss

What we did at the Shalem Institute was like an early version of this. It was silent meditation, an openness to God—and, of course, my understanding of the word "God" had changed over the years.

Here I want to talk about an important break from my former religious life. It was Christmas Day of 1980, during the noon service at Blessed Sacrament Church, in Seattle. I was suddenly hit hard by the blatant sexism that surrounded me—it was like a punch in the gut. It wasn't the first time I'd been aware of sexism at this church, but there was something about this time that thrust itself into my consciousness. I felt compelled to do something about it. I thought about the whole thing for a few days, let the raw emotion pass, and then penned the following letter to the priest:

* *The Cloud of Unknowing with the Book of Privy Counsel,* trans. Carmen Acevedo Butcher (Boston: Shambhala, 2009).

I am writing to express my anger and deep frustration about the incredible lack of sensitivity to women evident in the liturgy at noon on Christmas day. If you have doubts, please look at the songs selected. One of the early songs, Lo, How a Rose E'er Blooming, had a last line "she bore to <u>men</u> a savior . . ." NO effort was made to replace the line with inclusive language. Just when I had recovered from that song, it was announced that we should all sing Good Christian MEN Rejoice!!!!! GOOD GRIEF!!!!! Minimal sensitivity would have dictated selection of any number of songs with less sexist content. . . .

Frankly, I am in almost complete despair of any possibility that this institutional church cares to or is able to include women as full human beings. Non-inclusive, male-oriented language, a god only called Lord, Father, or the masculine he/him, liturgies on holy days with an array of ordained men arranged around an altar, suggest little awareness or concern for the needs, cares, rights, and value of women. . . .

I have mentioned once before that the sexist, non-inclusive language of the morning office prohibits my taking part. The experience is simply too oppressive. . . .

Peace and joy in God!!!!
May her blessings be with you.
Marsha

I was done with the church as institution, an institution run by men. It was a place that considered women to be lesser than men. And I considered it immoral to continue to give that institution money, because it would be like giving money to a group that refuses to ordain African Americans or Hispanics. It cannot be justified. For a long time I stopped going to Catholic Mass, with a very sad heart. It was one of the biggest losses in my life. Losing your church is like losing your family.

Unable to Look into the Mirror

During my first year at Shalem, in the mid-seventies, classes in contemplative prayer were once a week. We sat in a circle. Sometimes we meditated or did other spiritual practices. Sometimes we were given simple questions that in reality were rather deep, somewhat like koans (riddles meant to provoke enlightenment) in Zen training. I had no idea what was going on most of the time.

For instance, one question was "Who am I?" Well, that was easy, I thought. "I am a teacher." It took me a while to get that the question was more like "Who . . . am . . . I?" The question they were really asking me to consider was "How do I see myself in connection with all things and beings around me, in a spiritual sense?" Another question was "Where do thoughts come from?" I said, "What are you talking about? They come from synapses firing between neurons in the brain." Again I was being too literal, too prosaic.

In one exercise, we had to find a partner, sit opposite him or her, and then gaze into each other's eyes for half an hour. Saying nothing, expressing no emotions in any manner. It's a pretty intense experience, and it is often hard to stop even the merest hint of a smile from migrating across your face. Try it. You will see what I mean.

In the last class, the exercise was to sit in front of a mirror for an hour, looking at yourself. Simple: look at yourself without moving. But as I sat there, watching myself in the mirror, without warning I started to cry and couldn't stop. I had to leave. To this day, I have no idea what was really going on. It was just an experience.

Because I had not completed that class, I decided to take the entire course again the following year. This time, when they said, "Where do thoughts come from?" I said, "From right to left." Just that. It didn't mean anything. It just was. I knew I had advanced from the year before. The idea is to observe your mind, see what thoughts emerge. I made it through the entire course on this second try.

A Second Enlightenment Moment

That had been my experience of Shalem when I was living in D.C. in the mid-1970s, and it left a deep impression on me. After I moved to Seattle and needed instruction in becoming a spiritual director, I decided to return to Shalem for guidance.

I don't remember a lot about my visits to Shalem from Seattle. I do remember that I went for a three-week extension course, over two years. I failed to complete the final paper, so I never did get my certificate. But that didn't stop me from acting as a spiritual director for a number of people.

One incident at Shalem stands out very clearly, however—a lightbulb moment.

My first enlightenment experience had come in the chapel at the Cenacle Retreat Center, in Chicago, back in 1967. It was an ecstatic moment, and the experience of oneness, of being thrown into God, lasted at least a year. When I was with Ed, the deep feeling of love I had for him was identical to the feeling I had had in the chapel.

In the chapel, I had thought the ecstatic feeling was the experience of *God loving me*, which was what I had been desperately seeking for so long. But when I experienced the very same ecstatic feeling while lying next to Ed, which was an expression of *me loving Ed*, I realized I had been mistaken. The ecstatic feeling in the chapel was an expression of *me loving God*, not of God loving me. That was it. My year of ecstasy came to a sudden end, evaporating in mere seconds. Spiritually and emotionally, I was back to where I had been before my mystical experience in the chapel. I was forced to resume my search for God.

More than a decade later, on one of my visits to Shalem from Seattle, my search was still unfulfilled, in the dark night of the soul. I was sitting in class during one of these summer sessions at Shalem when my attention drifted from the speaker at the front of the class, and I turned my gaze to the window. Just through the window, moving gently in the breeze, was a big flower, a blue hydrangea. As I looked idly at it, a certainty flooded through me. It was undeniable. It was the sudden realization that God had never been gone after all. God had been here the whole time. God is *everywhere*. God is *everything*.

My search was over. I had found God. God had found me. It was a second enlightenment moment—my hydrangea moment.

It may seem like a mundane setting, but people commonly have enlightenment experiences in everyday settings. Driving down the street or just looking at the big clock in the train station—*ticktock*—and suddenly you know some profound truth, perhaps an eternal truth about yourself, the world, God.

In Zen they say, "Act compassionate and you will find that you've always been compassionate. Act enlightened and you will find that you've always been enlightened." It's this notion that you've always been there; you just didn't know it. That's what had happened for me that day. God had never left me. I realized right away, I had never been left.

Everything Is Love, Everything Is Good

This second enlightenment moment was one of the treasures of my Shalem experience. The other was what Gerald May taught me about willingness.

Willingness is about opening yourself to what is. It is about becoming one with the universe, participating in it, doing what is needed in the moment. It is doing the dishes when needed, helping someone up who has fallen, letting go of battles you will never win and even some you could win. It is letting go of being right, even when you are right. It is when you do things you might not want to do, but you do them because they are needed. With willingness, you accept with grace what is happening. You could say it is throwing yourself into the will of God, or into acceptance of the causal factors of the universe. It is giving up tantrums. "Willingness," says Gerald May, "is saying yes to the mystery of being alive in each moment."

The opposite of willingness is willfulness. With willfulness, the focus is on controlling reality, it is "my way or the highway," it is about being right. It is a battle with reality, and that consumes emotional energy and gets you nowhere. Willfulness is doing the opposite of what is needed.

The concept of willingness resonated strongly with me, and I realized it could be very effective with the clients I work with, helping them create a life experienced as worth living. Willingness later became part of the DBT distress tolerance skills.

Some years back, I had an amusing—in retrospect—struggle with willfulness that led me to see clearly that you cannot fight willfulness with willfulness.

Here's what happened. I had proposed a project in my lab with high-risk clients (opioid addicts) that I had to get approved by the department. I knew that getting approval was by no means certain and that I would have to be very diplomatic, something that can be a challenge for me, especially with something I'm passionate about, as I was in this case. The details of the project are not relevant here, just the fact that I was facing an upcoming meeting with the department chair and several other luminaries from the clinic, who I knew were very leery about the project because of the risk involved.

I knew that I could scuttle my project if I let my passion push me to anger about their resistance. I decided to employ opposite action so I would understand their point of view.

The night before the meeting, I started practicing understanding their point of view. Every time I started going down that path, a willfulness would erupt and say, "No, you can't do that." And I would say, "Down, willfulness! Down, willfulness!" I kept doing that over and over. "I am right, they are wrong." "Down, willfulness!" None of it worked. This was bad news.

At the meeting next day, we were sitting on chairs with rollers. I had two colleagues with me. When I started to get worked up, I would move my chair back a little bit, and my colleagues would move theirs up and talk until I calmed down. I managed to get through the whole thing without losing my composure, though it was a struggle.

After it was all over, I had to figure out why opposite action had not worked. I realized that you can't treat willfulness with willfulness (commanding it to get down like a dog, my saying, "Down, willfulness! Down, willfulness!"). Then I thought, "What am I afraid of here?" It was that they could take away my academic freedom, and that is my highest value. The minute I realized that, I thought, "Oh, no, they can't take that away from me. They can take space away from me, but they can't take academic freedom away from me, because I have tenure." I calmed down. It worked out.

When a skill won't work for me (opposite action in this case), I have to figure it out to be effective. The skill that would have worked was willingness—to see their point of view. Willingness is entering into the world and doing what is needed.

The Power of the Body

One of the more fascinating insights in psychology is the (unexpected) power of the body over one's feelings. Not just in the way that intense exercise and paced breathing change feelings by changing the body's chemistry, but merely through effects of posture and facial expression.

You are well aware that when you feel angry, it shows in your body. It manifests as downward-curled lips, a furrowed brow, an overall tenseness in your facial muscles. Your whole body is rigid, and your fists are clenched. And when you are happy, your face is relaxed, your lips curl up as you smile, and your body and fists are open and relaxed.

In other words, your feelings sculpt your overall posture. That is the power of mind over body. Research shows that the reverse is also true—that if you adopt the posture of anger or happiness, you have a tendency to experience that same feeling. The power of body over mind.

Half-Smiling and Willing Hands

I decided to incorporate the power of body over mind in the service of willingness in two specific distress tolerance skills in DBT. I call them half-smiling and willing hands.

I tell my clients that half-smiling is a way of accepting reality with your body. For instance, if you half-smile when you are thinking about someone you dislike, it helps you feel more accepting of that person, more understanding. Sounds hard to believe, but it is true.

Here's how you do it. First, relax your face, from the top of your head down to your chin and jaw. Let go of each facial muscle (forehead, eyes, and brows; cheeks, mouth, and tongue; teeth slightly apart). If you find it hard, try tensing your face and then letting up.

Second, let both corners of your mouth go slightly up, just so you can feel them moving. A half-smile is slightly upturned lips with a relaxed face. Third, try to adopt a serene facial expression. The whole exercise is one of your face communicating with your brain. It works. Research and experience confirm it. Try it.

Willing hands is another way of accepting reality with your body. Anger is often opposite to accepting reality, a motivation to change what is. And sometimes that is appropriate. But in a crisis, you often need to find a way to accept reality for what it is. Willing hands is a way to do that. I co-opted the idea from the practice of the Vietnamese monk, author, poet, and peace activist Thich Nhat Hanh.

Here's how you do it. If you are standing on the floor, drop your arms down from your shoulders; keep them straight or bent at the elbows. With your hands unclenched, turn your hands outward, with thumbs out to your sides, palms up, and fingers relaxed. You can also do this while sitting, by putting the backs of your hands on your thighs. Or even lying down on your back, arms by your sides, hands unclenched, palms turned up. Each of these positions is very peaceful, and that is part of the goal: to be accepting of what is, not fighting it.

Half-smiling and willing hands take practice, and you can do them at any time of the day. The effect is wonderful. Not long ago a teenage client told me how it had helped her. She was in a public place and someone was being unhelpful to her, disrespectful even. The girl was getting angrier and angrier, and her impulse was to react angrily to that person. "Then I remembered what you said about willing hands, Marsha, and I did willing hands," she told me. "I couldn't believe it—all my anger went down." If you can change your emotions like this—using half-smiling and willing hands—you can change your actions and avoid impulsively doing something you might later regret.

The Need to Accept the Unexpected

I used to tell Ed that I wanted my tombstone to read, "She said 'Yes.'" Meaning that I lived my life willingly, doing what God wanted me to do for the betterment of people's lives and the world.

In his book *Will and Spirit,* Gerald May wrote, "As long as science is a servant of willfulness it can lead only to the gateway of meaning. To move through this gateway, willfulness must give way to willingness and surrender. Mastery must yield to mystery."[*]

If you approach scientific exploration with willfulness—that is, seeking to control outcomes, or believing you know what the outcomes are going to be—you will get only so far. To be successful,

---

[*] Gerald G. May, *Will and Spirit: A Contemplative Psychology* (New York: HarperCollins, 1982), p. 8.

science requires willingness to accept findings in your research that go completely against what you predicted—a willingness to be open to mystery, if you like. It requires the flat-out humility to be wrong, which can sometimes be more fun than being right. It requires willingness to admit that someone else's research is better than yours when it is, willingness to share authorship with others who have worked hard with you. And, most important, it requires a willingness to share the truth of your research findings ahead of politics, public and professional opinions, ahead of getting more grant money, becoming rich, and so on.

I went through a long period when I said, "My spiritual self will be on the weekends and in the mornings, when I go to church; and my scientist self will be during the weekdays." I did this for years. Then one day I decided this was ridiculous. With the guidance of a wonderful teacher (Willigis, whom you will meet before long), I began to see that the universe is what it is. They say that all physicists are mystics. They say that out of nothing came something. Essential mass, essential reality—it is all one. I tell my clients that everything is caused. The fact that we don't know the cause doesn't mean there is no cause.

There is the domain of experience, and there is the domain of articulation. Science is the domain of articulating with words. Spirituality is the domain of experiencing.

You can't describe the experience of taste in such a way that another person experiences it as you do. Not unless they have tasted it themselves. The spiritual path has led me to value being nonjudgmental and to value radical acceptance. Spirituality was having a huge beneficial impact in my own life, and I wanted to translate that into behavioral terms for effective treatments for my clients.

But first I had to get tenure.

CHAPTER TWENTY-FOUR

My Fight for Tenure

GETTING TENURE IS essential in academia, both for job security and for the freedom to pursue out-of-the-box research. Your colleagues on the tenure committee weigh several factors in their decision, such as the number of grants you've been awarded, the number and quality of papers you've published, and the quality of your teaching. Letters of reference matter, too, as does the committee members' judgment of how you will fit in as a long-term member of the department.

Playing politics matters, too. Unfortunately, I am not good at playing politics.

I was up for tenure in 1982, toward the very end of the year. At UW, there is no second chance: either you get tenure or you are looking for a job elsewhere come the next academic year. My publishing record was adequate, and included the chapter on suicide. I wasn't what you would call a shoo-in, but I would have given myself favorable odds. Although some people in the psychology department were uncomfortable with my being there, doing the kind of work I was doing, I also had strong allies, in particular Bob Kohlenberg.

"Part of Marsha's problem had to do with the patient population she was working with," Bob now says. "People probably wouldn't admit it, and I don't know how conscious it was. But I know that many were just uncomfortable with having these highly disturbed patients around. That's point one. Point two is that Marsha needed to be hard-driving to pull off this incredibly difficult work. She was very demanding of faculty and students. So it's not surprising that she necessarily ruffled feathers." As I said, I am not a very good politician, or at least I wasn't then.

Clinical people had very strict rules about the "appropriate way" to interact with patients. Bob explains this well. "Their idea was that patients should be well behaved, appear on time, leave on time, see you in a week, and don't bother you," he says. "They don't have the right to call you whenever they want. To do otherwise would be what they called 'boundary violation.' It was said to be for the good of the patient, give them structure. Marsha said, 'You are basically protecting yourselves, and this does not help the patients.' She was very explicit in the way that is very Marsha. People didn't like that. She had strong ideas about what was most helpful for patients, and her patients didn't fit neatly into their system."

"The board that would approve tenure would be 'hard' scientists," recalls Ed Shearin, a doctoral student of mine at the time, "and Marsha was doing clinical research, which some saw as not very worthy of respect."

André Ivanoff, part of the team from the beginning, says, "There was a lot of tension around Marsha's getting tenure, and it permeated all of the activities we [the research team] were working on at the time. From the perspective of a twenty-two-year-old, it was hard to understand how the department might not want her. Marsha was extremely active, and her research, while certainly of life-and-death importance, I think may have been off-putting to some of her then more sedate-topic colleagues."

My housemate Kelly Egan remembers that I was not favored on campus. "She was a woman, relatively new, she was ambitious," says Kelly. And the entire faculty was male at that point. "Male faculty were very critical of her, didn't recommend you work with her, and weren't impressed if you were working with her. It didn't seem to bother Marsha. She expected to have to fight her way, and she did."

There were four of us up for tenure that month. At one of the early tenure committee meetings, one of the members launched a fierce attack on the statistics I had been using, saying I had used the wrong kind, that they were terrible. It was blistering. Fortunately, Allen Edwards, who had written the all-time best statistics book for psychology, happened to walk in on this scene, and he came to my defense. He said, "Her statistics are really good. What are you talking about?"

I ultimately got a near unanimous vote, with only one abstention, from the faculty. It looked promising. All I needed was a positive vote from the College Council. The job of the College Council is to make sure that departments don't give tenure to cronies, people with poor references or research, or with other drawbacks that should prevent tenure.

But this was the early 1980s, when Washington, like the rest of the country, was in a state of financial crisis. The state was looking to cut down numbers in university departments. After the near-unanimous vote by the tenure committee members, the College Council turned me down for tenure, saying, "She's clinical, not a real scientist—she's in the wrong place. She should be in the psychiatry department at the medical school." There was another woman up for tenure that year, and she was turned down, too. What about the two men in our group, who had something like a 60 percent rating? How did they fare in all of this?

They both got tenure.

You Can Bend but Never Break Me

My chair said, "Don't worry, Marsha, you'll get it. They're going to vote again. I'll be there. You'll get it." You could get a second vote if the faculty insisted on it. So I went around to every member of my department and said, "Look, they are saying I shouldn't get tenure in this department because what I am doing is 'applied' research, not real research. What do you think? What do you think I should do?" I felt fully centered during this episode, didn't yell and scream and say "It's not fair." I just calmly talked to my colleagues around me.

Bob was standing up for me. "I presented a strong case at the faculty meeting, talking to colleagues, saying it would be to our disadvantage if she were to go elsewhere," he says. "There was some muttering about how her research hadn't progressed very far. I told them that Marsha was treating patients that no one else would treat, and that they were not recognizing how difficult it is to do research on this population."

The dean refused to step in and overturn the council's negative decision. The director of clinical training supported me and tried to intercede with the dean. The dean again refused. There was a lot of refusing going on by this time. But eventually the dean agreed: "Okay, I'm going to read everything she's written and I'll make my decision, but I'm going out of town for two weeks." It was torture.

The dean returned to town. It was late December, a Friday, the last day for a yes-or-no decision. I was beside myself, on edge waiting for word from the dean. My chair tried to reassure me: "Don't worry, Marsha. You'll get it." By midmorning we'd heard nothing. By now I was seriously beginning to doubt I'd get a yes decision. Noon came and went. Nothing.

Three o'clock and we were still waiting. "I've had it," I said. "I'm going home." I walked the twenty blocks to my house. It was already getting dark. And I was beginning to feel strangely calm.

At home, I put on "I Am Woman," by Helen Reddy, a favorite call to arms:

You can bend but never break me
'Cause it only serves to make me

More determined to achieve my final goal
And I come back even stronger
Not a novice any longer
'Cause you've deepened the conviction in my soul.

I sat on my couch, in the dark, and said to God, "If you want me to do this work, you have to give me tenure. If I don't get tenure, I'll accept that this is not what I'm supposed to be doing now. Either way is okay with me, but if you want me to do this, I have to get tenure."

The doorbell rang and I went to answer it. It was my chair, holding a bottle of champagne.

He extended it toward me, beaming. And said, "Congratulations, Marsha."

CHAPTER TWENTY-FIVE

The Birth of Dialectical Behavior Therapy

THE GOAL OF my NIMH-funded research study was to determine whether behavior therapy would be effective in treating highly suicidal people. And, specifically, to see whether behavior therapy was *more* effective than the standard treatment of the time, which was principally psychoanalysis. Here's what happened.

The Search for the Right Balance in Therapy

There were four research goals. The first was to develop a reliable and valid measure to assess intentional self-injury and suicide attempts; this is called an outcome measure. Second, conduct a pilot study to develop the new treatment, to determine whether it has promise. Third, develop a treatment manual, a how-to guide, that I could use when conducting a randomized clinical trial and that could then be used by others treating the same population of patients. The final goal was to carry out a randomized clinical trial, based on the first three goals, to properly evaluate the new treatment.

The treatment plan was to combine problem-solving, assertiveness training, and standard behavior therapy. I would be the principal therapist in the study, working one-on-one with participants, who were mostly female, for about an hour once a week. I would talk through issues that had been bothering them in the past week, exploring what new exercises might be helpful. A fairly typical behavior therapy. Other team members would watch the therapy sessions through a one-way mirror and take notes on what worked and what didn't work. They would know it wasn't working if the patient screamed at me, walked out saying I was invalidating them, and so forth.

After each session, our team (around seven or eight people) would discuss the treatment session. I used this input to decide which procedures should be kept in the treatment and which should be dropped. The manual evolved as we went along. As far as I am aware, it was one of the first manuals—if not the first—to be written this way. That is, by observing exactly what the therapist actually does in the therapy room, rather than basing treatment instructions on theory.

Standard Behavior Therapy—a Technology of Change—Doesn't Work

Once I had my outcome measure established, I began developing and pilot-testing the treatment. I immediately found myself in uncharted territory. The client would come in, we'd talk, she would tell me about her life problems and why life did not seem worth living. We had to discover which of her many problems was driving her suicidal behaviors. It might be her believing that no one loved her, that people hated her, that she just wanted to die. I would say, "No problem. I can find a treatment for that." I went through existing behavior therapy manuals to come up with the appropriate treatment.

The next week, I would review with the client what I thought was needed to solve the problem we had focused on, what changes we could make together. But a typical response to any attempt to change the patient's behavior was "What? Are you saying *I'm* the problem?"

They got very upset, sometimes retreating into silence, other times standing up, yelling, throwing chairs, stomping out of the room. "You're not listening to me," the client would say. "You're not hearing what I'm suffering. You're trying to change me."

Most of the clients had experienced intense suffering. They had tragic stories. In addition, they were extremely sensitive to anything that appeared to invalidate their pain, anything that suggested that they themselves needed to change. Standard behavior therapy, which is focused on helping people change, was a red flag to them.

For these clients, it was as if they didn't have emotional skin. As if they had suffered from third-degree burns all over their body. Even the lightest touch was excruciatingly painful, and they lived in environments where everyone kept poking at them. They perceived suggestions aimed at change as personal attacks or as further invalidation. It would whip them off the emotional charts.

Many Different Versions of Hell

I realized that what these people obviously needed was for me to be compassionate, to validate them, to show that the factors driving their suffering made sense to me. I had to see the world from their point of view. Before the study started, I'd had no idea how excruciatingly painful the lives of these people were. I would have to find a way for both the client and the therapist to accept the tragedies that had happened.

At the time, I didn't connect their suffering with mine. My past was so different from many of theirs. I understood pain, loneliness, rejection in general. But I didn't have to relate their experience to my past in order to understand their suffering. (That is hard to do anyway, when you are intently focused on someone else.)

When I heard and saw them, I felt with them. In a small but meaningful way, I went through what they were describing as they described it. This is not unusual among therapists. All of us have cried with our clients; all of us have felt stabbed in the chest with them. The specific thing from my life that was helpful was: I actually know what hell is, and I know how to get out. The path out of hell is hard work, a sea of misery, but I know a person can get out.

A New Focus on Acceptance: That Didn't Work, Either

So I dumped the emphasis on change and went full-bore for helping clients accept where they were in their lives. My new goal was to validate my clients' tragic lives. I knew about unconditional positive regard, a set of strategies developed by the humanistic psychologist Carl Rogers. And I knew of supportive therapy, an approach that focuses on providing a strong therapeutic alliance, where the therapist is both trusting and validating. "No problem," I thought, "acceptance is it. I am switching my strategy."

The response to this was as volcanic as it had been to my focus on change. "What? You're not going to help me?" the client would say. "You're just going to leave me here, in all this pain?" More tears, more sitting mute, more walking out of the room.

As the study progressed, I began dancing back and forth, back and forth, back and forth, trying to find the right balance in the dynamic between pushing for change and offering acceptance. It was like walking on a tightrope. Too much weight on either side and over you went.

Blackmail Therapy

My students jokingly called our treatment "blackmail therapy." I would spend a lot of time at the beginning on validation, and very little on change, other than a commitment to stay alive until the next session. Once I had a good relationship with the client, I would use it as a reinforcement, by increasing warmth toward the participant following effective behaviors or emotionally withdrawing it as a negative consequence of dysfunctional behaviors.

With suicidal clients, I would generally start by asking if they believed that they would be happier if dead. They seemed to think that their suffering would end if they killed themselves. I'd point out that there were no data proving that was true. There are religions that believe if you kill yourself you will go to hell, and others that believe you will have to live your whole life all over again. That could keep me from doing it!

The team continued to observe and offer feedback on therapy sessions. Before long we noticed a pattern. Clients had many tragedies, problems, and disorders, and they kept changing what they wanted to work on in therapy. They would say the problem from the previous week wasn't important, that some other problem was now more important. If I tried to work on one problem, the client would bring up another problem apparently even more distressing than the earlier one. "I can't stand it," "I'm going to kill myself," and so on. I realized that a core problem for my clients was their inability to tolerate distress.

Skills to Help People Tolerate Distress

I had to teach clients how to accept some suffering in the moment so that we could then focus on more important problems, such as life-threatening behaviors and dealing with interpersonal relationships. At that time, in the early 1980s, there were no protocols for teaching acceptance. No protocols for how to cope with the pain. Teaching acceptance was simply not part of the behavior therapist's repertoire.

This was the impetus for developing a series of distress tolerance skills, of which there are more than a dozen. I told you earlier about the TIP skills (temperature, intense exercise, paced breathing, and paired muscle relaxation), which would have helped me cope better with the fire in my Washington, D.C., apartment. Half-smiling and willingness are two more examples.

Others include the STOP skills, which help you to not make a bad situation worse. They stop you from acting on your first impulse. Parents of my clients say the skills have helped them enormously in difficult situations with their kids. It helps them to not lose their temper! And, I'm sure you will agree, there are times in many people's lives (perhaps all people) when the STOP skills can be very helpful.

These are the STOP skills:

Stop the urge to act immediately.
Take a step back and detach from the situation.
Observe, so you can gather information on what is happening.
Proceed mindfully, by evaluating the most effective option to take, given the goals, and finally following that option.

I'll go into each step in more detail.

Stop:

When you feel that your emotions are about to take control, stop! Don't react. Don't move a muscle! Just freeze! It can help prevent you from doing what your emotion wants you to do—to act without thinking. Stay in control. Remember: you are the boss of your emotions. Or at least you can become the boss.

Example: If someone says something that provokes you (insulting you or saying untrue and hurtful things), you might have the urge to attack this person physically or verbally.

That, however, is probably not in your best interest. Doing that might result in your getting hurt, being jailed, getting fired, or saying something that is also untrue and hurtful. So stop, freeze, and don't act on your impulse to attack.

Take:

When you are faced with a difficult situation, it may be hard to think about how to deal with it on the spot. Give yourself time to calm down and think. Take a step back (in your mind and/or physically) from the situation. Get unstuck. Take a deep breath. Continue breathing deeply until you are back in control. Do not let your emotion control what you do. Remember: you are not your emotion. Do not let it put you over the edge.

> *Example:* You are crossing the street and don't notice a car approaching. The driver stops the car, gets out, and starts cursing at you and physically pushes you. Your urge is to punch him in the face; however, you know that would escalate the situation and get you in trouble. So you first stop and then literally take a step back to avoid confrontation.

Observe:

Observe what is happening around you and within you. Who is involved? What are other people doing and saying? To make effective choices, it is important not to jump to conclusions. Gather the relevant facts to understand what is going on and what your options are. Try to be nonjudgmental.

Proceed Mindfully:

Ask yourself, "What do I want from this situation? What are my goals? What choice might make this situation better or worse?" Go into wise mind (see Chapter 32 for a full explanation) and ask it how to deal with this problem. When you are calm and in control, and have some information about what is going on, you are better prepared to deal with the situation effectively, rather than make it worse.

Example: You get home really late from work because you had a flat tire on the way. Your partner starts to yell at you, accusing you of cheating on him and calling you names. You get really angry, and your first impulse is to yell and call him names back. However, you want to deal with the situation skillfully. So you stop and then take a step back from your partner. You observe that there are a lot of empty beer bottles in the kitchen and realize that your partner has probably had a little too much to drink. You know that when he's drunk, there's no point in arguing, and he is likely to apologize in the morning. So you proceed mindfully by explaining the flat tire, pacifying your partner, and going to bed. You postpone a full discussion till the next morning.

I am sure that you won't have a lot of trouble thinking back to a situation in which, had you used the STOP skills, you wouldn't have gotten yourself into a situation you later regretted.

Is This Something New?

Within a couple of years, I had an embryonic version of what eventually would be called Dialectical Behavior Therapy. It was wildly incomplete and still lacked some of the major innovations that make DBT so very effective (balancing acceptance and change, providing a set of behavioral skills, requiring that all therapists work within a team). My major question at that point, though, was this: Is DBT something new and different?

I wrote to a few trusted colleagues and described what I was doing. I'd ask the straightforward question "Is this something novel, or is it simply a version of standard behavior therapy?"

Terry Wilson is now professor of psychology at Rutgers. When I wrote to him back in the early eighties, he had recently served as president of the Association for Advancement of Behavior Therapy. Terry said something to the effect of "Your emphasis on distress tolerance and acceptance is unique, and not part of behavior therapy." As it turned out, acceptance was a key difference.

Movement, Speed, and Flow

Throughout the development of DBT, I had to be prepared to go where my clients wanted to go. At other times, I had to guide them where I wanted them to go. It required a spaciousness of mind, dancing with what I call "movement, speed, and flow." Both the client and the therapist are moving forward into a new place, smoothly and quickly. It became a mantra for us. Knowing when to push. Knowing when to support. Going back and forth, an organic and loosely scripted flow. It's not easy to explain this process.

Beatriz Aramburu, a former student, has a different angle on it: "Marsha has a deep, deep blend of warmth and caring for her clients, and she couples that with telling them, 'That's not all right— stop doing that. I understand why you do it, and I know it comes from pain and is difficult to stop. Now knock it off.' Marsha has a very good clinical sense of getting into the client's mind."

This new therapy we were developing was more demanding than standard behavior therapy, not least because the client population the therapist works with are highly emotionally volatile and present the very real threat that they might kill themselves. You can imagine how emotionally draining that could be. The therapist needs to be compassionate without getting drawn into the horrors of her client's current crisis. In addition, clients are free to call their therapist at any time of day or night. Again, the therapist has to be compassionate, but completely focused on directing the client to the DBT skills that are relevant to the current crisis. DBT practitioners have to be willing to reveal themselves to some degree. It's not surprising, then, that there is a high burnout rate among DBT practitioners. Many therapists have to move on to other avenues of work after three years or so. At the same time, DBT is more liberating. "It is a treatment that allows me to be me, to use me, the person, as a therapist, as opposed to just supporting the client," says Beatriz.

Another student of mine, Anita Lungu, echoes this. "To be good at this therapy, you have to know the treatment components extremely well," she says. "Yet at the same time, it allows me to be who I am. I don't need to put on a therapist's hat and assume a different persona, because I am in the role of therapist. I can be who I am, very genuine, very straightforward, say what I think. And at the same time, having the treatments in my mind to guide my decisions. I don't have to become a different person to be a therapist."

The Role of Irreverence

One of the defining techniques is irreverence. I am naturally irreverent, saying what is on my mind, not censoring myself, calling a spade a spade. It's gotten me in trouble more than once. But the students noticed that my irreverence often had beneficial effects, getting the therapy unstuck after it had jammed.

Being irreverent is saying the unexpected. Research shows that unexpected information is processed more deeply than expected information. It gets the client's attention, maybe jolts them out of their mental rut—hating therapy, for example, or being consumed with self-loathing. An example might be:

CLIENT: I'm quitting therapy!
THERAPIST: Oh. Would you like a referral?

It is not being cold and unemotional. It has to be in a context of warmth and validation, letting the client know that you understand that they are miserable and why they are miserable. The population of people I work with often have a rather direct and intense way of communicating, and they often respond positively to equally direct communication.

> CLIENT: My life is so horrible. I am so miserable. I just want to be dead, to escape all this pain!
>
> THERAPIST: You know, there is absolutely no evidence that you will feel better when you are dead. Why take the risk?

For Charles Swenson, who was the first person outside the clinic whom I trained in the new therapy, in the late 1980s, it was a challenge. He had had psychoanalytic training, so he was stepping into very different territory. I'll let him tell his story.

Marsha supervised me in the beginning. I would videotape a session, send it to her, and she would talk about it with me over the phone. She'd always start by saying, "Okay, I've watched the tape. Do you want the good news or the bad news?" I said, "Let's start with the good news." She said, "You are unbelievably validating. I think your psychoanalytic training probably helped with that. You have a million ideas. I think your psychoanalytic training helped there, too."

I then said, "So what is the bad news?" She said, "Are you ever funny? You aren't in your sessions. You are like you are in church. That has to change. Do you have irreverence in you? Next week, I want you, at least once, to speak without thinking. Just speak. See what comes out." She was right. I thought too much. It was my psychoanalytic training.

I eventually figured it out. There was an adolescent boy I was working with, and adolescent boys can be very dark. He said to me, "Why should I do anything in therapy with an adult? Have you looked at the world lately? Have you seen how fucked up the world is now? Who has done that? Have children done that? No! Adults have fucked up the entire world, and they do that every day, and I am supposed to be in therapy with an *adult*?" My response was "I know what you are saying. But you are wrong. It is way worse than you are saying. It is worse than you can imagine. I can't even tell you how bad it is." The kid said, "Really?" It got his attention. I said, "Yes, but I can't go down that road or we'll both end up dead." That's pretty irreverent, because it's not what he was expecting to hear. He really turned around.

Most people are very serious when they talk about suicide. It is a serious matter, of course. But being serious all the time is not the answer. The occasional irreverent statement, spoken with humor, warmth, and support, can be an effective tool. It can produce fireworks, sometimes when you least expect them. It's all in the timing. A client might get angry, for instance, and scream at me that a friend will take care of her dog when she's dead. I would say, "Well, I am going to tell them not to. So if you want your dog to live, you have to stay alive."

Acceptance: For Both the Client and the Therapist

One of the reasons I developed a therapy that was out of the mainstream was likely because my academic training was in science and the methodology of scientific research. I hadn't formally trained as a clinician, dealing with clients. I was saved from "therapy-ese"— the approach to treatment that is highly rule-bound, overly "fragilizing" of clients, with oh-so-soft voices on the one hand, treating them as damaged human beings in need of coddling, and judgmental invalidation on the other. I learned to apply science-based treatment at Stony Brook, but I had arrived there with an already developed philosophy of treatment. That philosophy, of compassion and love, later drove my development of DBT.

You could say there were two realizations that set me on the path to DBT. First, I had to accept clients for who they were, as well as accept the tragedy of their lives. Second, clients *also* had to accept the tragedy of their lives. I had to accept the slow pace of change, the attacks and anger from clients, the refusal to do what I wanted them to do. I also had to accept the real risk that he or she might die; I could even be sued. I saw what was needed— acceptance—but I didn't know how to do it myself, and I didn't know how to teach it.

Therapist Teams

Working with highly suicidal people is extremely challenging. Your emotions pull you in different directions. At one extreme is trying to take control of the patient's life, to save them from themselves. At the other is wallowing in compassion and empathy, sharing in the patient's misery and despair. Neither response is helpful. Therapists who work with highly suicidal people need emotional support themselves. This was why I developed the requirement for therapist teams.

Teams have two main responsibilities: first, to keep therapists effective and in compliance with DBT therapy, and second, to provide support to reduce therapist burnout. Teams are like therapy for the therapist. They are coaches and consultants to one another. Therapist teams also agree that all therapists are responsible for all clients. If a client commits suicide, and a therapist on the treatment team is later asked, "Have you ever had a client commit suicide?" the therapist has to say yes, even if he or she did not personally treat the client. This is no small responsibility.

Six Rules to Guide Therapists

I developed a set of six consultation agreements for therapists. Of the six, my favorite is the Fallibility Agreement. No one therapist is perfect, or can be. This rule, then, is that we have to accept that all therapists are fallible and can make mistakes that cause clients pain and suffering. "Therapists are all jerks," as we express it in the agreement. This rule, which is called the Fallibility Agreement, and the five others* are vital for providing support for every therapist on the team.

We were making good progress at this point (the early eighties), and I was encouraged by our direction. The combination of change skills and acceptance skills was new to psychotherapy. Now we needed a name for this new therapy.

* The others are the Dialectical Agreement, the Consultation-to-the-Patient Agreement, the Consistency Agreement, the Observing-Limits Agreement, and the Phenomenological Agreement.

CHAPTER TWENTY-SIX

Dialectics: The Tension, or Synthesis, Between Opposites

Around this time, I had an executive assistant, Elizabeth Trias, whose husband was a Marxist philosopher at the university. One day, while I was talking to her about the therapy, she said, "Marsha, your treatment is dialectical!"

Dialectics? I had never heard of it. So I looked it up in the Merriam-Webster dictionary and found the following definition: "a method of examining and discussing opposing ideas in order to find the truth." I like to think of it as "the tension, or synthesis, between opposites."

Dialectical Behavior Therapy seemed an appropriate name, reflecting as it does the tension between seeking change in a person and encouraging them to embrace acceptance.

Dialectics Is Everywhere: Embracing Opposites

Everything in nature is a dynamic balance between opposing forces. Planet Earth has a tendency to fly off into space because of centrifugal forces, but the sun's gravity opposes that. Every movement of every limb is a tension between opposing forces, flexor and tensor muscles: your biceps muscles bend your arms while your triceps straighten your arms. These are concrete examples, but, more strictly speaking, dialectics is about seeking an answer through embracing opposites.

It had been this basic tension that caught Elizabeth's attention. After her observation, I learned that dialectics has been the underpinning of much of social and natural science for the past 150 years. "Okay," I said to myself. "If it's good for science, it's good for me. 'Dialectical Behavior Therapy' it is going to be." It was like an epiphany, like learning what intuitively I already knew to be true.

Shortly after that, I called the philosophy department and said, "Can you send someone over here to teach me and my students about dialectics?"

Dialectics allows opposites to coexist: you can be weak and you can be strong, you can be happy and you can be sad. In the dialectical worldview, everything is in a constant state of change. There is no absolute truth, and no relative truth, either; no absolute right or wrong. Truth evolves over time. Values that were held in the past might not be held in the present. Dialectics is the process of seeking the truth in the moment, drawing on a synthesis of opposites.

There are echoes of what I said about willingness in a previous chapter: "Willingness is about opening yourself to what is. It is about becoming one with the universe, participating in it, doing what is needed in the moment."

I told my students that I was going to embrace this new perspective and I needed them to help me. "All right," I said, "we have to find everything that is not dialectical in the treatment and change it to being dialectical." There might have been eye rolls, but they were well used to this kind of thing. I was always having new ideas about where we should be going with the therapy.

Embracing dialectics was a bigger change of direction than anything before. It felt like jumping onto one of those sleek European bullet trains as it rushes into the station. It's the *Dialectical Express*!

The doors open, I leap aboard, and the train roars off into the distance. And I am thinking, "Well, I'll see where this takes me. If it crashes into a wall, I'll just have to think of something else."

So far it hasn't crashed.

Transactions: Therapy Balancing on a Teeter-Totter

Many of us tend to see reality in polarized categories of "either/or" rather than "all" or "this and that." We are often stuck in either the thesis or the antithesis, unable to move toward synthesis. An inability to believe in both of these propositions: "I want to be with you, and I want time alone." Or, "You forgot to pick me up at the ferry, and you still love me." Or, "I want to finish this chapter before I go home, and I want to go home and stop working right now." All of us face this. It is the inability to ask, "What am I leaving out here?" and "Where am I being extreme?" that gets us into trouble.

In the dialectical worldview, because everything is connected, blame is taken out of the picture. Because everything is connected, everything is caused. From the non-dialectical point of view, A is blamed on B—a one-way street. In the transactional dialectical world, A influences B and B influences A, back and forth, back and forth. (Transaction was a new idea in psychology when I developed DBT.)

When you think in a transactional way, in which everything has a cause, there is nothing to blame. There is a reason for every action. If you know the cause behind a certain behavior—no matter how unpleasant or hurtful that behavior might be—then that behavior makes sense.

Many of my clients are severely traumatized by one or both of their parents. I believe that most people are better off loving their parents than not, no matter what the parents have done. So many of those traumatized by their parents still want to somehow love them. I try to help them grasp that both outrage and understanding can come together. Their parents' behavior was reprehensible, *and* it was caused, meaning that the parents behaved as they did because of something that happened in their own lives. (Like how my mother's efforts to "improve" me derived from Tante Aline's successful efforts to improve her.) I can love a parent and disapprove of her at the same time.

The therapist must help find the syntheses of opposites, to look for what is being left out. I have spent many a session saying to myself, "Look for the synthesis. What am I missing?" A patient wants to go to the hospital. I don't want him in the hospital. A battle ensues. What is the dialectic? The patient thinks he is likely to commit suicide if he doesn't get in the hospital (a point I completely fail to understand); I believe he is likely to commit suicide if he goes into the hospital (a point the client completely disagrees with). What is the synthesis? We have to find a way for him to be safe either way. We have a problem to solve.

It took me a long time to realize the dialectic inherent in planning a suicide or engaging in self-harm. Both make you feel better, and both make you feel worse. Both sides are true. When I can't get an agreement from a client to stay alive forever, then I try for a certain amount of time. If she's giving me a week, I try for two, and keep going until I am stopped. If I can't get an agreement, I search for a synthesis: "If we can find a way to get your life to be experienced as worth living, would you be willing to work on finding that?" Almost all say yes. For a person who intentionally self-injures, I might ask, "If we could find a way to solve the same problems that are upsetting you without self-injury, would you be willing to make the switch?" So far, all have said yes.

Therapy is like being on a teeter-totter, with me at one end, the patient at the other. Therapy is the process of going up and down, each of us sliding back and forth on the teeter-totter, trying to balance it so we can get to the middle together and climb up to a higher level, so to speak. This higher level, which represents growth and development, can be thought of as a synthesis of the preceding level.

Then the process begins again. We are on a new teeter-totter, trying to get to the middle, in an effort to move to the next level, and so on.

The challenge in doing therapy with a highly suicidal patient is that, instead of being on a teeter-totter, we are actually balanced on a bamboo pole, perched precariously on a high wire stretched over the Grand Canyon. When the patient moves backward on the pole, if I move backward to gain balance, and then the patient moves backward again, and so forth, we are in danger of falling into the canyon. (The pole is not infinitely long.) My task is not only to maintain balance, but to maintain it in such a way that both of us move toward the *middle* rather than toward the ends of the pole.

The therapist must be able to speak for both sides: "You are miserable and want to die; I can understand how you feel, how painful your life is at times and how hard it is to stay alive. On the other hand, I can also imagine the tragedy of your dying by suicide. I know you often think no one cares, but I am pretty sure you know that I care, that your cat cares, and, if you really think about it, that your parent cares. I totally believe that you can build a life that you will view as worth living. Even in your tears, you have to believe whether you believe or not, letting go of disbelief, holding on to hope."

Here's one very practical, almost mundane way in which accepting the notion of continuous change altered our therapy. In the 1980s, psychoanalysts insisted that it was vital for the patient's psychological well-being to keep therapy very stable. The room had to be the same for every session, everything in the same place. I said, "Absolutely not. We will not do this." Our task is to help clients feel comfortable in all environments. We all need to learn to live with change. Switching the room up was one small way to help.

An Unexpected Spiritual Journey Begins

Have you ever found yourself doing something as if propelled by a force other than yourself?

I was walking down the hall in the main psychology building. It was early 1983, not long after I had gotten tenure. The door to the chair's office was open. I walked in and said something like "If I can put all my teaching for one quarter into another quarter, and do double work in one quarter, can I take off the other quarter without having to have a sabbatical?" The chair said, "Well, what do you want to do?" And I just blurted out, "I want to go to a Zen monastery."

He said, "Does that have something to do with your work?" And I said, "Of course it does, it absolutely does. I've got to learn the methods of acceptance myself in order to be able to teach acceptance more effectively to my clients. I don't know a lot about Zen practice, but the one thing I do know is that it is about learning how to accept where you are in the world. I have to go to a Zen monastery and learn the practice of acceptance."

He agreed to it. I walked out into the hall and almost passed out. I'm not kidding. I thought, "Oh, my God, *what* did I just do?"

Elusive Mystical Experience

At that time, I was leading a meditation group at my church. Each week was the same. We sat in a circle, most people cross-legged on the floor. (Not me. I couldn't do that as a child, and I still can't do it, so I sat in a chair instead.) We meditated in silence for about an hour and then went from person to person, each of us sharing our experiences, anything we felt was important.

Each week, I was bored. It wasn't that hearing other people's experiences bored me; no, I always enjoyed that. I was bored with *me, me, me.* While meditating, I was expecting some type of spiritual experience to lift me out of myself, just like the mystical experience I'd had in the chapel at the Cenacle Center almost two decades earlier. I was expecting a new enlightenment moment and was annoyed when it didn't happen.

I had learned from the hydrangea moment, a few years earlier at the Shalem Institute, in D.C., that God is all around, in everything and everyone. So I wasn't looking for God in that sense. What I was expecting and waiting for was a mystical experience of God, and I was bored when it didn't happen. I needed spiritual advice to help me accept my life for what it was. (I eventually learned that when it comes to spirituality, the more you actively want it, the less likely it is to happen. You have to throw yourself into your life as it is, and be open to whatever might be. That is acceptance.)

A decade earlier in D.C., I had embraced Gerald May's concept of willingness, which is a form of acceptance. But obviously it wasn't enough. I needed more, so that I could let go of my constant expectations of some new and mystical spiritual experience, and so that I could teach my clients acceptance. So I called my friends at Shalem and asked, "Who are the best contemplative teachers in the world?" I figured that if I was going to do it, I might as well go to the best. There were two suggestions: Shasta Abbey, a Zen Buddhist monastery in northern California, whose abbess was Roshi Houn Jiyu-Kennett; and Willigis Jäger, a Benedictine monk in Germany. I decided I would try to go to both.

I was a very spiritual person at the time, often going on silent retreats at Kairos House of Prayer. From time to time, I kidded around with friends, saying something like "Oh, I should go to a Zen monastery." I had little idea what Zen was, and now here I was, preparing to do just that.

Two things must have been fomenting in my mind. One was the practical need to do a better job of teaching acceptance. The other was a deep but barely articulated desire to discover a more profound spiritual identity. It was these two things that had propelled me into the chair's office that day. And I had simply followed my instinct.

I called Shasta Abbey and said, "I would like to come down for a three-month stay." They said, "No, you can only come for a weekend." I asked why and they said, "Because you might not like it. And we think it is important for people who have not been here to try it out before deciding to come to our long-term training program." I thought to myself, "How is that relevant?" I couldn't care less whether I *liked* it or not.

In truth, though, I had little idea of what I was getting into. I was terrified. Judith Gordon, a friend of mine, kept saying to me, "You know, Marsha, not every moment is going to be terrible and painful."

I asked myself, "What do I have to lose, really? Nothing as important as what I have to gain." So I packed up my office, told the director of clinical training what I was doing, packed my camping gear and three months' worth of clothes, and, on August 20, 1983, set off on the five-hundred-mile drive to Shasta Abbey.

....

CHAPTER TWENTY-SEVEN

Learning Acceptance Skills

I COULD HAVE TAKEN Interstate 5 all the way to the town of Mount Shasta. The drive would have taken me maybe ten hours if I'd pushed it. But I chose instead to meander along back roads, enjoying the spectacular scenery and looking for suitable spots to camp overnight. It took ten days. I kept a diary of my trek, and it reads like a musing hiker's travelogue of the Pacific Northwest.

Here's an early example:

8.22.83: McKay's Crossing Campsite, Oregon

Well, here I am sitting by my fire a stone's throw from a rushing creek, my lantern on, a book close by, tent up & ready for me, dinner eaten (I even made bran bread by putting muffin mix—mixed—in my camp skillet with a pot upside down over it & one under it—sitting on my fire—it turned out good)—

Last night I stayed at a site on a lake just across from Mt. Hood—it was beautiful! A family to my left, 2 gay women to my right, a group of young boys/men up a space, couples & families & good cheer—& I didn't need my ear plugs, I went to sleep at 10 & slept until 9 am! Only waking once . . .

On the Road to Freedom

Shasta Abbey is a Buddhist monastery in the Serene Reflection Meditation (Soto Zen) tradition, which focuses on paying attention to one's thoughts without being drawn into them. It is a training monastery open to visitors who, like me, want to learn about Zen Buddhist meditation and spiritual training.

At an elevation of four thousand feet, half a dozen rustic stone buildings nestle among tall pines and flowering and fruiting bushes on sixteen acres. A few miles to the east, the majestic Mount Shasta towers a further ten thousand feet above the abbey. It is a truly spectacular setting, both peaceful and breathtaking. The buildings were raised by Italian stonemasons in the 1930s, as a motor lodge. Other structures, with Buddha statues and brass bells and gongs, are scattered among meandering walkways.

Roshi Jiyu-Kennett founded the abbey in 1970. She was born in England in 1924 and grew up questioning gender roles in society. She was called by God to be a priest in the Church of England, but church rules didn't permit women to be ordained, so she turned to Buddhism. She studied in Japan, the first female to be sanctioned by the Soto School of Japan to teach in the West. She was an ardent feminist. She set traditional Buddhist liturgy to music based on Gregorian chants.

End of the first day:
    Notes while at Shasta Abbey

I am here at a Zen monastery
Feel at once very alien
    & kind of at home

We are to meditate with our eyes open nine times a day each time it has been a total struggle against closing my eyes I keep seeing double, one eye moving to the other side. When I told the director he said to stop worrying and just decide which eye to focus on and keep going, so I did.

    —In addition my back hurts at all times

I feel so utterly alone
I really want to go to Kairos, in Washington [Spokane], with Florence
    —perhaps I will stay here only a month
    —then go to the sesshin in Spokane

Perhaps I will come to be at peace here
I must give it a whole hearted try
    I must do my best here, & remember I am always uncomfortable when I feel new

Days were very regimented, beginning at four thirty with bells ringing in the darkness, followed by the soft shuffle of monks in their sandals and robes, heading to their first meditation of the day. There were eight people in our lay group, mostly men. The women slept on the floor of the meditation room, or Zendo. We had fifteen minutes to get ready in the morning. We had to roll up our sleeping bags and blankets and stow them in a drawer, do our ablutions, get dressed. It's amazing what you can learn to do in fifteen minutes.

An hour or so of meditation was followed by breakfast, served on long wooden refectory tables. It was the best vegetarian food I have ever tasted. We each had our own pots and silverware and a cloth, which we took from our allotted spots on kitchen shelves. Before we sat, we put our palms together and bowed, *gassho*, to the cosmic Buddha, and went to our assigned place at the table. (In Eastern religions, the *gassho* gesture involves the palms of the hands pressed together in front of the chest. It is a gesture of respect and reverence.) Someone would ring a bell. We raised our hands in *gassho*. Prayers were read as we uncovered our plates. Food was passed down the table from person to person. *Gassho*. We were expected to take what we were going to eat, no more, no less. All in silence, eyes down, focusing on the moment. All very ritualized. The head director told me, "Marsha, we have noticed that you are not staying in your practice during breakfast." (I kept looking along the table to see what was coming.)

Then there was work around the farm. Jobs were handed out after breakfast. I loved the entire experience. When we passed another member of the crew, we were expected to look down, not catch their eye, and remain silent. When a lot of people live as close together as in the monastery, the only privacy is that others do not look at or attend to you, nor you to them.

Lunch had the same rituals. More meditation. Zen instruction. Sometimes we listened to tapes of Roshi Jiyu-Kennett. One of the guys always fell asleep during these sessions and snored loudly. This was a great chance to practice acceptance. Another work period, then supper, then vespers sung in Gregorian chant. Then casual time, which for us laypeople was in a very small sitting room, reading, sewing, writing letters, drinking tea, just being. We could talk then. Finally came the last meditation of the day, and then to bed.

It felt very alien to me. I'm sure I wasn't the only one who was wondering what we had gotten ourselves into. At the same time, I knew it was part of that spiritual journey that I had embarked upon a couple of years earlier when I was at the Kairos House of Prayer. It felt like refinding the essential me.

Adjusting to a New Routine

What I quickly became most excited about was the work around the farm. Sometimes it was moving sheep dung in a wheelbarrow. Sometimes picking green beans or digging trenches or pouring concrete for a new path round a garden. One week, a friend and I were caught talking while picking beans. This led to our entire group's losing our evening tea time, including our fabulous desserts. Fortunately, everyone else in our group practiced acceptance.

Had a wonderful time at work today. Got assigned to the construction crew & helped pick & shovel for a new sidewalk. What fun! Had learned to pick 2 days ago while digging a garden (fun also). Was the only woman on the crew. Felt very macho!
  "I am woman
  I am strong . . ."

What was thrilling about the work—about everything, really— was the gender equality. It was the single most nonsexist environment I've experienced in my entire life. It felt like going back to the womb, so safe, so comforting. I was so ecstatically happy that within a few days I was seriously considering giving up my life back in Seattle, training to be a Buddhist monk, and living right there at Shasta Abbey. It became something of an obsession, as is clear in my diary entries. These thoughts kept insinuating themselves during meditation—a no-no. I struggled with that.

Meditation was hard enough for me physically without having this mental distraction. My back hurt terribly during meditation. My whole left shoulder was tight. I couldn't figure out where to focus my eyes. I was so tired. My hands felt uncomfortable. It was all I could do just to keep awake. Hardly the image of spiritual serenity that comes to mind when one speaks of Zen meditation, is it? My Zen teacher told me that the back pain and tiredness were likely due to my resistance to accepting or dealing with something in myself, some kind of blockage. I doubt that. I likely needed a better way of sitting.

Another challenge was keeping my eyes down, not looking around. I am a scientist, and scientists by their nature are curious people. I knew this was going to be difficult for me.

On the very first afternoon, a junior guest master told me I was looking around too much. I was humiliated at first, but eventually I accepted his comment as valuable instruction. It took a lot of practice, but eventually I learned to focus. I had to be completely in the moment. It is the notion of not doing all the time what you want to do. It is letting go of having to know everything. Letting go of what you want. This was the road to freedom. It later became part of DBT, where I employed it in distress tolerance, just one of many translations of Zen practice into DBT skills. Acceptance is the freedom from needing your cravings satisfied.

Acceptance Demands Practice, Practice, Practice

At Shasta Abbey, you had to work hard while at the same time not seeing any particular job as a "good" job, better or more deserving of your time than another. So if you were sweeping and the bell rang, the signal to go to the next thing, you stopped sweeping right away. It was considered egotistical to think, "No, I have to finish what I'm doing and then I'll go to the next thing." You would be obeying what you wanted to do, not what you should be doing.

Another thing: you don't help another person unless you're asked, because if you're helping them, you're probably really doing it for yourself. This can definitely be true for a therapist. I am always telling my therapists to make sure they are doing what is good for the client, not what makes them feel good as a therapist.

"June" (another lay trainee) annoys me
    —she bows too deep
    —does everything precisely & "too good"
    —& I feel she is being "better than thou"
    —she scrapes all her food off her plate with her fingers going too far I am sure! At everything
    —she takes all foods and eats it in layers (the cheese off the cheese on the toast, filling out the pie, etc. probably as a way of eating one food at a time)

—I find myself just annoyed

—I also am sanctimonious myself, and very much a snob.
June was a library clerk before coming here & somehow I
see her coming here to be a monk (she will enter soon) as a
way of

        Get this

Unfairly jumping up the hierarchy! Or something like
that!!!

The above diary entry, with my allergic reaction to "June," demonstrates that this learning process didn't come easily. In my defense, the anti-June rant happened not long after I entered training. But if I had absorbed and assimilated the core principle of Zen right away, June would not have gotten under my skin. There were several other similar entries about her later on in the journal. I tried my best to take my negative reaction to June as an opportunity to practice acceptance.

But the learning process was slow. I think that is most people's experience. It takes practice, practice, practice, and is never-ending, really. It is like learning how to do anything that is new and challenging. Even now, three decades later, after many years of being in Zen practice and eventually becoming a Zen master, it is still practice, practice, practice.

DBT Skills Are Life Skills

When I think back to my early years in Seattle, believing I could help highly suicidal people out of their trough of suffering and anguish with just twelve weeks of behavior therapy, I am humbled. DBT doesn't offer a "cure" for people whose lives are unbearable, in the sense that antibiotics might cure a bacterial infection, or immersion therapy might eradicate a specific phobia. Instead, DBT is a path to building a life experienced as worth living.

I've already introduced you to a few DBT skills in earlier pages, including opposite action, distress tolerance skills (such as TIP), emotion regulation skills, and STOP skills, and I will describe more—in particular, mindfulness and radical acceptance—as we go on through my story. These skills, which help my clients realize a life experienced as worth living, are also skills for life. In fact, they are skills for *all* lives, for each and every one of us, not just those individuals with severe behavioral disorders. These "life skills," as you might call them, will help you lead a more fulfilling and spiritually aware life, and enhance your connectedness to yourself and to others. Whatever their context, DBT/life skills need to be practiced, practiced, practiced. It gets easier as time passes, but it still requires constant practice.

Like Zen.

In fact, I wrote in the diary, "Being here is like being in therapy." Shasta Abbey offered support and gave nonjudgmental feedback. I knew very quickly that this experience would be very healing for my clients. Not healing in the sense of curing an illness, but healing in the sense of nurturing the person for who they really are— welcoming their soul. And it comes with a challenge, because, as I put it in my diary, "Here, as in therapy, one must confront oneself!" And I sure tried to.

But I was struggling mightily with where I was going and what was expected of me in life.

I feel bewildered. On the one hand, I feel called to do the work I do. I promised to return to hell to get (help) others out & I feel the way I am doing it is the best way to go about it.

I believe I have something to contribute & that for it to have an effect, I need to stay in the scientific community.

Light bulb: If I went on half salary—that would be more than enough to live on
     & I could come down here, train to be a monk
       & still keep my job

I went back and forth trying to figure out how to juggle these competing parts of my life. About a month after I arrived, a truly wonderful woman, Sunder Wells, joined our lay group. Like me, she was Catholic, and on a spiritual journey. She planned to become a monk and wanted to establish a contemplative community of some kind.

Sunder and I spent a lot of time talking about how we might do such a project together. (Actually, too much time talking—she was the one I was talking to when we got reprimanded for causing "a ruckus" while picking green beans. I'm sure it was nowhere near what you and I would understand a ruckus to be.) We continued to scheme and spent a lot of time writing up plans for how to make the project come to life and discussing them during casual time in the evenings.

But these ideas, ideas of training to become a monk, of setting up a contemplative community, of working half-time—all of this came to an unequivocal end with one simple but powerful realization. As I expressed it in my diary:

NO! my clients!

I couldn't do anything that would take me away from my clients. Yes, I had left them for my stay at the abbey, but I did that so that I would be more effective in helping them. When someone is in distress, the best compassion you can give is to be effective in helping them.

About two weeks after I got to the abbey, I called the clinic and learned that Angela (not her real name) had been in a very bad way since I left. She had been hospitalized and was so completely out of control that she had to be transferred to another unit. She wrapped herself in blankets and set them on fire. They had no idea what to do with her. Angela told them I was her therapist, but she hadn't told them I was away.

I wrote the following in my diary:

> I FEEL her pain!
> She is out of control, & yet I know that somewhere deep inside
> her is all that she needs to regain it.
>> —I can feel with her
>> —I have been there
>> She is still looking outside herself for what she needs
>
> God! The emptiness that she is experiencing, I know!
>> I know it well!
>
> I want to cry her tears for her, to take her place—yet I could only
> take one person's place—& then what of the others left? Only
> god can take everyone's place—& so, I have to leave it to him/
> her.

Getting Re–In Touch with Who I Really Am

My mother had been diagnosed with cancer shortly before I went to
Shasta Abbey. I wrote her postcards as often as I could, which was
almost every day. She occasionally wrote me letters, which were
both somewhat bewildering and heart-wrenching:

> She is writing me all these wonderful, loving special letters & I
> wonder what I will do when I know I will never get another
> one—(well, of course, I am crying again). I don't want her to
> die! She may be awful in person—but she is wonderful in let-
> ters—so perhaps, it is her core that writes. Oh! This is making me
> cry too much.

When I was with her, she focused on how I looked, how I talked,
how I ate ("Eat slower, Marsha"), and usually disapproved—she
would never validate or accept me for who I was. She loved me, I
am sure, but she didn't really like or admire the kind of person I was.
Marriage and children were most important to her, as they were to
most women of her generation from Tulsa.

But then, those letters, those loving letters. So sad.

In my postcards, I gave her whatever news I had. Shortly after I left the abbey, I wrote in my diary:

The Shasta Abbey experience got me re–in touch with who I really am—an expression of god in Creation. Who each of us is. Certainly the Kingdom of god is within each of us!

I always knew I was spiritual, but I had forgotten how integrated into my whole life spirituality really was.

I didn't know it at the time, but I was heading on a spiritual journey during the course of which that conception of me and God would change. A lot. Someone at the abbey said to me, "If you doubt your experience, you may lose it." Well, I am a psychologist, a scientist, so it is in my nature to be questioning. Doubting my relationship with God sure had a price. Remember my enlightenment experience in the Cenacle chapel, which I interpreted as "God loving me" but later came to realize was in fact "me loving God," just as I had loved Ed with a deep passion? At some point in my time at Shasta Abbey, I did indeed doubt my faith, and this further widened the gulf between me and God. I am now comfortable not having a personal God, as I did for so very long. I am me in the universe, and the universe is in me, in all of us together.

I think back to how fervently I used to pray, the feeling of ecstasy that flowed through me. The change is almost shocking. Although I throw myself into God almost every day, I don't pray very often anymore.

Okay, I'll admit I do pray sometimes, and that is when the Huskies—the University of Washington football team—are losing and need help. It is the one time I pray. I figure I should try it, just in case.

The Illusion of Freedom in the Absence of Alternatives

About halfway through my time at Shasta Abbey, I felt called by God to meditate for a very long time, just by myself. I thought I needed to have this intense meditation, and I guess God was going to show up or sit in the room or something. I couldn't break my schedule without permission, so I went to the director of training and explained want I wanted to do, what I *needed* to do.

He looked at me and then, with a small smile, said, "Well, if you need to do that, certainly you should do that." I was thrilled. Then he said, "Now, you know we don't do that here, but there's a Holiday Inn right down the street, and you can go there for three days and come back when you are finished." I was completely floored. Then I muttered something like "Maybe I made a mistake. Let me think about that."

Of course, I didn't go to the Holiday Inn. He had forced me to ask myself, "Okay, what do I really want? Do I want to go off by myself? Or do I want to be part of this community?"

I wanted to be part of the community.

The translation to therapy was easy. When a client says, "I'm done with this . . . I am going to get another therapist," she usually doesn't actually want to get another therapist. What she really wants is help in relieving her anguish. My response is "Would you like me to help you find one?" Or when the child says, "That's it. I am running away," she doesn't really want to leave home. She wants her mother to undo whatever it was that upset her. And the mother says, "Would you like me to help pack your bags?"

This is the illusion of freedom in the absence of alternatives. It is the illusion of having a choice—of accepting the offered assistance to achieve a stated goal—but not really wanting the stated goal. The client doesn't really want a new therapist. The child doesn't really want to run away. I do this all the time. Irreverent answers force clients to focus on what they really want. It can be very effective.

That was an easy lesson from Zen that I could implement in therapy. But I wanted more. I wanted to incorporate aspects of Zen meditation. My journey to Germany to be with Willigis would do that.

But before I go there, I need to describe what I mean by acceptance, and particularly *radical acceptance*.

....

CHAPTER TWENTY-EIGHT

Not Just Acceptance—
Radical Acceptance

I WANT TO TELL you a personal story about a failure of acceptance on my part.

Early in 1991, I had the good fortune to spend a vacation in Israel with my friend and colleague Edna Foa, who has a daughter there. I was on sabbatical in Cambridge, England, at the time, to write my professional book about DBT. By now you know that I love to travel, to explore new places. So I rented a car, planning to visit the area of the Golan Heights, where there was a good deal of conflict at the time. Edna and her daughter were concerned for my safety, driving around alone. They gave me all kinds of directions. "Don't stop for anyone, not even a policeman," Edna said, "because you might get yourself kidnapped."

I set off. Ahead of me, I saw a road that seemed to be going in the direction I had planned. I took it, and drove with purpose. And drove. And drove. The neatly paved road began to deteriorate. I found myself bumping along a dirt track, and then there was no track at all. There were cars in the distance, up the hill, but I couldn't see how to get there. I started to think that I must have taken a wrong turn somewhere and that this wasn't the right road. *Brilliant deduction, Marsha.* I became afraid and turned back. Then I stopped the car and said sternly to myself, "I don't approve of your acting on fear. You have to turn around and go back along that road." So I did. I kept going.

After a while I came across a kibbutz, and I stopped and chatted with the people there. Dusk was approaching, and I had to think about getting back. The problem was, I couldn't find my way. Every road seemed to end up at the edge of a cliff. I began to worry that I might run out of gas. Then I began to worry that Edna might come looking for me. A man on horseback swept past at great speed. It was getting to be a bit nightmarish, and I began to fret that I might go to jail and my friends would find out what a bad person I am.

Finally I stopped the car and said to myself, "Okay, Marsha. You have a PhD. That means you should be able to figure out how to get out of here." I gave myself a new rule: "If you go down a road once, and it is the wrong road, you cannot go down that same road again, because it will still be the wrong road." But the roads that looked right were all the wrong road. And all the other roads looked like they were going toward a cliff. I had been driving for hours.

But I finally made it back safely.

That new rule I imposed on myself—"If you go down a road once, and it is the wrong road, you cannot go down that same road again, because it will still be the wrong road"—was an example of *radical acceptance*, which, until that point, I had failed to follow. The same thing happens when you've mislaid your keys and you go looking for them. You look in all the obvious places. You don't find them. You start looking in less obvious places. You still don't find them. Then you check the obvious places again. No luck. You have to accept the fact that once you've checked the obvious places and not found your keys, looking again in those places is a waste of time, because they still won't be there. We've all been guilty of this one, I should think.

The following is a story about acceptance that I adapted from one told to me by my Zen teacher, who read it in a book by another spiritual teacher, Anthony de Mello:

A man bought a new house and planned to create a beautiful garden. He worked hard, did everything the gardening books instructed him to do. But dandelions kept showing up on his lawn. The first time he saw them, he thought simply pulling them out would do the trick. It didn't. Then he used weed killer. That worked for a while, but then they returned. He worked harder, pulling them out *and* killing them with weed killer. They were gone. Or so he thought.

The following summer, they came back. He decided the problem lay in the type of grass he had used for the lawn. So he spent a lot of money and had all-new sod put down. It worked: no dandelions. He was very happy. And he began to relax in his beautiful garden. Then they returned yet again.

A friend told the man that the source of the offending weeds was other people's gardens. So he went around to all his neighbors and convinced them to kill all their dandelions. They did. But to no avail. The dandelions returned just as before.

By the third year he was exasperated. After failing to find solutions with local experts and more gardening books, he decided to write to the U.S. Department of Agriculture for advice. Surely they could help.

Several months later, an official-looking envelope arrived. He was so excited. Help at last! He tore open the envelope and read the letter: "Dear Sir. We have considered your problem and have consulted all our experts. After careful consideration, we think we can give you very good advice. Sir, our advice is that you learn to love those dandelions."

I often tell this story to my clients. My idea is to get them to the point where they can say, "I know this is a dandelion." In other words, a problem that isn't going to go away easily, so the best way forward is to work with it as best you can.

Radical acceptance is complete and total openness to the facts of reality as they are, without throwing a tantrum and growing angry.

What is the difference between acceptance and radical acceptance? This is what I tell my clients:

> Acceptance is acknowledging or recognizing facts that are true, and letting go of fighting your reality (and of throwing tantrums).
>
> Radical acceptance is accepting all the way, with your mind, your heart, and your body—accepting something from the depths of your soul, opening yourself to fully experiencing reality as it is in this one moment.

One client preferred the phrase "radical acknowledgment" to "radical acceptance." Same thing.

The following is a typical description of radical acceptance by clients who have experienced DBT:

> One of the skills that helped me early on to get through this was radical acceptance. That meant I had to accept that I was depressed, but that I was still okay. I learned I could be depressed but still go to work. You have to radically accept that you are right here right now, but you can still function in the world. Learning to accept that you can be depressed and still have a life. And you can be good enough. Learning that bad things and good things coexist. I can have a really bad day today and still go out and take my dogs for a walk. And that is really pleasant. It's learning to find a life that's worth living. It's knowing that maybe I will have depression or sadness, but that doesn't mean there aren't pleasurable things in my life, or that it won't end. "This too shall pass": that was a very important lesson that DBT taught me.

Teenagers like radical acceptance best; it's their favorite skill. Because it is "What is, is." That everything is caused. They want their parents to radically accept that they are who they are. They realize that you have to accept things in order to change things.

Acceptance for Therapists and Clients

The therapist has to accept the client—this means not just accepting but *radically* accepting. Accepting the client has to come from the depths of the therapist's soul. That isn't always easy. These are people whom most therapists won't treat; most therapists kick them out of therapy. So I have to accept my client for who she is. I have to accept the unbelievably slow rate of progress. And I have to accept the fact that she could kill herself the next day, and I might be sued.

When I came to this realization, this was the point at which I was truly on the path to developing DBT.

For my clients, acceptance is very, very hard, because their lives are often unbelievably tragic. They are the most miserable people on earth, unbelievably angry, unbelievably anguished, and they often attack their therapists. I've been the target of many such attacks. Often students come into my office, sobbing and sobbing. "They yell at me, they abuse me, how can they say these things to me, they're so terrible, I can't stand it." And I say, "Look, you can't dislike your clients for having the problems that we're here to help them with. That's all this is. The problems we're here to treat have shown up in your office. That's good news. It's not bad news. But, yes, it's hard."

For clients, acceptance is the first step toward change. In order to change who/what you are, you must first accept who/what you are. You have to accept reality in order to change it. Reality is what it is. If you don't like it, you can change it. The following are the six key pointers about radical acceptance:

- Freedom from suffering requires acceptance from deep within of what is. Let yourself go completely with what is. Let go of fighting reality.
- Acceptance is the only way out of hell.
- Pain creates suffering only when you refuse to accept the pain.

- Deciding to tolerate the moment is acceptance.
- Acceptance is knowledge of what is.
- To accept something is not the same as judging it as being good.

If you surrender and radically accept life as it is—with willingness, without resentment, without anger—then you are in a place from which you can move on. Don't say, "Why me?" Whatever has happened has happened. To radically accept something is to stop fighting it.

The problem is, telling you what radical acceptance is and telling you how to do it are two different things. Radical acceptance can't really be completely explained. It's something that is interior. It's something that goes on inside of you. You could say it is the will of God. Accept with grace. You might not have an enlightenment experience like I did, but you can move forward in your life, grow, and be transformed through embracing radical acceptance.

People who have been in DBT treatment often say something like this:

Radical acceptance changed my life. My therapist was constantly asking me, "Do you want to escape from your hell?" And I would say, "Well, yeah, of course." And she would say, "Well, you have to practice radical acceptance." Sometimes it is really, really difficult, especially if the suffering seems unbearable. But it works.

The next skill that's involved with radical acceptance is "turning the mind." Radical acceptance is not something you can do just once. You have to do it over and over and over. You have to practice turning the mind toward acceptance. It's a little bit like walking down a road, and you keep coming to forks in the road. One direction: accepting. The other direction: rejecting. Turning the mind is when you keep turning your mind toward the acceptance road.

It can be very hard. You have to practice, over and over and over.

It's like walking through a fog, seeing nothing, nothing, nothing. And then suddenly you emerge into sunlight. The good news is that if you practice turning the mind toward acceptance, eventually you'll practice acceptance more often. And if you do that, what happens? Suffering gets less intense. Suffering goes down to being ordinary pain.

Go Find a Tulip Garden

Radical acceptance is akin to willingness, Gerald May's beautiful concept that originally pointed me in this direction. Willingness is when you allow the world to be what it is. And, no matter what it is, you agree to participate in the world.

When I'm trying to explain willingness, I say that life is a lot like playing cards. Imagine that you are in a card game. You get dealt a hand of cards, as does everybody else. Now, what's the objective in a card game? The objective is to play the cards you get. Right? That's the game. You get the cards, you play them.

So you get your cards; other people get their cards. And one of the players gets mad about their cards, doesn't like them, throws them down and says, "I don't like my cards. I want different cards." You say, "Well, those are the ones you got dealt." And he says, "I don't care. It's not fair!" You say, "Well, those are your cards." He won't listen. "No! I'm not playing these cards."

What would you think? Would you want to play with that player? Probably not. And who do you think is going to win the card game? Not the person who threw their cards on the floor. In order to have a chance of winning the game, you have to be *in* the game, playing the cards you are dealt. Accepting that reality is willingness.

I used this phrase in an earlier chapter, but it captures the essence of willingness and radical acceptance so beautifully that I will reuse it here:

If you're a tulip, don't try to be a rose. Go find a tulip garden.

As I said in that earlier chapter, my clients are tulips, and they're trying to be roses. It doesn't work. They drive themselves crazy trying. I recognize that some people don't have the skills to plant the garden they need. But everybody can learn how to garden.

CHAPTER TWENTY-NINE

Good Advice from Willigis: Keep Going

WILLIGIS JÄGER, A German Benedictine monk, was described as "one of the great mystics and spiritual teachers of our time." He studied in Japan, and in 1981 he opened a Zen and contemplation center in northern Bavaria. He was a visionary and something of a radical, combining Christian mysticism with Zen traditions, as well as modern scientific insights. The result is a transconfessional, or trans-religious, spirituality. He played down the Christian concept of God as a person and stressed mystical experience over so-called doctrinal truths.

He so irritated the Catholic Church that in 2002, Cardinal Joseph Ratzinger (later Pope Benedict XVI) banned him from speaking in public in Germany. After a brief silence, he defied the authorities and continued to speak anyway.

My kind of leader.

But this notoriety was still in the future for Willigis when I met him at a retreat in Portland, Oregon, in November of 1983, a few days after I left Shasta Abbey. White-haired, tanned, solid in himself, Willigis defines the word "charismatic." Our meeting was in a small private room, and I was intimidated.

Willigis asked me, "How old are you?" Odd question, I thought. I told him, "Forty." He looked at me and said, "That's very boring." We both sat there for a minute, or maybe less, and then he asked me again. "How old are you?" This time I said, "Forever." He smiled and said, "Good. You have deep experience."

In Zen, there is no being born, no dying. Just forever. Willigis would describe it as experiencing that we are each an expression of essential being (God to some, Buddha to others). In essence, we are one.

I Am in a Very Different Environment

My friends at the Shalem Institute had advised me to study with Willigis, but the people in the lay group at Shasta Abbey said, "No, don't go. You will be in too much pain with that group." They meant that it would be so physically and emotionally demanding. I didn't listen. And so, on November 11, 1983, almost a month after I left Shasta Abbey, I set out for Willigis's Zen center, in Würzburg, excited but feeling some trepidation. I had expected to stay one month but ended up being there for four.

At Shasta Abbey, I had been surrounded by people who spoke and taught us spiritual classes twice a day, in English. A monk in training was walking around and watching our small group, which meant we got a lot of individual feedback. Being at Shasta Abbey was akin to being at a Catholic seminary, training to become a priest.

At Benediktushof (Benedictus House), by contrast, there was not a lot of feedback on our spirituality. Zen training, for the most part, took place in one-on-one meetings with Willigis. He gave half-hour Zen talks from time to time. The audience was always rapt, even if they had heard the talk ten times before.

But these formal talks were in German. In fact, most of the instruction was in German. I had no one to translate for me, so I learned nothing from them, but I still found them captivating. I could *feel* completely part of a conversation, without understanding a single word being said. It was a visceral experience, much like Zen is a visceral experience.

I had said to myself before going to Germany, "Either you can go to please the teacher or you can go to learn, but you can't do both. You have to choose." I chose to learn. This was definitely one of my best decisions. People see me as a leader, and of course I am from time to time. What many people don't appreciate is that I love being a follower, too.

The Challenges of Meditation

Willigis ran retreats, or sesshins, every couple of weeks at Benediktushof. "Sesshin" means, literally, "touching the heart-mind," and it is the expression of the core Zen principle that heaven and earth and I are of one spirit, that all things and I are one. The goal of the six-day sesshin is to *be* that oneness, together with your fellow participants—not necessarily to achieve some personal goal of enlightenment, though that might happen as a fringe benefit.

I explained in a note to Mother toward the end of my time at Benediktushof: "It is hard to describe what has happened to me here. There is little to say. I am so deeply into this experience & words do not play much part in it."

The core of the sesshin is intensive meditation (zazen), done three or four times a day, each time for about half an hour. Most people sit cross-legged on a mat on the floor, back straight, eyes open, in silence, perhaps elevated a little on a meditation cushion, facing a wall. The purpose is to go within and notice reality as it is in the present, noticing without analyzing (which is hard for a psychologist). Observing without analyzing is the essence of meditation.

Since, as I said before, I have never been able to sit cross-legged without extreme pain, I found a chair and did it that way. Your hands, maybe palms up, rest in your lap or on your thighs, and you begin meditation practice. Sometimes this is simply Zen breathing, which is counting your inhale (one), your exhale (two), your inhale (three), your exhale (four), and so on, up to ten; and then you start over, repeating this throughout the meditation period. I teach my meditation students that the exercise is about paying attention to one thing at a time, whatever it is, with the goal of reaching mental clarity and emotional calmness.

Walk Like a Buffalo

Traditionally, periods of zazen are interspersed with walking meditation, for about five minutes. When I asked one of the house teachers how I should walk, without hesitation she said, "Walk like a buffalo," as if I was supposed to know what that meant. So I just made up a rule: *Do what the person on my left is doing.*

Willigis is a big believer in walking. Sometimes during sesshin periods, he would send us to walk the paths through the gardens or the forest, eyes down. "Just be the walk," Willigis told us. It's harder than you might imagine—not thinking, not looking, not listening; just walking and becoming the walking. It is hard if you get distracted. At times my experience was one of being walked rather than of walking myself, of being the walking.

One day, while walking during a sesshin, I remembered how many times I had seen people in mental hospitals walking around, wringing their hands. As I walked, I would wring my hands, too, for all the mental patients of the world. "Today you don't have to wring your hands, because I am doing it for you," I would say. I still do it, in sesshins that I run in the States.

The Practice of Sesshins

Sesshins at Benediktushof lasted six days—same routine every day. Rise before dawn, sitting meditation, breakfast, more sitting meditation, walking, lunch, and so on until the end of the day. Sesshins are completely exhausting. The reason is that, odd though it might seem, it takes an enormous amount of energy, burning a lot of calories. Focusing the mind is hard work for the brain. Research proves this. My friend Martin Bohus said to me about his first sesshin, "I was more tired doing this than I am climbing mountains."

Sesshins are held in almost complete silence, except when you interact with your Zen teacher. There were typically more than a hundred participants at sesshins at Benediktushof. We lined up for our turn to talk with Willigis or another teacher. Willigis would ring a little bell, you would go in and ask him a question or raise a concern, he would respond, then he'd ring the bell again and the next participant would come in.

There was a hierarchy. The more advanced students were at the head of the line. They were working on koans, which are Zen paradoxical stories, or parables, for learning and going deeper into your true self, learning to express to the teacher (generally without words) Buddha nature, God nature, Jesus nature, essential nature, or whatever you want to call it. Next were the students who had yet to embark on koans. And then there were those who were not official students. That was me, at the end of the line. I loved being at the end of that line. At home, I was first in line in my lab, and being last in line at Benediktushof balanced that. I loved it.

Learning Through Koans

Here are some examples of simple koans. "How many stars are there in the sky?" "Stop the sound of a temple bell." "Make Mount Fuji take three steps." And there is the classic one "Does a dog have Buddha nature?" I can hear you say, "Well, Marsha, what are the answers?" I am not going to tell you, just as I don't tell my Zen students. If I were to tell my students the answers to koans, they would learn nothing.

Koans don't have answers in the way that normal questions do, such as "What is the distance between the Sun and Earth?" Or "How many continents are there?" Nor are they ethereal, supernatural visions. The student doesn't analyze the question but instead comes to an answer through meditation and holistic thinking. It's not an intellectual exercise. You must be open to allowing the answer to come. And when you do see the answer, you feel ecstatic. It's like "I can't believe I did that. Wow!" (The koan "How many stars are there in the sky?" doesn't have a numerical answer, by the way.)

Thinking about koans is a way to gain insight into the nature of reality, a reality that we typically perceive in a fragmented way. It is to see Buddha nature, the fundamental nature of all things, the oneness of the universe.

The student presents her answer to the teacher as if it were the only solution, because koans can have many solutions, as long as each captures the essence of its universal truth. The student conveys his or her answer to the teacher through acting or miming. Occasionally I got too intellectual, too analytical, and Willigis would admonish me, saying, "Concepts, Marsha, concepts." He'd ring his little bell and I'd leave to try to think of another way.

My Time with Willigis Is a Blessing

I loved the simplicity of Münsterschwarzach Abbey. Everything was beautiful, inside and outside. Large golden gongs faced the Zendo. Inside, there were beautifully arranged ikebana flowers placed thoughtfully throughout the very simple rooms, and small flowers on the tables at meals. Outside, there were flower gardens with flowing creeks and various statues. Very Zen.

The abbey was built in the late 1930s, but an abbey has stood on this site since the eighth century. The previous one was destroyed by fire in the early eighteenth century. The River Main is less than a mile to the west, and the surroundings are quite rural.

Most of the time I was very happy. I was happy here just as I had been at Shasta Abbey. One person at Benediktushof was very depressed and seemed angry at me for being happy. I said to him, "I can't help it if I am happy." Remember dialectics? At one and the same time, I could be very happy and very sad about aspects of my life and my journey.

But my poor back. I tried every strategy. Walking helped but did not solve the problem. One day, during a particularly painful sit, I suddenly realized that pain was irrelevant. I didn't have to pay so much attention to it if it wasn't dangerous, and mine wasn't. It was a great breakthrough, and it got me through many more painful moments.

Talking about physical pain was not what I wanted to do, but when I finally told Willigis about it, he jumped right into solving the problem. He told me to lie down on the floor in the upstairs chapel. I did that, and promptly got bopped on the leg by someone who told me I was not supposed to be lying down. I refused to open my eyes or respond and stayed there for the meditation period, but I didn't want to do it again. Next we tried a chair with arms and a back. There was a cushion on my lap, my arms rested on top of the cushion to support my shoulders, and it got me through without so much pain.

Now, sitting like that during zazen takes a fair amount of humility. Your natural tendency is to conform, to do what you are supposed to do. During meditation you are "not supposed" to sit in chairs with arms and backs; you sit cross-legged on the floor. But was I there to impress others, or to learn? I opted to stay in chairs with arms and backs and to learn meditation practice in relative comfort. When they saw me, the staff always said, "Get out the queen chair, Marsha is here," and they hauled down this huge red chair with arms.

Willigis spoke very good English when we met one-on-one. Soon my times with him stretched from five minutes to ten to fifteen, longer than any of the other students. Partly it was his way of making up for my not understanding his talks in German. So many times he said, "Marsha, I wish you could have understood my talk today." Over time, a bond grew between us, very much like my bond with Anselm, my spiritual director at Loyola.

I was, by turns, in states of both ecstasy and deep sadness. On one occasion Willigis said, "You have suffered, Marsha. I've never suffered, but I understand it." It was such a loving and validating embrace, as if he'd looked into my soul, seen my pain and anguish, and cradled it in his hands. I felt nurtured by Willigis, but I struggled mightily with the challenge of being there—going deeper into Zen, grappling with koans, the physical pain of meditation, the volcanic upwells of emotional distress. At one point I must have complained about this to Willigis. "So you want to quit, do you?" he said to me. "You don't want to come back here?"

In fact, I really had wanted to quit. But as soon as Willigis said it, my immediate, visceral response was "No, I absolutely do NOT want to quit. I am not a quitter. I am your most loyal student." I practically yelled at him. It was a pivotal moment for me.

Zen and Oneness

The experience of sesshins is just that: experience. It is nothing intellectual. That is Zen. It is more that you just *are*, the experience of "is-ness." Maybe you are at the railway station and you look up at the clock and realize that this is it, the is-ness—everything just is, there's nothing else.

We think of the universe as being a collection of separate entities that interact in a creative manner. But in Zen—in reality—everything is connected to everything else, as one. We are an expression of the one, God, grounded being, essential reality, Buddha nature.

Simple but Important Lessons Learned

I had gone to Shasta Abbey and Benediktushof to learn acceptance. The essence of Zen, after all, is acceptance of what is, of where you are in life. Two simple, practical activities during sesshins at Benediktushof had a big impact on my developing practice of radical acceptance.

First, all of us, including Willigis, had to stay seated until every single person in the dining room had finished eating. Now, to Mother's everlasting chagrin, I am a very fast eater. Every mealtime at Benediktushof was the same for me. I was completely exhausted from sitting and meditating and wanted nothing more than to finish eating and drop into bed for a quick nap until the next sitting meditation. Alas, there were some very slow eaters in the room, and we had to wait until every last person had finished. *Click, click, click*—the sound of a knife on a plate. *Click, click, click*. I had to wait until there was silence, finally. If anything taught me radical acceptance, this was it.

This rule of waiting until everyone has finished eating was such an effective practice that I carry it on in my own sesshins.

The second practice that reinforced my radical acceptance involved work in the kitchen. Everyone had a job, and mine often was washing dishes. I am very systematic and therefore very fast in tasks such as these. But, you guessed it . . . the people working with me were often completely nonsystematic, and slow, slow, slow. Radical acceptance again. I had to be patient, like it or not. In honor of this experience, I installed a large spray faucet in my kitchen at home, just like the one with which I washed dishes in sesshin. The faucet reminds me each day to practice.

Part of a Family, at Last

The simple, delicious vegetarian meals were sometimes taken at "the family table," a long table where Willigis and other teachers could see all the participants in the room. There were staff and short-term visitors and me, the first and only long-term visitor. When meals were taken at the family table, everyone would stand at their place until all were there, and then together we would bow and sit down.

Sitting at the main family table was no small thing for me. Willigis often told me to sit by him, particularly in the years following that first visit in November of 1983. "Come sit next to me, Marsha," Willigis would say, and that would be my seat until I left. It was a very embracing gesture. This was the most healing thing that had happened to me, this profound experience of being part of a family, being completely accepted.

Aline, my sister, later said to me, "You didn't have a home with a family growing up, Marsha, not in the way you needed it." She was absolutely right. For the first time, I understood what people meant when they said they were "going home" for Christmas. For many years, I did indeed spend Christmas at Benediktushof. To this day they are still family to me.

Over the years that followed that first visit, I got to know most of the other people at the abbey. Particularly important was Beatrice Grimm, a teacher of contemplative prayer and spiritual dance. I fell in love with the dancing. After dinner, the group would go outside and dance on the large driveway on warm days. Much of the dancing was to spiritual, prayerful songs called Taizé songs. It was a glorious experience.

The dance is done in circles, holding the hands of the person next to you. Dance is now an important component of the retreats and other gatherings I run in the States. The reason I get people to dance—I pair therapists with therapists and clients with clients—is to bring them together. I do a dance with clients because I believe that it gives them (if we can get them to do it) an experience of oneness, reminding everyone to stay mindful. The music we use is "Nada Te Turbe," a beautiful, soulful, meaningful piece that translates to "Let Nothing Disturb You." Later, in Chapter 36, you will learn about its meaning. When I have groups of therapists together, I get them to dance, too. For this one we use "The Shepherd's Song," which has a strong beat and is easy to dance to. Everyone calls it "the DBT dance." I urge therapists to follow this model when they are back home working with clients, to dance with them just as we did together.

(I got both pieces of music for my dances from my visits with Willigis.)

A Selfish Moment with Good Intentions

All too soon after I arrived in November of 1983, my planned one-month stay was coming to an end. I couldn't bear the thought of leaving. And I needed to learn a lot more if I was going to eventually translate this into an effective treatment for my clients.

Without thinking much, I called the department chair and asked for a three-month extension of my leave of absence, without pay. I thought it was a very reasonable proposition. I would be enhancing the quality of treatment for my clients, and the department wouldn't have to give me my salary during my extended absence.

But, of all the insensitive things I have done in my life, this undoubtedly was one of the worst.

First, I was completely ignoring the fact that I was supposed to teach specific courses the next semester. Second, I had students who now did not have an adviser while I was gone. Who was going to take them on? My student André Ivanoff, who is now a professor at Columbia University and president of the Linehan Institute, was so angry at me for ditching her in the middle of her dissertation that she did not talk to me for five years. (We have repaired our relationship since then.) Third, I had just gotten tenure, and my colleagues were wondering why they had given me tenure if I was going to run out the minute I got it.

Believe me, I paid a subtle but big price over the years for this blunder.

The chair's initial response was something like "What? Now that you have tenure, you are going to take off and leave everyone to pick up for you? How very selfish of you." Eventually, however, he did agree to an extension of my leave of absence by three months. And later he said, "You know, Marsha, you don't have bad intentions, but sometimes you don't appreciate the impact of what you do or say on others around you." He was right. I had focused only on myself and what I needed, how my research would benefit. I hadn't given a thought to how my action would affect others.

A Mysterious and Eerie Sensation

If a sesshin got to be especially intense—if I found myself crying about my mother or yearning for God—Willigis would order me to go outside, to walk, be in nature. It was so beautiful in that valley, with snowcapped mountains in the distance. It was the first place I'd seen that challenged Seattle for its claim on natural beauty. All my senses were flooded during those walks. The colors of the flowers, the smell of them, the breeze on my face. The sound of birdcalls in the trees. If I put my mind to it, I could literally taste the profusion of nature around me. Each of my five senses was touched by that valley.

That flooding of the senses could not have happened on that first visit to Benediktushof because it was November, winter. But over the years, my memories of being there at various times have become bundled as one. So it has become easy to imagine that, on that very first visit, I could indeed see and smell the flowers, feel the breeze on my face, and hear the birds. That is the magic of human imagination.

Staying four months and participating in a sesshin every couple of weeks was indeed intense. I wasn't going to miss a chance at learning everything I could. But that was a whole lot of work for my brain, as I found out later. One day, while facing the wall during meditation, I suddenly felt as if my body was being pushed into the floor. At the same time, it felt as if my head was going to fly off my body. I desperately wanted a scarf to hold my head on. I threw myself into my meditation practice as if that would keep me from falling through the floor. This went on for a few weeks. The one positive thing is that, when you think your head might fly off and your body might go through the floor at any minute, you definitely stay focused.

As these disconcerting sensations continued, I started to get worried. I said to myself, "You are a psychologist. You can do something about this." I took a long walk. I went into town and walked for hours, and counted every stone on the walls, block after block after block. I reminded myself that this was just part of the meditation practice. As long as I stayed focused, I was okay. Eventually, everything calmed down.

I Had to Let Go

At Shasta Abbey, the teachers had told us that the ultimate goal of Zen was to experience enlightenment. Never mind that I had actually experienced enlightenment in that transformative moment in the chapel at Cenacle Center, in Chicago. I didn't know that my experience back then was the experience they were talking about. Once again, I was looking for what I already had.

I often walked at night because I couldn't sleep. One night, I was walking back to the abbey and stood for a moment at a corner. Just standing. It dawned on me that what was going through my mind all the time was just soap operas. I was ruminating all the time, the way depressed people do, ruminating, worrying, feeling guilty, feeling bad, being self-critical. All of a sudden I felt, "Wait a minute. I don't have to turn this damn soap opera on. This whole thing is meaningless." I had such a sense of freedom. At this time, I was still searching for the experience I'd had in the Cenacle chapel. But I realized I had to let go. I knew I had to let go of that, let go of God.

A Journey to Be Weathered, Not Navigated

From time to time, Willigis suggested that the two of us take day trips, or even overnight, me playing the tourist. I continued writing postcards to my mother. Looking at them now, I can see that I had quite a travel adventure. January 17, Zurich. . . . January 23, Lucerne. . . . January 24, Tyrol. . . . February 1, Munich. . . . February 4, Garmisch. . . . February 18, Innsbruck. You get the idea. Some of the postcards showed landscapes or mountains. Mostly, though, they were of churches and other beautiful old buildings. The nave of the cathedral in Würzburg, for example. The royal chapel at Innsbruck. The famous main street in Munich, with its medieval gate. Every church I went into, I lit a candle for Mother.

My messages were mostly simple observations:

Hi—I am in the car driving back to Würzburg. The course ended this morning & afterwards, we stayed for Willigis to baptize 2 children. You would have loved it! The little girl (3 yrs) in a long white dress & pink ribbon around her neck. The little boy (5) in blue velvet pants & bolero vest over a long white blouse with pleats & also a pink ribbon. A 9 yr old girl played the flute & we all sang and lit candles, etc. . . . the next course (contemplation) starts wed night for 4 days & then we have a zen sesshin for 6 days (they are, of course, the same to me) & then I go home.

This one was toward the end of February, just a couple of weeks before I was due back in Seattle. I had weathered quite a journey, and was in a very different place from when I'd arrived four months earlier. I say "weathered" the journey rather than "navigated," because in truth I had little or no control over what was happening to me.

I was wrestling with an unruly surge of negative-self-worth emotions, as well as the ache of unfulfilled spiritual longing, and I often found myself awash with tears.

And then I got a letter from Mother, which she opened with "Marsha, dearest daughter of mine." It was like being hit by a truck. I started crying in each subsequent meditation session. And when I say crying I mean *really* crying, for one whole day, including morning, afternoon, and evening sittings.

Close to the end of that evening, I went to see Willigis. Through my tears I said something like "I'm crying, and I don't know why." I had no idea what I was crying about, because I didn't connect it at all to my mother. I am still not sure it was about my mother. Willigis just looked at me and said, "Keep going," and rang his bell, and out I went. His position was "It didn't have to have meaning. You didn't have to think about it. You didn't have to do something about it. Everything is what it is."

Eventually, after several days, the crying passed. I must have been exhausted, physically and emotionally. I went back to Willigis and said, "I've stopped crying." He said, "Oh, do you know what was going on?" I said, "No." He said, "Okay." And rang his little bell. Out again. It was the same thing. You don't think in Zen. Everything comes and goes, comes and goes. Zen is seeing and experiencing reality as it is.

Alas, I missed this particular point a lot of the time. When I did, Willigis would say to me, "Marsha, it's just this," and then he would make a gesture as if he were holding and playing a violin, and say, "It's just this, nothing else, just this." One evening, I was feeling agitated or blue. I called him and said, "Willigis, will you come and play the violin for me once?" He came to me, and did. He lifted his arms as if he were moving the bow back and forth. "It's just this, Marsha," he said. "Nothing else, just this." That was all I needed.

My sessions with Willigis weren't all focused on my dark night of the soul. Sometimes they were very practical. There was a guy who often sat next to me. He hadn't shaved, and kept rocking in his chair and stroking his chin. I heard every stroke of his fingers against his coarse stubble. I said to Willigis, "Can't you do something to stop this?"

He told me a story. "Okay, Marsha. In olden times, the Zen masters would go down to the stream, where the waterwheel was turned by its flow. They sat down and could hear the waterwheel go *clickety-clack, clickety-clack*. They sat there, with this noise going on in front of them. *Clickety-clack, clickety-clack, clickety-clack*. They did this just to practice letting go. For you, that man and his annoyances are *clickety-clack, clickety-clack*. Just practice letting go. Go back, keep going. This is a waterwheel."

As I said earlier, it is practice, practice, practice.

Two Gifts to Take Away

I took away precious gifts from my time with Willigis, that first year and in subsequent years.

First, I had recognized early on that Zen practice contained elements that could be translated into clinical practice. That confidence was a little misplaced, however, because the translation process was a lot more complex than I ever imagined. And my first attempts to do so ended in complete failure. Eventually, after several years of going back and forth to Germany, consulting with Willigis to get feedback on what to try next, I did succeed in translating Zen practice into the foundation of DBT skills. What I came to call mindfulness skills are so important that they are the first skills taught in DBT—they are the core skills of DBT. Mindfulness is focusing on where you are in the present moment and accepting where you are in the present moment, without being judgmental. Achieving mindfulness is the gateway to acceptance. I will talk more about mindfulness in a later chapter.

The second gift I took away was profound, and completely unexpected.

I had gone to Benediktushof with no thought that I wanted to be a Zen teacher or a Zen master, but over the years I ended up becoming both. That, as you can imagine, was a major and unexpected phase in my spiritual journey, one that I'll tell you about in the following chapter.

No Longer Homesick

But I took away something more personal than that, too.

When I first went to Benediktushof, I was racked by virtually incessant feelings of inadequacy, questioning my self-worth, despair, all combined with the constant ache from the unfulfilled longing—for God, or whatever it was. Much of the time I felt awful, not knowing what was wrong with me.

I had been quite lucky in my earlier years in Chicago, with my spiritual advisers Ted Vierra and Anselm. They both saw the spirituality that is the essence of me, and they both loved me. But it had never been enough. When I started talking with Willigis, I knew this was something different, something important. I could talk about my longing in a way that I hadn't been able to previously.

And Willigis recognized it as no one else ever had.

Once, I said to Willigis, "Why do I feel this way? What is wrong with me? What is my problem?" He was quiet for a little while, and then he said, "The problem, Marsha, is that you are homesick." I said earlier that I had found my home at Benediktushof, and I had. But that's not what he meant. He meant I was homesick for God. I used to lie in bed at night and feel as if there were a veil, or some barrier, between me and God. I'd try to make the veil go away, but it never did.

So when Willigis used that simple word, "homesick," it suddenly made sense. I said to myself, "Oh, okay, this is all right, I'm just homesick, there's nothing wrong with me. I'm not mentally ill. I'm just longing—it's a longing." The dark night of the soul didn't exactly disperse at that point, but it definitely eased.

Love was the other treasure that Willigis gave me. "Gave" isn't the right word to use, of course, because love is not an object you can give to someone, like a box of chocolates. Love *is*. And I came to feel loved by Willigis in a way that felt like the first time—the first time I had experienced being loved. Ted Vierra and Anselm loved me, but it wasn't the same, and Anselm rather put me on a pedestal, so it was more an adoration than pure love. Ed had loved me, of course, but that, too, was different. With Willigis I had a sense of belonging, of coming home. He saw the spiritual part of me, the essence of me, as if for the first time.

His love was pure and strong, coming from his radical acceptance of me. It transformed me. I was no longer without family, no longer homesick, no longer alone and lonely.

I was Me at last.

CHAPTER THIRTY

Becoming a Zen Master

ONE DAY IN June of 2010, I went into Willigis's room at the abbey. By this point I had done many, many koans. He pulled out a piece of paper and tossed it at me. "Now you are a Zen teacher," he said. I was completely startled and said, "I can't be a Zen teacher. I haven't finished my koans yet." He responded, "If you can do this many koans, you can do all you need to do. Now you are a teacher."

At this point, a student is expected to go to another Zen master, to be checked, so to speak. Willigis sent me to Pat Hawk, who was a Catholic priest and Zen master, just like Willigis. Pat was based in Tucson, Arizona, and before long he was leading Zen retreats for psychotherapists for me.

The Redemptorist Renewal Center, on 150 acres of desert scrub, is on the edge of Saguaro National Park West, northwest of Tucson. It is stunningly beautiful. The mountains are splashed with lilac and crimson rays at sunrise and sunset. The Hohokam people found the place to be holy and long ago left sacred petroglyphs all around the center's grounds.

The Church of Our Lady of the Desert is part of the center. On the church's wall is a saying that paraphrases Hosea 2:14: "The desert will lead you to your heart where I will speak." I love that little church.

The goal of Pat's retreats was to bring to psychotherapists the kind of mindfulness I had discovered for myself, and to guide them into Zen as far as they wanted to go. I was Pat's assistant, along with Cedar Koons, an experienced Zen student and therapist. Pat became very important in my life; our relationship was similar to the one I had with Willigis.

Pat agreed to help me become a good Zen teacher. What I didn't ask was to be made a Zen master. (A Zen teacher is like a Catholic priest, while a Zen master is equivalent to a bishop. Of course, there is no equivalent to a pope in Zen.)

But Pat did make me a Zen master in 2012, about ten years after I started working with him. Pat was dying, and he wanted to make four Zen masters, including me. He said I represented him. At the time, many students wanted to be Zen masters. Pat's close friend once said to me, "Marsha, you are the best teacher here." I asked him what he meant. He said, "Because you are the only one who does not care if you become a Zen master or not."

It was a beautiful ceremony, with a lot of ritual. Pat wasn't there, because he was too sick. He died soon afterward. But he is always with me now when I lead Zen retreats. He comes to me like a veil descending over me, his presence a comfort.

And when I think of Pat, as I often do, a particular exchange comes to mind. I used to believe that an important goal of therapy—after dealing with life-threatening behaviors and behaviors that interfere with therapy itself—was to achieve joy. Everyone wants to have joy in their life. One day when I was talking with Pat, this idea came up. I said, "Pat, you are a Zen master. Aren't you joyful all the time?" He responded, "Marsha, wouldn't you rather have the freedom to not have to have what you want, whatever it is? Wouldn't you feel better if you were free not to have to have all the things you think you want?"

Pat was right. We are better off accepting what life has to offer, rather than living under the tyranny of having to have things we don't yet have. This is not to say that we are to be completely passive—not at all. It means that we should strive for important goals, but we must radically accept that we might not obtain them. It is letting go of having to have.

And accepting what is.

This is a wonderful message, one I give to my Zen students. I also give them the Four Great Vows of the Bodhisattva at the beginning of our session, repeated three times:

> *The many things are numberless,*
>   *I vow to save them.*
> *Greed, hatred, and ignorance rise endlessly,*
>   *I vow to abandon them.*
> *The gates of learning are countless,*
>   *I vow to wake to them.*
> *The pathless path is unsurpassed,*
>   *I vow to embody it fully.*

No Need to Search for Meaning

I am an unorthodox Zen master. I'm not like the others. I integrate dances into Zen practice, and there are many traditional rituals that I don't follow. I once asked Willigis if he would watch me practice, listen to my talks, see if he approved. He said, "I don't have to, Marsha. There is no need to. I know you are good."

Being a Zen master is like jumping into a pool of water. I used to go down, come up, go down, come up. But now I just sit on the bottom. I don't have to come up for air anymore. These things are things that are impossible to talk about with words. So now I am what I am, and I don't need to come up for air anymore.

There's a phrase in Zen: beginner's mind. Beginner's mind means that every single moment is the very first experience you have had of that moment. Every new moment is a beginning. Right now, the only thing that exists is this one moment. Miraculous, when you think about it. Only this moment, there is nothing else. Beginner's mind is the recognition of this. The entire universe is this moment. That is amazing to me. I just throw myself into it.

Initially, I analyzed everything. "What is the meaning of this?" "What is the meaning of that?" I think of it as very Catholic, the search for meaning.

Now I don't search for meaning anymore. Everything just is.

CHAPTER THIRTY-ONE

Trying to Put Zen into Clinical Practice

I RETURNED FROM GERMANY with the zeal of a convert. I wanted my graduate students to learn what I had learned from Zen practices so that we could incorporate it into DBT skills.

I invited a roshi (Zen master) to come teach my grad students. Before he came, I gave my students instructions: They should take off their shoes before coming into the room; they could not come late. And if they did come late, the door would be closed and they would have to wait until a bell rang.

The roshi came, wearing his long robes. He sat down, very still. The students came in without their shoes, and no one was late. The roshi gave a talk about Zen practice and philosophy and then invited questions. A student asked, "Marsha told us we would be disturbing things if we come late. Is that true?"

The roshi answered, "What is there to disturb?" Of course, he was right. There is nothing to disturb. Everything is as it is, nothing more, nothing less. I should have understood that, but obviously I hadn't fully gotten it, given what I had said to my students.

I have often told this story about the roshi to my Zen students and to those learning DBT. I also say, "If your phone rings during mindfulness practice, do not turn it off. If you start coughing, do not get up to deal with it. If you start sobbing or crying, do not start to focus on how you are disturbing other people. Just sit there."

I was venturing into very sensitive territory. Shasta Abbey was Zen Buddhist, Willigis was Zen and Christian, and I was a professor teaching psychology and developing a rigorously scientific mental health treatment while teaching at a secular state university. As my colleague Bob Kohlenberg now says, "In those days, it was heretical. I would have said to Marsha, 'This is crackers.' But now it is mainstream." My mentor Jerry Davison, from Stony Brook, advised me against talking about Zen in behavior therapy circles.

I was careful not to talk about Zen with my clients, not to talk about contemplative prayer. Unless, of course, I knew a client to be spiritual. But I wanted my clients to experience what I had experienced. I had felt in my soul that it was what they needed. I had to find a way of bringing that experience into the clinic.

"I Don't Do Breathing, Marsha"

I decided to test my new ideas for DBT skills at Harborview Medical Center, in downtown Seattle, which is affiliated with the University of Washington. Patients with all sorts of behavioral disorders had volunteered to be in my skills group.

I asked everyone to take off their shoes before entering the room, as is usual practice in Zen. This did not go over well. Most did not want to, and I was unable to give reasons for why they should. So I let that go. Next I asked them to sit on the floor. The answer again was no, and once again I could not remember why that was a good idea. A client told me later that sitting on the floor was embarrassing. I suppose she had felt conspicuous or foolish. It wasn't something people did, in her experience.

Once we were all seated in our chairs, I explained that we were going to practice a very short meditation that involved watching our breath as it came in and out. Before I could even finish my instructions, someone said, "I don't do breathing, Marsha." Then another person said something like "I do breathing, I die." So that was the end of that.

I thought, "Okay, forget breathing." We would do walking meditation. "Everybody please stand up," I said. "Let's all walk together in a single line. The idea is to walk slowly, focusing your attention on the sensations of your feet, letting go of thoughts that might arise." I got everyone in a line behind me and started walking very slowly down the hall, just as I had so many times in walking meditation. A few minutes after starting, I glanced behind me, only to discover that no one was behind me. All of them had stayed in the room!

Not an especially good start to my new venture!

The Challenge of Translating Zen Practice into Treatment Practice

What I learned at Shasta Abbey and with Willigis was important. But I didn't know how to describe what I had learned. I had to translate everything into concrete behavioral steps. I had to come up with a set of skills that everybody could do, and that would not alienate people.

I was testing skills with patients at Harborview, and I was also asking Willigis to give me feedback. He pointed out where he saw shortcomings, where I had gotten things right, where I had gotten things wrong. Back and forth. Back and forth.

Eventually, after a couple of years, I was able to write up in the training manual the core skills of DBT, the foundation on which all other skills rest. I describe them as the "psychological and behavioral translations of meditation practices from Eastern spiritual training." The core skills, as I told you in the previous chapter, are mindfulness skills.

CHAPTER THIRTY-TWO

Mindfulness: We All Have Wise Mind

THERE ARE MANY variants on the definition of mindfulness. Here's how I look at it.

Mindfulness is the act of consciously focusing the mind in the present moment, without judgment and without attachment to the moment. Mindfulness contrasts with automatic, habitual, or rote behavior. When we are mindful, we are alert and awake, like a sentry guarding a gate. When we are mindful, we are open to the fluidity of each moment as it arises and falls away.

Mindfulness practice is the repeated effort of bringing the mind back to awareness of the present moment; it includes the repeated effort of letting go of judgments and letting go of attachment to current thoughts, emotions, sensations, activities, events, or life situations.

It is very difficult to accept reality with our eyes closed. If we want to accept what is happening to us, we have to know what is happening to us. We have to open our eyes and look. Now, a lot of people say, "I keep my eyes open all the time." But they are not looking at the moment. They're looking to their past. They're looking to their future. They're looking to their worries. They're looking to their thoughts. They're looking to everybody else. They are looking absolutely everywhere except at the present moment.

Mindfulness is the practice of directing our attention to only one thing. And that one thing is the moment in which we are alive. The very moment we are in. The beauty of mindfulness is that if we look at the moment, we will discover that we are looking at the universe. And if we can become one with the moment—just this moment— the moment cracks open and we are shocked that joy is in this moment. Strength to bear the suffering of our lives is also in this moment. Going through the practice just once doesn't get us there. Mindfulness is not a place we get to. Mindfulness is a place we are. It is going from and coming back to mindfulness that is the practice. It's just this breath, just this step, just this struggle. Mindfulness is just where we are now, with our eyes wide open, aware, awake, attentive.

The Meaning of Wise Mind

Psychologists have long recognized that each of us possesses two opposing states of mind: "reasonable mind" and "emotion mind."

You are in reasonable mind when reason is in control and is not balanced by emotions and values. It is the part of you that plans and evaluates things logically. When you are completely in reasonable mind, you are ruled by facts, reason, logic, and pragmatism. Emotions such as love, guilt, and grief are irrelevant. While in reasonable mind, your cognition may be described as being "cool."

You are in emotion mind when emotions are in control and are not balanced by reason. When completely in emotion mind, you are ruled by your moods, feelings, and urges. Facts, reason, and logic are not important. In emotion mind, your cognition may be described as "hot." Some may say you are being unreasonable.

Reasonable mind and emotion mind are both capable of making good decisions, but there are limited circumstances where *only* rational inputs or *only* emotional inputs are relevant. Most circumstances are more complex than that and require broader inputs.

Mindfulness skills help to balance emotion mind with reasonable mind, with the goal of making wise decisions. There is a third state of mind that takes the middle path; this is what I call "wise mind." Wise mind is the synthesis of emotion mind and reasonable mind. Wise mind adds intuitive knowing to emotional experience and logical analysis. Intuition eludes easy definition, but each of us knows what it is. It is that sense of *knowing* something in a particular situation, without knowing exactly *how* you know. You meet someone, and within seconds you feel somehow that you can't quite trust this person. You walk into a room and immediately sense danger lurking somewhere.

Being able to practice mindfulness and wise mind is a key step in the journey toward building a life experienced as worth living. It opens a person to being able to embrace the more practical skills of interpersonal effectiveness, emotion regulation, and distress tolerance, which are the life skills that make DBT what it is.

Clients often find mindfulness difficult to grasp at first, but when they get it, they love it. Here's a typical comment a person might make when she grasps mindfulness:

I had known about mindfulness, but I hadn't known how it might help me. But, doing DBT, I learned how it could help me. It helped me handle the ruminating and self-hating. Instead of feeding into all that, I was able to slow down my thought processes, slow down the bad thoughts, just reset and ask, "What was the first thought that started me down this sad thought process?" And then you understand what got you to a bad place.

Origin of the Concept of Wise Mind

I came up with the concept of wise mind from two different perspectives.

First, I wanted my clients to understand that they are much more than the disorders they present with. Too often, this is how people view those who are diagnosed with certain behavioral conditions: "Oh, she's schizophrenic," "He's a borderline individual," "She's a depressive," and so on. It's a label that sticks and seems to define. My message to clients is "No, you are more than that. You have made bad decisions in the past, no doubt about that, but you still have the capacity for wisdom, you have the capacity to know what is right for you. You just don't know how to access it yet. I will help you."

Clients often say, "Absolutely not. Not me. I don't have a wise mind." I respond by saying, "All humans have wise mind, and the fact that you don't feel it does not mean you don't have it." It is like saying you don't have a liver just because you don't feel it.

One client described it like this: "At first it was 'How do I know what I need?' But in the end, I did. I know what I need to do to stay safe. I know what I need to do to be not lonely."

Second, I looked at my clients' dysfunctional behaviors. "What is the dialectic here? What is the functional opposite of these behaviors?" The opposite of dysfunction, I decided, is wisdom. Hence the concept of wise mind, which very quickly became entrenched in the mindfulness skills of DBT.

But I had made an error in my calculation. The opposite of dysfunctional behavior is not wisdom; it is functional behavior. By the time had I realized this distinction, though, the concept was firmly rooted in our DBT practice.

After clients' initial skepticism, most of them come to love the idea of wise mind. It is personally very validating, and my clients are hungry for validation. In truth, we all are. It was too late to let go of wise mind as a skill, because wise mind not only was quite effective for clients, but also it may actually be true: we all *do* have the capacity for wisdom.

One event really sold me on wise mind. In the middle of group skills training, a client suddenly jumped up and said, "I'm leaving," and started walking toward the door. "Okay," I said, "you can leave, but first tell me if this is wise mind." The client stopped, breathed in and out, looked at me, and said, "NO!" Then he added, "But I'm leaving anyway." His wise mind knew what he *should* do, which was stay, but it wasn't what his emotion mind wanted right that second, so he left. It was amazing that a person so highly emotional in the moment could, at the same time, access wise mind. Wise mind creates a new context where a person can access effective behavior or wisdom. Whether or not one chooses to follow wise mind is a separate question.

There was nothing spiritual about wise mind initially. That would come later.

My therapists also love the concept. Something about it resonates strongly in the client–therapist relationship. Katie Korslund, my former associate director at the clinic, talks about the power of wise mind:

> Thinking of suicidal clients, the darkest night of their life, hoping they can feel the connection, the clarity of purpose, that they can open themselves up to a connection with the universe by practicing wise mind, by practicing other DBT skills—what an amazing thing to be able to offer somebody. Connection with the universe. By practicing skills. I can tell you, with clients who have been acutely suicidal, on the phone, that has brought comfort and brought them through the night.

Wise mind fits perfectly with what I had learned from Willigis. The idea of going into wise mind is the same as recognizing and going within our connections to the universe as a whole.

Learning to Recognize Wise Mind

Finding wise mind is like searching for a new station on the radio. First you hear a lot of static and you can't make out the lyrics of the song, but if you keep adjusting the dial, the signal gets louder. You will learn to know right where the station is, and the lyrics become a part of you.

But it's difficult to know for sure if you are in wise mind. When I teach my clients, I draw a picture of a well, and this is what I tell them:

> The well is in you; it goes down to a lake or ocean, which is the wisdom of the universe. You can go down the well to reach wise mind. Except that on the way down the well, there is a trapdoor. When it is open, you go straight into wisdom. If it is closed and it is raining, there will be water there on top, and you might mistake the rainwater for wisdom. This means you can't be certain you are in wise mind without giving it time, and without getting feedback from other people. If you believe you are in wise mind, it doesn't always mean you are. You have to check to make sure you are right.

Some Ideas for Practicing Wise Mind

- Imagine that you are by a clear blue lake on a beautiful sunny day. Then imagine you are a small flake of stone, flat and light. Imagine that you have been tossed into the lake and are now gently, slowly floating through the calm, clear blue water to the lake's smooth, sandy bottom.

  - Notice what you see, what you feel as you float down, perhaps in slow circles, floating toward the bottom.

  - Notice the serenity of the lake; become aware of the calmness and deep quiet within.

- Imagine that within you is a spiral staircase, winding down to your very center. Starting at the top, walk very slowly down the staircase, going deeper and deeper within yourself.

○ Notice the sensations. Rest by sitting on a step, or turn on lights on the way down. Do not force yourself further than you want to go. Notice the quiet. As you reach the center of yourself, settle your attention there—perhaps in your gut or your abdomen.

• Take a deep breath in and say to yourself, "Wise"; breathe out and say to yourself, "Mind."

○ Focus your entire attention on the word "wise," then focus it again entirely on the word "mind."

○ Continue until you sense that you have settled into wise mind.

How I Came to the Term "Mindfulness Skills"

I was determined to keep my spiritual journey separate from DBT. The last thing I wanted was for DBT to be perceived as a treatment based on religion or spirituality; that could be a distraction from the efficacy of the therapy. But when I was casting around for a suitable descriptive term for this new set of skills, I read Thich Nhat Hanh's book *The Miracle of Mindfulness*. It is one of the best introductions to the practice of meditation and is now a classic.

Here are a couple of quotes of his:

To be beautiful means to be yourself. You don't need to be accepted by others. You need to accept yourself.

Breathing in, I calm body and mind. Breathing out, I smile. Dwelling in the present moment I know this is the only moment.

You can see how I would resonate with what he was saying, and I was immediately attracted to his use of the term "mindfulness." It seemed to capture exactly the goal of the skills training, which is to give people a means of being effective in their worlds—in the relational world and the practical world.

There is an important "but" here. Thich Nhat Hanh is a Buddhist monk, and he is teaching meditation. That seemed to be firmly in the spiritual arena, and I wanted to avoid that. I thought, "That's too bad." And kept looking.

I then came across the work of Ellen Langer, a social psychologist at Harvard. Since the late 1970s, she had been working on the notion that most of us operate from a position of mind*less*ness, and that to be effective in the world one needed to be mind*ful*. Stanford psychologist Philip Zimbardo had this to say about her work: "Her extensive innovative research and compelling writing took mindfulness out of Zen meditation caves and into the bright light of everyday functioning."

"That makes a difference," I mused. "If there's a science around mindfulness, I can be comfortable with the term." Langer had also published a book titled *Mindfulness,* which garnered great acclaim. "That does it," I thought. "I can use that term. I didn't coin it, but that doesn't matter to me. It captures so completely what the skills do." They engender mindfulness.

Later, I learned about the work of Jon Kabat-Zinn, a psychologist in the Department of Medicine at the University of Massachusetts Medical School. In 1979, he introduced a program called Mindfulness-Based Stress Reduction. He was onto the power of mindfulness before I was, but in a different realm: that of physiology and medicine. He was in the secular world. I had gotten into mindfulness exclusively through the spiritual realm. I am not a mindfulness *researcher*. I am a mindfulness *practitioner*. And my claim here, if I have one, is that I was the first to introduce mindfulness into psychotherapy, in DBT. These days, mindfulness is common in many different forms of psychotherapy.

Mindfulness as a practice is thousands of years old. It exists in both Western and Eastern spiritual traditions—it just goes by different names. Recently, Western science has been looking at the very same practice. In other words, ancient spiritual traditions and modern science arrived at the same insights. Mindfulness is now being recognized as a source of great power in many, many realms of human activity.

Mindfulness permeates the whole of DBT. And it begins with the therapist practicing mindfulness herself. Saying to the therapist "Be mindful" is saying, "Be aware, lock into the session, focus on your client, don't be planning dinner or thinking about the last session you had."

For the client, the idea is that we often don't experience the moment we are in, because we are focusing on something different from the moment. Teaching clients mindfulness skills will lead to other behavior changes that help clients function more effectively in the world.

Teaching clients to be effective is the goal of much of DBT.

* * *

I want to end with a few of my favorite quotes about our connectedness with nature:

> Are not the mountains, waves, and skies a part / Of me and of my soul, as I of them?
>
> LORD BYRON, poet

> We invent nothing, truly. We borrow and re-create. We uncover and discover. All has been given, as the mystics say. We have only to open our eyes and hearts, to become one with that which is.
>
> HENRY MILLER, novelist

> There are sacred moments in life when we experience in rational and very direct ways that separation, the boundary between ourselves and other people and between ourselves and Nature, is illusion. Oneness is reality. We can experience that stasis is illusory and that reality is continual flux and change on very subtle and also on gross levels of perception.
>
> CHARLENE SPRETNAK, a writer on women and spirituality

CHAPTER THIRTY-THREE

DBT in Clinical Trial

To DETERMINE WHETHER DBT was effective in helping highly suicidal individuals, I needed a randomized clinical trial that would compare the outcomes of DBT with "treatment as usual" in the community. Thank God our friends at NIMH supported us all the way, awarding me a grant in 1980 to carry out the trial.

I started with a pool of about sixty women between the ages of eighteen and forty-five, all of whom met certain criteria for borderline personality disorder and had had at least two episodes of parasuicide (serious self-harm, with or without the intention to die) in the previous five years, with at least one of the episodes occurring in the previous eight weeks. We did various pre-treatment assessments, during which some candidates dropped out.

We ended up with about fifty women, whom we randomly assigned to either the group that would receive DBT or the group that would have standard behavior therapy. (That's the "randomized" component in a randomized clinical trial.) The study was to run for a year, with assessments of how patients were faring at four, eight, and twelve months. (A year was a lot longer than the twelve weeks I had optimistically planned for when I embarked on the project. Input from our friends at NIMH, plus my experience trying to apply the treatment, brought about that change.)

It is appealing to imagine that the trial would come to its natural end, the data would be crunched, we would exclaim, "Too fabulous for words!" in unison, and then we'd break out the champagne. Unfortunately, none of that happened. My student Heidi Heard was brought into the study in 1989. She had a tremendous amount of expertise in evaluating clinical research outcomes, so her role was to analyze the raw data we had obtained from the trial. "We didn't even know for a time if the study was going to be a success," Heidi says. "None of us was confident that it would have a positive outcome. It looked like it would, but there have been plenty of studies that looked promising but came to nothing in the end."

Scientists have to be attentive to the danger of seeing a positive outcome in their work when in fact it is not there. The most productive approach is to be dispassionate about data, examine it objectively, and listen to what it tells you. If it tells you something you didn't expect, then be grateful, because you have learned something. There's a twist on an old adage: "I wouldn't have seen it if I hadn't believed it." See what I mean?

But our outcome was very positive—mostly, anyway. This is how we drafted part of the conclusion:

> First, we found a significant reduction in the frequency and medical risk of parasuicidal behavior among patients who received DBT compared with that for control subjects. Subjects who received DBT had a mean of 1.5 parasuicide acts per year compared with nine acts per year for control subjects. Second, DBT effectively retained subjects in therapy. The 1-year attrition rate [i.e., dropping out of the trial] was only 4 (16.67%) of 24 patients, one of whom committed suicide. Control subjects who started with new therapists had an attrition rate of 50%. Third, days of inpatient psychiatric hospitalization were fewer for subjects who received DBT than for control subjects. Patients who received DBT had an average of 8.46 inpatient days per year compared with 38.86 for control subjects.

In other words, the trial had demonstrated that patients who receive DBT are far less likely to injure themselves than patients who receive conventional therapy and are much more likely to stay in therapy. We did note, however, that these differences occurred despite the fact that people in the two groups reported about the same degree of depression, hopelessness, thoughts of suicide, and absence of reasons for living. This was a surprise, but I realized later that developing a life worth living takes longer than developing a reduction in self-injury.

What makes DBT effective, where other conventional therapies fail, in helping highly suicidal people? It's a good question. DBT is unusual in its combination of a human touch (close, genuine relationship between therapist and client) with practical skills that help the client navigate every aspect of his or her life. DBT puts heavy emphasis on treating clients as equals and not viewing them as somehow damaged goods who need to be coddled—what I call fragilizing them. Clients are validated for who they are. As clients gradually master the practical skills that help them solve problems, they feel more in control of their lives and probably feel better in themselves. You could say that skills are central to the effectiveness of DBT.

I am sometimes asked, not completely jokingly, whether there is a "magic" to DBT. That is best answered by those who have been through it. A typical answer is something like the following:

The answer is "Yes and no." The "no" part is that a lot of it is learning simple, practical skills that help you get through the day. And the next day. And the next day. The "yes" part is that it works. It's like no other therapy I know. It is written in a way that is easy to understand. It changes your thoughts. The acronyms make it easy to remember. Perfect for me. I can see how they would work for others. It's not scary. It's not boring. It really applies to you. It helped me find a life worth living.

When some scientists write up their results, they tend to leave out the flaws. I wanted to put all the mistakes in so that people could see the whole picture and maybe learn from my mistakes. We drafted the paper, flaws and all, and set about deciding where to publish. I submitted the paper to *Archives of General Psychiatry*, a mainstream psychiatry journal. This was the audience I needed to convince of our new and effective therapy. I got a very quick response.

A flat rejection. This was in mid-1990.

I wasn't going to take no for an answer. I called the editor and said, "Well, I know you rejected this, but I'd like to resubmit it." There ensued a half hour of conversation, the tone of which was— how best to put it?—combative. I'll paraphrase it. "We have no intention of taking anything from you," he said. "You obviously don't know how to write." They had a point. So I said, "Well, that might be true, but I think the research is really important and psychiatrists would like to hear about it." He didn't agree. "No, it's just junk, and we're not wasting our time on your research. You're just a waste of time."

Growing up with two older brothers is good training for life's bumps. I learned with John and Earl that when I got knocked down by them—by anything—I should bounce right back up like a Bobo doll.

"Okay, so the writing's not good," I persisted. "How about if we do this? I'll rewrite it, but I wouldn't want to waste your time, so I'll find some reviewers and I'll get it reviewed before it comes to you and it'll all be redone. It'll be very good. And then you can look at it, so it will hardly take you any time at all. How about that?" I persisted along these lines for a while. Eventually he relented, probably out of self-preservation, to get me off the phone.

I recruited a lot of help to rewrite the paper, including Mark Williams, a psychologist in Cambridge, England, with whom I had spent some time on sabbatical. "Oh, Marsha," he said, "you can't tell them all the mistakes in your research. Just write the research." I followed his advice, cut out a lot of the unnecessary detail, and submitted the paper a second time, in early 1991.

It was rejected again.

Another conversation with the editor, shorter this time. Another promise to resubmit, an even better version this time.

Less than a week after I submitted version number three, I got a note saying that the paper had been accepted. It was April 4, 1991. The paper was scheduled for publication in the December issue.

"The whole episode was a good example of Marsha's tenacity," said my student Heidi. "If it had been me, I would have given up. . . . But she soldiered on. She always does."

DBT on Trial by Psychiatrists

Otto Kernberg is the kindest of human beings, as I discovered when I spent some months in mid-1991 at the Weill Cornell Medical College, in White Plains, New York, where he is based. Kernberg is the author of the prevailing psychoanalytic theory of borderline personality disorder. One day during my stay, he looked at me with concern and said, "Can I talk with you privately, Marsha?"

We went into his office and he closed the door and sat down behind his desk. I took the guest chair. Then he said, in a caring voice, "Have you been in a mental institution, Marsha?" I said I had. He said, "I thought so—the scars. Don't tell anyone." He gave me advice about how to handle it.

It was a very kind moment.

Kernberg had thirteen inpatient programs at Weill, and the one treating borderline patients was the hospital's flagship unit. Charlie Swenson had run that unit for some years prior to my sabbatical there, in 1991. This is how he describes the unit.

Everything was very formal, very efficient, run like a Swiss watch. Group meetings were rigid and followed a strict formula. Patients were expected to follow rules: how to behave on the unit, how to interact with the therapist. They were not supposed to be friendly or intimate in any way, not ask personal questions. So if the patient were to ask the therapist where they planned to vacation this year, they would be told, "It's fine that you ask that, but you know the rules; we have to maintain a definite distance between staff and patients. This is not something to share."

The therapist was supposed to maintain a neutral attitude toward the patient, being neither positive nor negative. You were not supposed to make practical suggestions for how the patient might handle their anger. Like doing an energetic stint on an exercise bicycle, for example, or making a drawing of the subject of anger and then ripping it apart. Nothing like that. Being friendly or in any way demonstrating care was absolutely taboo. [Anger was at the core of Kernberg's model for BPD.] The idea was that if you got close to the patient, she wouldn't be able to unload her negative feelings on you. And then the treatment wouldn't work.

Unexpected Outcome of a Chance Meeting

You are probably thinking, "What? Have you lost your mind, Marsha? What Charlie Swenson describes is the absolute antithesis of everything you believe about therapy. And yet you went there on sabbatical. Why on earth would you do something like that?" It's a good question. Here's what happened.

A few years earlier, a chance encounter had occurred between Charlie and a prominent psychiatrist, Allen Frances, on the borderline unit at Weill. Again, I'll let Charlie tell the story.

There was a meeting that day in the hospital, and a famous psychiatrist, Allen Frances, happened to be visiting. He was on the Cornell faculty but based at the Payne Whitney Clinic, on the Upper East Side of Manhattan. He was an expert on personality disorder and had helped draft the *DSM-IV*,* which outlined cri-

---

* The fourth edition of the *Diagnostic and Statistical Manual of Mental Disorders* (Washington, DC: American Psychiatric Association, 1994).

teria for borderline personality disorder. He is very open-minded, willing to challenge everybody, and is a furious critic of the controversial most recent edition of the DSM. He was also familiar with Marsha's work.

At one point in the meeting, I stepped out for a short while, and ran into Al in the hallway. I said to him, "Al, can I talk to you for a minute? Can I get a curbside consultation about this particular patient? We don't know how to get out of the mess we are in. It is a constant struggle. We are doing everything we can. But it's not working. Are you interested?" He said, "Yes. I'm sick of this meeting I'm in. Can we go up to your unit? I can meet the patient."

The patient was in the seclusion room upstairs, had been for a while. She was notorious throughout the hospital. I thought she was very interesting. She was clever, funny, and had a tortured vibrancy about her. She was regarded as a troublemaker. When Al and I got to the seclusion room, the patient was sitting on the floor. Al sat down beside her and talked for a while.

About twenty minutes into that, Al said something to the patient that changed my career: "You know, I have a recommendation for you. It is going to sound crazy, because here you are in maximum security, practically. Do you have much money?" She said, "No, I have nothing." Al said, "I think you should get out of this hospital as soon as you can and hitchhike to Seattle and look up this woman, a psychologist called Marsha Linehan, and get in her treatment program. That's what you need. And if you can't do that, I will get you into my facility in Manhattan, if you really do want to get better."

What Al had said to the patient made a big impression on me, along the lines of "Hmm, if Al thinks this Marsha Linehan has a good and different approach to treating BPD, I think I should check it out for myself."

The patient did get out of the Weill unit, but she didn't come to me. Al had recognized that the anger-centered treatment she was getting, the Kernberg treatment, was absolutely counterproductive and harmful to her. It brought out the worst in her, and she brought out the worst in the hospital. So Al got her transferred to Cornell's Manhattan facility and arranged much more humane psychotherapy for her, which he supervised.

I did, however, have a different visitor from Kernberg's borderline unit. Charlie Swenson.

After his encounter with Al Frances, Charlie got hold of my 1987 paper on DBT, which had been published in a small journal before our randomized clinical trial. (I thought that no one had seen it, but I guess at least one person read that paper after all.) Although Charlie's entire background had been psychoanalytic, he did have what he describes as "a latent interest in behaviorism." He called me and said, "I am a psychiatrist, and I run a program in New York on borderline personality disorder. I learned about your work from Allen Frances. Can I come out and visit?"

Charlie came out to the University of Washington in early 1988, with his wife, who is also a therapist, and spent about a week with us. I remember clearly Charlie's initial reaction after we watched hundreds of hours of videos of DBT sessions. "Wow, that patient is really mad at you. Oh, my God, she's so angry." And I said, "Where? Where? I didn't see it. What'd she do? What'd she do?" I couldn't see what he was seeing. "She's not talking to you. That's an attack on you." I said, "I don't think so. Don't you think maybe it's more likely she's afraid?" "No, it's an attack! Don't you see?" We went back and forth like this quite a lot.

"My whole training with Kernberg was to look for and see expressions of anger, and that could be shouting and yelling or the silent treatment," Charlie recalls. On that first visit to Seattle, Charlie asked me, "In DBT, how do you deal with someone who is aggressive but she is suppressing it, and it is coming out as passive-aggressive, and you didn't say anything about it? In our model, I would have brought it up immediately. I would have said to the patient, 'The way you said that right now, it is unmistakably the case that you were mocking me.'"

I absolutely didn't see that, so I told Charlie that I saw someone who was trying to manage herself, somebody who was highly reactive. His response was "So you have no primary assumption that this was coming out of anger, hidden anger?" I said, "More than anything else, Charlie, my sense was that she had fear and shame, not anger."

Pretty soon, Charlie began to see that labeling every behavior as an expression of anger was probably not helpful. Not an interpretation of reality. He remembers one group meeting with new patients that had a big impact on his outlook.

Marsha had these six women sitting around a table. She was saying in a very friendly way, "I am so happy you are here. You are probably terrified, but don't worry, it's all going to be okay." She was being like a normal host in a normal social gathering. These are patients, their first session, all terrified, hands under the table, they are ripping their cuticles, looking like they are going to explode. "I'm just glad to have all of you here." It was just like she was hosting a Sunday afternoon tea party in Tulsa, Oklahoma, with genteel people. She starts teaching the general model, then she asks somebody, "What about you? Do you think this might be helpful to you?" Just starts interacting with them in this friendly, social way.

But she was clearly not just hosting a tea party. She is unbelievably astute about all the things that are going on. Catching everything. Sometimes she comments, sometimes she doesn't. But she misses nothing, takes it all in, thinking about what to do. Creating a validating atmosphere. She maintains her psychotherapy skills in the group. Watching Marsha, I could see that her model incorporates coaching and psychotherapy at the highest level—each of them. The coaching informed by evidence-based backing from behaviorism about the treatment of anxiety, treatment of depression, treatment of habits. Nothing like that ever happened on Kernberg's borderline unit.

Charlie became a DBT enthusiast and began training to become a DBT therapist. He said it resonated more with his true nature. Charlie eventually established a DBT unit at Weill, the first DBT unit outside of Seattle.

When I told Charlie I was going to spend a sabbatical in Cambridge, England, in early 1991, writing my professional book on DBT, and didn't have plans for the rest of the year, he said, "Why don't you come to Weill, Marsha, do the rest of your sabbatical there?"

I said, "Why not?"

A View from the Other Side

The campus of the Weill Cornell Medical College was designed by Frederick Law Olmsted, the same architect who designed the grounds at the Institute of Living, and there was a certain similarity between the two. (Olmsted also designed New York's Central Park.) Charlie lived in a house on campus, and there happened to be a vacant house just opposite his. He arranged for me to live there for three months, beginning in the late summer of 1991.

The professional book I was finishing that year described the theoretical background of DBT and laid out the components of the therapy. I was going to make it personal. I was writing it in the first person, which is unusual for a therapy manual. I described every component of DBT in complete detail. I wanted readers to understand the therapy through immersion, not just get a set of broad outlines. Again, that was unusual for a therapy manual. Jerry Davison had been my model for this approach.

I believe one of the reasons the book has done as well as it has is that it is written in a personal rather than a remote academic voice. It is not about my life; it is about DBT. People generally refer to its author as "Marsha"—not "Marsha Linehan" or "Linehan." It's "What would Marsha say about this?" or "What would Marsha do under these circumstances?" My clients know me as Marsha. I don't know of any other treatment that is so aligned with the person who developed it as DBT is with me.

Besides finishing my book, I had another reason to go to Cornell: to act as a consultant for Charlie's newly established DBT unit. That was very interesting, and a lot of fun, but I also got an opportunity to experience Kernberg's approach to treating borderline patients firsthand. The patients on his unit were long-term—there for eighteen months on average. They were mostly women, from prominent families, just like back at the IOL. Once a week, there were case reviews. Patients would be interviewed in the presence of a panel comprising Kernberg and his colleagues, and maybe a nurse on the unit. They would then be dismissed, and their case discussed.

Imagine the scene. A big room, chandeliers, dark wooden paneling, a long mahogany table with half a dozen people sitting on one side—mostly men, very formal, dressed in suits and ties, notepads and pens in front of them. Quite forbidding, really. On occasion, I was to be the interviewer. The first time, the patient was a young woman. I was sitting with my back to the table. She sat in front of me, facing the panel that was behind me. She said very little to me, just one-word answers. I wasn't getting anywhere. I said, "I think part of the problem is that you are sitting here, having to face all these people—it must be difficult for you. Why don't we change places?" We did, and she talked a lot more. It went well, I thought.

When she left, the first thing the panel said was "Wow, she was angry at you." "Hmm," I thought. "Where have I heard that before?"

Someone said, "Look at her, she hardly talked to you. She was really angry." I said, "I don't think she was angry. I think she was afraid. Why do you think she was angry?" "Because of what her father did to her when she was young." Or some such psychoanalytic interpretation.

I said, "Think about it. The whole setup is intimidating. Anyone would be nervous in that situation." Ed Shearin then spoke up. He said, "You know, when you look at the patient, every behavior is a behavior of fear. Her facial expression, her slumped body. Had she been angry, and Marsha suggested switching places, she might have grumbled about it, but she didn't; she did it immediately. She did everything Marsha asked her to do."

No one looked convinced.

The next week, the setup was the same, except that I had already switched positions so the patient wouldn't have to face the panel. There was a knock on the door at the appointed time. A young woman came in and sat down. Someone said, "Where's the nurse?" The young woman said, "The nurse didn't come, so I just walked over here by myself because I didn't want to be late." She was a new patient on the unit.

When she left, someone said, "She was acting out to make trouble." I said, "What do you mean, acting out?" "She didn't wait for the nurse. Patients are not supposed to go anywhere without a nurse." I said, "Doesn't her behavior make sense? She had an appointment here, with us. The nurse wasn't on time, so she made the decision to come on her own so as not to be late for the appointment." "Absolutely not . . ."

I was thinking, "You've got to be joking." It was like a reprise of everything that had happened to me at the institute. No matter what she did, it was interpreted as abnormal. Motives were imputed based on a psychiatrist's own model of what the world should look like. It seemed that with the Kernberg model, if you tell a patient she is displaying aggression and she denies it, you then tell her that's just because she isn't aware of it, and pretty soon that patient really *is* going to get angry.

Then you sit back and say, "See what I mean!"

Conflicting Theories of Borderline Personality Disorder

Although my DBT paper wouldn't come out until that winter, word of it was beginning to get around. But my 1987 paper had published my theory of borderline personality disorder. You can't develop a therapy for a disorder unless you understand the basis of the disorder. I had developed my understanding by listening carefully to my clients as they talked about their lives. I realized that one of the things clients need most is validation, an understanding of why they behave the way they do. I saw that my clients very probably had experienced an invalidating environment for much of their lives, and probably a *traumatic* invalidating environment.

The Biosocial Theory of Borderline Personality Disorder

So that's one part of it. The other part of my theory is that one of the toughest challenges borderline individuals face is regulating their emotions. They are quick to become very emotional in response to some trigger in their environment, and slow to come back down. Emotion dysregulation is known to have a strong biological component, probably including a genetic one. I came to the conclusion that borderline individuals have biologically based emotion dysregulation, and have been and often still are exposed to an invalidating environment. People who have a tendency toward emotion dysregulation will have problems in an invalidating environment but will fare quite well in a validating environment. I call that the biosocial theory of borderline personality disorder.

Many people think that Kernberg and I have similar theories, inasmuch as we both posit a biological component interacting with an environmental component. We just disagree on what those components are. Kernberg assumes underlying aggression. I assume underlying emotion dysregulation. We both assume difficult environments.

The initial reaction to my theory was, shall we say, muted. Behaviorists weren't interested, and psychiatrists ignored it.

And now I had a paper in the pipeline of a major psychiatry journal, claiming effective treatment for people at high risk for suicide as well as for individuals meeting criteria for borderline people, all with behavior therapy. The response was something like:

"Who do you think you are?"

And "How is she having this impact?"

And "She has to be wrong."

And "We've been in this for fifty years. We know what we're doing. She doesn't."

I was poised to become the target of criticism from psychiatrists for many years, and I still am in some quarters.

Skeet Shooting, and I Am the Target

It started in earnest while I was at Weill. I was invited to give a major presentation—grand rounds, as it is called—on DBT at the Payne Whitney facility, in Manhattan. Al Frances had invited me. The head of psychiatry, Bob Michels, was in the front row. Kernberg was there. And a lot of other people who can safely be described as non-fans of DBT. Charlie Swenson was there, so he was a friendly face. I'll let him tell you what happened.

Grand rounds is a big deal, not pleasant. It's a skeet shoot, and you are the target. If you do a bad job, then they are nice to you. If you do a good job, then watch out: you are going to get slammed, because you are a threat to them. Marsha gave her talk. Someone asked a question about dialectics, and she answered it as if she had invented the concept, as if there were no such thing as Marx, Engels, and so on. Someone in the audience happened to be a scholar of dialectics, so he tore into her, saying, "It was there before you, Dr. Linehan." He was very rude. Marsha was very polite and replied, "I know that." Then Bob Michels said, "Look how much you are making out of such little data." Marsha shot back, "And how much data are there in psychoanalytical treatments of patients at this point?"

They knocked holes in the biosocial theory, saying it was oversimplified. They said, "You don't take into account the internal world, which we all know exists. Psychoanalysis is the ego, the superego, and the id, so what is new under the sun?" They treated her that way because they saw she was really good. You don't get that unless they feel challenged.

I went to lunch with Marsha afterwards and said, "What was that like for you? They were nonstop, tearing at you." Marsha's reply was "Oh, it was great! You will never make your model better if people don't constantly challenge it. You want skeptics. That guy Bob Michels is very smart. He said things that I am going to have to think about. You want people to attack your model with all their brain. So I felt pretty good up there. It is being able to take shots and make use of it." Marsha is the same when she gets research data that don't support the model. She is the only one in the lab who is happy at that point. When research shows that maybe she's not right, it is "Oh, my, we have a chance to improve it."

Evolution of the Criticism

The lines of criticism developed over time. The first was that I was just a teacher. Shortly after my paper was published, I went to a psychodynamic meeting in France, where I'd been asked to give a presentation. During the first break, someone came up to me and said, "You know, everybody's talking about your stuff. They're saying you're just—you're like a teacher." My response was something along the lines of "Oh, really? Thank you." I took it as a compliment. I love teaching my students. I love teaching my clients skills, teaching them how to put aside all the negative, anti-self emotions, and how to see themselves for who they really are, which is good people who are capable of receiving and giving love.

This person shook her head and said, "No, Marsha. You don't understand. It's not a compliment; it's an insult. They are saying that you aren't treating the disorder. You are just teaching them skills." It's true, in a way: I have never been interested in borderline personality disorder as a "disorder" in itself. I have never targeted that. I target suicidal behavior, out-of-control behavior. I don't think of myself as treating a disorder. I treat a set of behaviors that gets turned into a disorder by others.

The data in the 1991 paper, and in a follow-up paper two years later, were strong enough to demonstrate that whatever I was doing, my clients benefited. That was undeniable. So the line of criticism shifted to "Okay, we accept that you get good outcomes with clients, but that's because you are a really good therapist—you are charismatic—not because DBT is good therapy."

I am a good therapist; I knew that. And I am charismatic; I knew that, too. I also knew that DBT was a good therapy. So my team did another study, in which I was not directly involved in the therapy. Same outcome. That would convince them, I thought. It didn't. They suggested that I must have influenced the study somehow—my charisma, you know!—simply by being in the same building.

My next step was one of the wisest moves I've made in my research career. I invited every single researcher in the world who had any interest in DBT to join what would come to be known as the DBT Strategic Planning Group. We meet once a year in Seattle, at the University of Washington, and share what we've learned during the previous year, what we don't know, and what we need to know, and we plan out strategies for future research. A vital part of the group's work is to ensure that researchers in other labs and in other countries test the efficacy of DBT, just as my team and I have. If DBT works in my hands only because I am a good therapist, then other researchers wouldn't be able to get the same positive outcomes.

By now there have been sixteen independently run, randomized clinical trials of DBT, and all yielded the same outcomes as our very first trial. You could argue, I suppose, that these sixteen trials worked only because the therapists involved just happened to be really good therapists. But I think you can agree that argument is a bit of a stretch.

There were actually two battles going on simultaneously. There was the battle around borderline personality disorder, its causes and appropriate treatment. And there was suicide, its causes and appropriate treatment. The psychiatrists thought they had stumped me when they started to claim that suicide is a biological disorder. Now, of course, that's actually true, because there's no such thing as a nonbiological disorder in a human being. But their idea was that if it's biological, then you have to treat it with a drug, electroconvulsive therapy, or something like that—not with behavior therapy.

I used to get invited to be on panels: three psychiatrists and me. "This is biological," the psychiatrists would proclaim. And then they would trot out all these reasons why behavior therapy was irrelevant. They would sit down, believing they had won the argument. I relished these encounters. I'd stand up and say, "I see how suicide must be biological. I have a biological intervention, and I can tell you that right now. It's DBT, of course. It changes the biology. If it's a biological problem, and I can change it, then how could I be doing that except by changing the biology?"

You have to remember, this was psychiatrists' territory. They have a long history with suicide, whereas psychologists do not.

The argument became "Okay, your treatment works, but you are just treating symptoms." This barb was tossed at me in scientific meetings and in papers in the psychiatry press. It would be the equivalent of treating a bacterial infection by using cold packs to reduce someone's fever rather than going to the source of the condition, by giving antibiotics. Psychiatrists have the idea that there is a disease underlying these dysfunctional behaviors, and you have to treat the disease, not just mitigate the symptoms.

So I said, "All right, give me a measure of something that is not a symptom but is what you consider to be fundamental to the condition. I will then test to see if DBT changes this measure. If the measure improves, you have to agree that my treatment is effective, and you will stop saying I only treat symptoms. So I'll take whatever measure you select—anything you select. Anything. Give it to me."

The Introject

This provoked complete silence. Finally, John Clarkin, a colleague of Kernberg's, gave me a measure that was at the heart of the psychoanalytic perspective on borderline personality disorder. It is called the "introject," which essentially is a measure of an individual's self-esteem, or one's relationship to oneself. Now, you really don't have to tie yourself in knots trying to understand this term. Just know that if we found that DBT improved the introject in borderline patients, we would have demonstrated that DBT is indeed treating the cause of the condition, not just the symptoms. Our hypothesis was that DBT would indeed improve the introject.

Jamie Bedics, who is now at California Lutheran University, and two colleagues in my department, David Atkins and Katherine Comtois, joined me in a study in 2009 to test that hypothesis. This time we had a pool of a hundred women, again between the ages of eighteen and forty-five, who met criteria for borderline personality disorder. Half of them had DBT, half conventional behavior therapy. We assessed them at the end of a year and did a one-year follow-up assessment.

This is what we found:

DBT patients reported the development of a more positive introject including significantly greater self-affirmation, self-love, self-protection, and less self-attack during the course of treatment and one-year follow-up relative to community treatment by experts.*

We also demonstrated that patients receiving DBT had a stronger relationship with their therapists than did those in the control group. This had been another annoying criticism of DBT—that behavior therapists were more interested in their behavioral tools than they were in developing a good relationship with their clients. But establishing a caring relationship with clients is a top priority at the beginning of DBT.

When we submitted our manuscript about the introject measure for publication in 2011, it was initially rejected. The reasons were along the lines of "This is an irrelevant question," "We already know DBT works. You are just trying to rub it in," and "This is unimportant research." We persisted, of course, and the paper was finally published in the *Journal of Consulting and Clinical Psychology* in February of 2012.

Our first public presentation of these results, before the paper came out, was at McLean Hospital, outside Boston, where John Gunderson, one of the great experts on borderline personality disorder, was based. I stood in front of a very large audience, most of them psychiatrists, and described our methods, our measures, the results—the usual framework for a presentation.

I finished. I looked out at the audience, paused, and said, "I think I have made my point." They all stood and applauded.

What of Otto Kernberg? He has told me that I am the only person he's met whose treatment matches the theory on which it is based. That was a wonderful statement to hear from such a luminary in his field of psychiatry.

---

* J. D. Bedics, D. C. Atkins, K. A. Comtois, and M. M. Linehan, "Treatment Differences in the Therapeutic Relationship and Introject During a 2-Year Randomized Controlled Trial of Dialectical Behavior Therapy Versus Nonbehavioral Psychotherapy Experts for Borderline Personality Disorder," *Journal of Consulting and Clinical Psychology* 80, no. 1 (February 2012): 66–77.

Part Four

CHAPTER THIRTY-FOUR

The Circle Closes

CAMANO ISLAND IS about an hour's drive north of Seattle. On a clear day, you can see Mount Baker in the far distance. It is one of the highest mountains in the northern Cascades, and one of the snowiest places in the world. It is majestic—it takes your breath away.

When you turn off the highway toward Camano Island, the road is lined with tall Douglas firs, forming a kind of tunnel. You feel the serenity that lies ahead, the press of urban life receding. Early in 1992, I bought a house on Camano with money my father had left me. It is the only island in the region that doesn't require a ferry ride. Instead, access is over the Camano Gateway Bridge, which these days is adorned with metal sculptures of eagles, salmon, and herons. Just forty-five minutes north of Camano on the mainland is Skagit Valley, famous for hundreds of acres of tulip fields that draw a million visitors each year during the month of April. It is beyond fabulous.

The house is on the west side of the island and sits on a bluff above the water. "House" is too grand a term, really. It is small, with two bedrooms and an open living area, one half of which is devoted to cooking and eating, and the other half to sitting in front of the woodstove on cool evenings. We call it "the cabin."

But the outside world is where the magic is. I built a huge deck that reaches close to the edge of the bluff. I don't know how many hours I have sat on the deck, looking west over Saratoga Passage and Whidbey Island and (on a clear day) marveling at the peaks of the Olympic Peninsula in the far distance. Or watching the eagles hunting. They nest in the big pine tree to the left of the deck. Great blue herons, too, patiently fishing at the water's edge. The sunsets are spectacular.

I always have intentions of exploring the island and doing things. But once I get to my cabin, I throw open the doors and windows, put on some loud music, pour a glass of chilled wine from the refrigerator, sit on the deck, and exhale. It's a place of peace and connection to nature, of being rather than doing. The most active I get is long walks along the pebble beaches, good for contemplation.

I used to go to the house quite a lot with my friend Marge, particularly when we had grants to review. I would sit in a comfy chair on the deck, with Marge in the hot tub. She joked that she could tell how good or bad a grant application was by how wet the paper ended up. When her attention drifts from a poor proposal, she finds herself slipping down into the tub, and the paper falls into the water.

Every summer, I organize a party at the cabin with all my research staff, graduate students, and friends. I encourage people to bring their children. At the end of it, I give each postdoc and graduate student a framed copy of the Rilke quote that we four fellows at Stony Brook presented to Jerry Davison when we graduated. I told you about it earlier, but it is so germane to the lives of therapists (and other people, actually) that it bears repeating here. The poem reads:

> Do not believe that he who seeks to comfort you lives untroubled among the simple and quiet words that sometimes do you good. His life has much difficulty and sadness. . . . Were it otherwise he would never have been able to find those words.

A Birthday, a Time for Reflection

On May 4, 1993, the day before my fiftieth birthday, I drove up to the Camano house. I had decided to spend my birthday alone at

Camano as a time to reflect on my life, as well as enjoy the beauty of the place.

The next day, I walked along the beach for hours and then drove home. I was hoping my DBT book would finally be there, in time for my birthday. The publisher of the book had said the title should include the phrase "cognitive behavioral therapy." I said, "Absolutely not. We are not doing cognitive behavioral therapy; DBT is something different. No one will buy it if you call it that."

In the end, we compromised and called it *Cognitive-Behavioral Treatment of Borderline Personality Disorder*. By this point I was less obsessed with what the book would be called and more with the fact that it wasn't yet released. I told the publisher that I absolutely had to have the book by my fiftieth birthday, because, I explained, no one writes anything really good when they are over fifty. (Where I got that idea I don't know.) They said they would try.

It was still light out when I got to my house in Seattle. I saw a big box sitting on the back stairs. I lugged it inside, got a knife, cut the seals, and opened it up. It was my book—a dozen copies. I was thrilled.

As I did that, I suddenly heard a message from God. It was like a voice, saying to me:

You have kept your promise.

I was shocked. So then I thought, "Okay, I can die now." I thought, "Okay, it's over." I'm not kidding. I was expecting a car to hit me on the street and that would be the end of me. I didn't know where it would come from, but I was ready for it.

After a month or so, I realized that I wasn't going to die. So what was I going to do now? Then I thought, "Well, why not just keep doing what you're doing, Marsha?"

And that's what I did.

CHAPTER THIRTY-FIVE

A Family at Last

Early in 1992, I posted an advertisement seeking a live-in assistant. Veronica, who was a student at UW, answered the ad. We hit it off right away, and she moved into the guest room. Veronica and I became quite close. Our relationship blossomed quickly. A few years later, Veronica met Preston, who is a wonderful person, and I soon came to adore him also. The two of them had an unbelievably volatile relationship, but they finally got married and moved into the apartment in the basement of my house.

After a few years, they decided they wanted to buy a house, but they didn't have a down payment. I agreed to lend them the money. The house next door came up for sale, they bought it, and we had ourselves a mini-community. We tore down the fence between the two houses and erected a little arbor in the backyard, so that we flowed back and forth as one.

Veronica and Preston had a network of Hispanic friends, and they knew how to party. It was always fun. I was caught up in their vibrant social life; their friends were my friends. We spent Christmases together, we spent birthdays together, and we went on vacation together. And then Veronica became pregnant, with a due date of June 1996. All of us were thrilled. We were like family.

My Sister and I See Each Other—for the First Time in Years

It wasn't long before this that more than a dozen years of estrangement from my sister Aline had come to an end. Aline had visited me in Seattle around my fiftieth birthday, in 1993. We started to talk—nothing premeditated; it just flowed out of each of us. This is how Aline recalls that moment:

We were standing at the sink in the kitchen talking and I broke down sobbing, telling her how sorry I was that I had never been there to help her when she was younger and under such duress from Mother and Dad and disapproval all around. I had gone the other way and had shunned her, too. I begged for her forgiveness and told her how guilty I felt for not having helped her when she had needed a friend. I had not been there for her at all. In fact, I had done everything to steer clear of her. My mother had always, for whatever reason, told me to "stay away from Marsha." It was as though something she would say would influence me in the wrong way. I did stay away.

As I sobbed and asked for forgiveness that day in May, Marsha was, as ever, her wonderful, accepting self, and we hugged and she said she understood and how could I have been any different as I was so under the influence of Mother, etc., etc. I felt a real sense of cleansing/relief after our talk that day.

For the first time, each of us truly saw the other. Now we talk every day. We are so close. At some point I said to Aline, "To demonstrate how much I love you, Aline, I am willing to let you die first." She knew what I meant. We are so attached to each other that we know that whoever is left behind, when that day comes, the other will be completely devastated. We are terrible when we say goodbye after any visit. We realize that this is silly, but that's who we've become.

So with this beautiful rapprochement with Aline, I felt blessed to have this family in my life—both the family I'd been born with and the family I'd chosen.

Isabella, Veronica's daughter, was born in the summer of 1996. Veronica and Preston asked me to be Isabella's godmother. You can imagine what that meant to me.

A Family No More

I cherished the Christmases I had shared with Veronica and Preston, as the family I'd never had. And this year there would be the new baby, making it especially wonderful. I so looked forward to celebrating it together.

But that year, out of the blue, an unbridgeable chasm opened between Veronica and Preston and me. The reasons are complex, and I don't want to go into them. But the immediate consequences were that the family I had so come to treasure was torn asunder.

The arbor that we had built together between our two houses—a symbol of our oneness as a family—was taken down, and the fence between them rebuilt. The period of happiness that came from loving and being loved, as a family, was over. Even to this day it feels so sad.

But soon, a new and more permanent family slowly began to blossom in my life.

The Accident That Led to a Home at Last

Geraldine had arrived in Seattle in February of 1994, with the aim of going to school in the United States. She was the daughter of Veronica's father's boss, who was a high-ranking officer in the Peruvian army. The initial idea was that until she went to college, Geri would stay with Veronica and Preston; this was when they were still living in the basement apartment of my house.

But Veronica and Preston didn't have room, so they asked if I would take her in. They told Geraldine's dad not to worry—she would be fine with me. But what did I know about teenagers? Nothing.

Geraldine was an independent and determined sixteen-year-old girl when she arrived. Growing up in Peru, in a fairly financially comfortable household, she had been expected, when she turned fifteen, to celebrate her transition to womanhood with a grand party, a quinceañera. After that, she'd be expected to get married, stay close to her parents, have children, and be a good wife. Geraldine would have none of that. She wanted a professional career, a bold stand in which she had full support from her mother.

"When I was a young girl, I said to my dad, 'I don't want a quinceañera party. I want to go abroad,'" Geraldine recalls. "'I want to go to Paris, study at the Sorbonne.' My dad spoke French, and I did, too. He agreed I could do that. So when I was going to turn fifteen, I said to my dad, 'Remember your promise? Well, I don't want to go to France. I want to go to the United States.' I had realized that speaking English was probably going to be of more use to me in my career than speaking French. He said, 'Okay.'"

Geraldine had originally wanted to go to Boston University. "It just sounded nice to me," she says. "I think I heard about it on television or something." She applied to BU, only to discover that she was too young to be accepted. Coming to Seattle was a fallback option. "I didn't know where Seattle was or even how to pronounce it," she says. "I thought, 'When I am eighteen I will transfer to Boston.'"

Learning to Be a Parent—Fast!

Preston picked Geraldine up at the airport, from a very late flight. I was already asleep when they arrived, so Preston showed her the bedroom I'd prepared. The next morning, I peeked around the door. Geraldine was completely invisible under a menagerie of twenty or thirty stuffed animals, mostly bears. "Hmm, that's odd for a girl who's just about to go to college," I thought.

Geraldine had arrived with two small suitcases, one with a couple of pairs of jeans, a few shirts, underwear, and not much else, the other bursting with her zoo of stuffed animals. She had very little English, and far fewer years than I had imagined. "Sixteen!" I said to myself when I found out. "What am I going to do?" I was well used to dealing with freshman college students, but there's a world of a difference between sixteen and eighteen. I was like every other new parent, having a major responsibility thrown into my lap with absolutely no training. Even when she asked me that first morning, "Where is the person who will pick up my room and make my bed?" (Okay, her father was a high-ranking general after all.) I told her that I did not have a nanny to help her.

I immediately changed my life around. I made breakfast every morning and came home by five every evening to cook dinner. As best we could, we started to get to know each other. I spoke only English, and she only Spanish. It took a long time for us to have an easy conversation. I wanted to hear her life story, and she was willing to tell it to me in Spanish with a little bit of her new English.

When Geraldine was a baby, she had to stay with her aunt while her family rushed to Lima to save her older brother's life. He was only two years old and had developed kidney disease. Her parents couldn't take care of the three siblings at the time, so Geraldine stayed with her aunt. Later, I would meet her aunt, who was so emotionally warm. I understood how Geri had become such a loving person herself.

At night, I went to check on her in her room. Often I found her halfway out the window, looking at the moon. I worried about her—I knew so little about what was going on. I knew she had had a boyfriend back in Peru, so I worried that the loss of him was a problem.

Parenting Rules

I had to come to grips with this parenting thing. Her parents did not call me, and I had no way of contacting them. Geri constantly called her dad, who just as constantly supported her financially. Not long after Geri arrived, I said to her, "You know, Geraldine, I think we should have some rules of behavior." She said, "Oh, yes, we should." I said, "Well, what do you think they should be?" I was very naïve, because I thought she was going to tell me what would be a good set of rules. Instead she said, "You are supposed to make them up, Marsha."

I came up with a set of three rules. Rule one: *If you have sex, be on birth control*. Rule two: *If you are in a car, the person driving cannot have drunk any alcohol*. Rule three: *If you are going to come home later than the time we had agreed on, you will call me*. That last one she kept, I know that. The others, I can't be sure. No parent can.

Soon Geri started making friends at the school where she was learning English. Sometimes they drove her home after classes. I was in shock when I saw that these wealthy young men often drove fast and very expensive cars. But I thought it would be important for her to be able to invite her friends back to our house, so she did.

The problem was, I had absolutely no idea what I was supposed to do. Her friends would come over, often in their fast cars, and I'd go upstairs to call a friend. "I'm up here, they're down there, what do I do?" I'd say. My friend tried to calm me down and explained that I should go downstairs and just be natural. I did that and was surprised to discover that a lot of Geraldine's friends were considerably older, in their twenties and thirties, maybe. I said to each of them, "How old are you? If you are not twenty-one, you may not drink alcohol in my house." "How old are you . . . ?" And so on. It still humiliates me to think of me at that moment.

Home for the Two of Us

Geraldine completed her English course and got accepted at Seattle University to study business administration. In her sophomore year, she decided that she wanted a true dorm experience. This was two years after she had arrived for what I had expected to be just a few days. Geraldine, daughter of a general, never did learn to make her bed or clean the kitchen or make rice without destroying the pots.

Even though she was living in a dorm, my house had become home for both of us. It was evident that Geraldine wasn't going to go through with moving to Boston. I just wasn't quite sure what our relationship was going to be, long-term.

She often came home on the weekends and holidays. She called often, when she needed advice or just to talk. We went to church together. I became her godmother for her Catholic confirmation. We were close, but it was nothing like the enthralling, if somewhat tumultuous, relationship I'd had with Veronica. With Geraldine there was a calmness, a distance, an ease. She said I was like her house mother. "Not a guardian, but someone you can call if you have trouble" is how she describes those days now. One time, she called me to come and get her and her friends from a party. I was too tired, so I sent a car service, like the one I use to get to the airport. Later, I felt very guilty that I hadn't been a good mother who would go and get her daughter. But she said, "Marsha, we loved it. It was so special to be in a limousine."

I threw a big party for Geraldine when she graduated from college, in 1998. Her parents came. Geraldine's mother was very quiet, but her father was a huge presence, and I liked him a lot. He absolutely adored his daughter. I felt that he appreciated the role I was now playing in Geraldine's life. I had met him two years earlier, when I went to Peru. He took me to Machu Picchu and we had a fabulous time, despite the fact that I spoke no Spanish and he spoke no English. There was a connection you sometimes have with another person, where language doesn't matter.

Morphing into an American Mother

Geraldine eventually moved back into the house, first into the guest room, then back into her old room, and finally into the apartment in the basement. I sensed our relationship gradually deepening. Geraldine did, too. "I was opening up more with Marsha," she recalls. "We got more and more close. Before, I used not to tell her where I was going, because I felt the need to be an independent person. But now I was including her more in my life." She got a job at a bank and did very well, and then a job at an investment firm, where she stayed for almost ten years.

A turning point came when Geraldine started dating Nate, whom she had met at work and had been good friends with for a while. I liked him a lot. Now it was getting more serious. This was around 2001.

Of course, I was hoping that Geraldine and Nate would get married. I had a feeling it would happen when the three of us were in the car waiting for a ferry, and I turned around to see Geri using an eyelash curler to curl Nate's eyelashes. Nate, happy as a clam, just letting Geri do as she pleased.

Geraldine and Nate got married in July of 2005. I had an engagement party for them. Geraldine explains:

My parents, sister, and one brother came. There were so many emotions that night. I felt how much my mom and dad loved Marsha. My mother is very quiet. "I show you that I love you. I don't have to tell you as well." That's my mom. But that night, it was very emotional for both of them. Mom and Dad couldn't be more thankful to Marsha. I now felt that Marsha was my mom, too. It was impossible for me not to have her name on my wedding invitation. I asked her if I could, and she said yes, so my wedding invitation read:

GENERAL DE DIVISION (EP) HOWARD RODRIGUEZ MALAGA
MAGDA TORRES DE RODRIGUEZ
MARSHA M. LINEHAN, PhD
INVITE YOU TO THE WEDDING OF THEIR DAUGHTER . . .

How wonderful it was for me.

That same year, I sold our small house on Brooklyn Avenue. Nate, Geraldine, and I looked for a much larger house in a nicer neighborhood where the three of us could live. The house I bought, where we live now, was four blocks up the hill and several blocks south on Eighteenth Avenue. We had the third floor converted into a self-contained apartment for Geraldine and Nate.

Geraldine is an accident in my life, and would that everyone could be blessed with so happy an accident. I'll let Geraldine put it in her words:

I grew up in an environment where living with your parents when you are thirty years old is more the norm than the exception. And I am proud and blessed that I am able to continue a tradition that perhaps even [our daughter] Catalina would follow. I asked Nate about it, and he was fully on board. He makes dinner for all of us every night and we watch the news together. I knew I could not leave her. I will live with Marsha until the end of time.

And what is most important is that Marsha is at peace, living with family who love her and cherish every moment she can give us. She is my American mother, my mother, and I know how fortunate I am.

CHAPTER THIRTY-SIX

Going Public with My Story: The Real Origins of DBT

I ALWAYS THOUGHT THAT one day I would "go public" about my past. "Are you one of us?" was a question I'd been asked many times, in many different ways. The scars and burn marks on my arms aren't always completely out of view, so it's not surprising that people might be curious, especially those who are familiar with the signature in the flesh of anguish.

I occasionally told clients about my history. On one occasion, in the spring of 2009, I elected not to be direct. "You mean have I suffered?" I said to the young woman, who looked at me earnestly. "No, Marsha," she replied. "I mean one of us. Like us. Because if you were, it would give all of us so much hope."

I went public about my history for the very reason that this young woman touched upon: it could be a message of hope to others who find themselves in hell. I had toyed with the idea in my mid-thirties, when I was running to be president of the Association for Advancement of Behavior Therapy. I imagined myself delivering the presidential address, saying, effectively, "Look at me. I've been there. I know what it is like. And I know how to help." It would have been very dramatic. When I told my mentor Jerry Davison what I was thinking, he strongly advised against it, saying it could derail my young career. Otto Kernberg said much the same thing two decades later, advising me not to tell anyone.

When my client asked me that simple question, "Are you one of us?"—it was a plea, really—I realized that the time had probably come to act on my intention. Another motivation came from a conversation with Aline around that time. My sister is always looking for ways to make a difference for those in need. I had recently become involved with NAMI, the National Alliance on Mental Illness, an advocacy group whose goal is to raise public awareness of shortcomings in the country's mental health system. I thought Aline could make a valuable contribution, and I asked her if she would also become involved.

An Initial Denial

I should step back for a minute and describe the first NAMI gathering I attended. The meeting was in Washington, D.C., and it included clients. There were mental health professionals of various kinds, and NAMI staff, too. The chairperson opened the meeting and asked us to go around the table, each of us introducing ourselves. There must have been twenty of us around this large oval table, so it would be a few minutes before it was my turn. Others said, "I'm so-and-so. I had borderline personality disorder." "I'm so-and-so and I've been in the hospital." "I'm so-and-so. I'm a parent, and my daughter has had multiple suicide attempts." "I'm so-and-so, and I'm an expert on schizophrenia." And so on.

I listened to these brief introductions with growing alarm, thinking, "Who am I?" and "What am I going to say when they get to me?" I contemplated coming out right there. There couldn't have been a more sympathetic audience, after all. But I hadn't prepared what I might say, and therefore I decided this wasn't the right time. "I'm Marsha Linehan. I'm at the University of Washington, and I am a clinician and researcher with highly suicidal individuals." The moment passed. But the disconnect between the public me and the private me struck me powerfully.

When I made my suggestion to Aline about joining this group, she said, "I can't work for NAMI, Marsha. I can't work in any area of mental health, because I can never tell anybody why I'm doing it. I can't tell them about you, Marsha."

It came in a flood, what I had been doing to Aline all these years but had been blind to. She had gone through all of this trauma as my only sister, feeling guilty that it was me instead of her. I've talked to a lot of sisters of borderline individuals, and I knew that the trauma of being the sister can be so hard. And no one pays attention to their plight. Someone ought to write a book on the topic.

No More Denials

I determined that the time had come to tell my story. I did not want to die a coward.

My siblings' reactions were decidedly mixed. Marston was adamant: "You are not a coward, Marsha," he would say. Marston is very passionate and protective of me, and I appreciated that in him. My younger brother Mike took a completely different position. "Listen, Marsha, if you're going to do it, you have to make sure you do it big," he said. "The worst thing that can happen is you go public about your life and—"

I finished his sentence for him. "Nobody notices?" Yes, that would be painful. Aline simply said, "Marsha, it's up to you. You have to do what you think is right."

Returning to the Institute of Living

The only question was where and how I should deliver my message. And the perfect venue would be the Institute of Living, the mental institution where I had spent two years as a girl, where hell had found me.

It would be closure.

I had visited the institute a couple of years earlier to deliver a lecture, my standard description of DBT. We had time to spare on one of those occasions, so I asked the person who was organizing my visit to show me their DBT unit. He was, of course, completely unaware of my history, and what other motives I might have. "It's in the Thompson Building," he added. (The Thompson Building, if you recall, was where I had spent most of my two-plus years at the institute.)

My friend Sebern Fisher, from my days at the institute, had joined me on the visit. There we were, the two of us poised to take a tour of the very same unit where we were in hell all those years ago. I didn't know quite how I would react. Would I find it overwhelmingly emotionally painful? Would I be indifferent?

My relationship to my past is one in which it feels like it was another person who went through hell, and I feel very sad for her. It's just so sad that anybody would go through what I went through. I'm a very different person now than I was then.

The Seclusion Room—Again

My experience during the tour was that it was surreal, as if I was in a movie, not me but someone else. At one point we were standing near what used to be the seclusion room in Thompson Two. I looked inside. So many times I had been in that small room, with the chair and the table, a nurse often watching over me. Being in there was supposed to be a punishment, but for me it had been a haven of safety from myself. Although I did manage to launch myself off the table and onto my head many, many times.

Now I was standing where Sebern used to stand when I would sit on the little bed and she'd be chatting with me, sometimes blowing cigarette smoke into my mouth. It was a factual recollection, not emotional. I asked if I could take photographs. Bizarre, I know, but I actually had a good time. The seclusion room was now a small office, and they had enlarged the windows. It is much lighter than it once was.

Meeting Former DBT Clients

Early in 2011, I emailed David Tolin, director of the institute's Anxiety Disorders Center, and told him I would like to make a major presentation at the institute on the history of DBT. "Would that be possible?" I asked. He said it would be. In fact, it was more like *"Yes, please!"*

There was a small lecture hall where academic presentations are usually held, but it was too small for what I had in mind. I asked David if I could give my lecture in the larger auditorium. (I told you some of this story in the first chapter, if it sounds familiar.) He called me back and said, "Well, we'd love to have you do it there, but I need to know why, because that's not usually what we do. What would be the reason?" I told him that I was going to go public about my history and that I planned for a large audience. I made him promise that he would tell no one.

David called back again and said, "Unfortunately, I have to tell the chair of the department, because it is such an unusual request. I have to explain why you want this room. Do I have your permission to do that?" I said, "Okay, you can tell him, but you have to have him promise complete secrecy. No one else must know. It is very, very important to me."

My lecture was scheduled for June 18, 2011. It was to be called "The Personal Story of the Development of DBT." Holly Smith and Elaine Franks, my assistants, took on the job of organizing the invitation list. I told them I wanted people I was close to, former and current students, colleagues, friends. I said, "Don't tell me who's coming. I don't want to know." I was very reluctant to ask my brothers, because I thought some of them might not come, and that would have been humiliating and hurtful. Aline went ahead and invited them anyway.

It was agony, trying to compress my life story into ninety minutes. What should I include? What should I leave out? Might I tread on some people's toes, even hurt some feelings?

I was to give my presentation in the afternoon. But I had also asked that I have the opportunity to talk to a group of the institute's former clients, those who had been in the DBT program, either as inpatients or outpatients. I wanted them to hear my story of hope, just them and me, in an intimate gathering. This was scheduled for the morning, just before lunch.

There were about thirty of us, in a small, bright room, with flowers in vases on either side of me. "You may be wondering why I am here today," I began. "I am here at the Institute of Living to give a major talk at one o'clock. You are invited to that talk, but I didn't want you to hear what I have to say at that talk. I wanted to tell you myself right now."

No one moved. I felt an expectancy in the air, almost electric. "When I developed this treatment, it was to fulfill a vow I had made when I was very young," I continued. "And the place that I made that vow was at the Institute of Living, because I was a patient here—always on that lowest unit, always on the locked unit. I rarely got out of the locked unit. I was supposed to be here for just a few weeks, but I didn't get out for two years and one month, so I was locked up for a very long time. I was where you are now. And here's where I am now. You, too, can get out of hell. You can be where I am. I want to tell you this because I want you to realize how much hope there really is and how important it is not to give up."

This was a collective jaw-dropping moment, heads shaking in disbelief. A former institute patient who was in the audience and had been in the DBT program after a series of suicide attempts remembers the moment this way:

I hadn't been back to the institute in a few months, since my weekly program stopped. Being there brought up all kinds of emotions—sadness, guilt, fear all welled up in me. I think it did for others, too. It was very bonding for us all, just being there together, each of us having gone through the program. It was very exciting being there, because we were going to meet the woman who we'd all seen on the DBT training videos, who had started it all. We would get to see what she is like.

When she got to the point of the revelation, I was completely astonished, incredulous. We all were. That she was one of us had never entered my head; none of us imagined she was one of us. Her story was so sad, because I think she had a harder time than I ever did. And because she had had to keep quiet about it for so long, because it would have ruined her career if she'd spoken up. So very sad, but it is also, as she said, a message of hope—for all of us. The most touching moment was when we danced together. . . .

I told you about the dance I had learned from Beatrice Grimm on my visits to Germany. A few years back, I developed a new dance. It is done to a beautiful song called "Nada Te Turbe," which I had also heard about while in Germany. The title means "Let Nothing Disturb You," from a poem by a sixteenth-century Spanish mystic, Saint Teresa of Ávila. I find it so very moving and meaningful, and so do the people who dance to it with me. Dancing in a circle as we do is a way of bringing people together, which is an important component of DBT.

Here are the words of the poem. I think you will see what I mean:

Let nothing disturb you,
Let nothing frighten you,
All things pass away:
God never changes.
Patience obtains all things.
He who has God
Finds he lacks nothing;
God alone suffices.

When I was first developing this dance, I practiced by myself in the house. Poor Nate; I forced him to practice with me when he was around. I wanted to get it right so I could teach it to anyone.

One day when I didn't have anyone to dance with, I decided to invite all the mental patients in the world to dance with me. That's right. I was surprised to find how moving that was, my hands out in front of me, imagining them dancing with me, inviting them to come with me. I was giving them an experience they weren't having, but now they were, with me.

I do a dance at the end of all my DBT workshops. I tell people they can invite anyone they want who wasn't there to join them—friends, loved ones, people who had died and were greatly missed. I tell you, by the time the dance is finished, almost everyone is in tears. It turns out to be a very powerful dance.

That's how I ended the gathering with the former DBT clients, that morning at the institute. All of us in a circle, one step to the left, two to the right, moving slowly, bodies swaying slightly, tears falling down many cheeks.

Including mine.

Giving the Talk

After lunch, David Tolin took me to the lecture room. He gave a brief introduction. That was followed by another, more personal introduction by my friend and colleague Martin Bohus.

I went up to the dais, more nervous than I had been in years. My brothers John, Earl, Marston, and Mike were sitting together in the front row, with my sister, Aline. I beamed at them and began.

"My biggest fear is that I won't make it through this talk." As I said those words, there was a very real possibility that I might actually cry, which would have been beyond embarrassing.

In the moment, I was reminded of a little story about me and my mother, and I decided I would tell it to the audience. "Mother used to cry all the time when she was upset," I said, exaggerating just a little. "But she also cried sometimes when she was happy. In one of my poverty-stricken years, I gave Mother an onion as a birthday present. I said, 'I know when you are happy you cry, and I know this will make you cry, so I am giving it to you.' She started crying."

Fortunately, on the podium that June day, I did not.

I quickly swung into "speaker mode" after my initial shaky start to the talk, but I remained emotional. I was about to reveal publicly what had remained intensely private for five decades. I looked at the audience for a few seconds, at this wonderful gathering of friends, colleagues, students, and former students. And family. I thanked them all for coming, and Linda Dimeff, Holly Smith, and Elaine Franks for organizing the event. "And I especially want to thank my brothers for coming," I said. "Jeepers," I thought to myself, "am I going to cry *now?*" Before I knew it, I had told my wonderful audience my story, the one you have been witness to in this book.

* * *

After I had finished, and the question-and-answer period came to an end, Geraldine got up from her seat and walked to the dais. This is what she said to me:

> You are a star in my life, Marsha. You always give me light. Thank you for loving me, and I love you very much. I am very proud of you.

We hugged for a long time.

It was one of the sweetest memories of the day. And forever.

Home at last.

Afterword

WHAT HAS HAPPENED since the day of my talk? My family keeps growing. I am now a grandmother to Catalina, the smartest child I've ever known and the prettiest little girl you can imagine. You may be wondering how smart she is? Well, she speaks three languages—English, Spanish, and Mandarin Chinese—while I, on the other hand, speak only one, and that's on a good day. We also adopted a rescue dog, Toby Choclo Boyz, a terrier mix.

Nate's parents come for visits often. For me it is just wonderful when they are here. I often wonder how Nate survives living with three girls—Geri, Catalina, and me. He makes us fabulous dinners every night. Nate takes care of Toby, a wonderful little dog—sometimes a little excitable, but we love him.

At home, Geraldine and I decided to build an entire new room for Nate in what used to be a dark and sad basement. It is now a beautiful room, a true "man cave."

Spiritually, I have recently begun to go to church regularly, as I once did. You will recall my disenchantment with the Catholic Church, and how I separated myself from the institution, though not its beliefs. For a time, I went to a local Episcopalian church, which I enjoyed for its inclusion of diverse thinking. One Sunday, my friends Ron and Marcia invited me to go with them to the neighborhood Lutheran church. I immediately loved the music, the food, the people. I love the talks they have, linking the gospel with everyday problems and giving guidance on how to be in one's everyday life. To top it off, one of my former students is their pastor, which makes the whole experience even more fulfilling. You can just imagine what a shock it was for me to discover that about my former student. And, last but not least, the Lutheran Church invites everyone to communion, which, sadly, the Catholic Church does not. From my point of view, attending the Lutheran Church doesn't mean I am not still a Catholic. I figure God loves me just as much regardless of what church I go to.

I have been spiritual throughout my life, in different ways. And now I have friends I go with, and a wonderful community of friends in the church. It's a combination of a community of friends and a love of God that now feeds my spiritual self. I love God, and I love to pray. So I am happy with all of that. And as I think about it, of course, I have such faith because my mother gave it to me in the beginning. She always said I could drop it, but once I had it, I wouldn't want to drop it. I can't imagine my life without faith. The single most important gift my mother gave me was faith.

Professionally, I think I can say I have fulfilled the vow to God I made while at the Institute of Living all those years ago. But I haven't stopped; I haven't given up. I want to make sure we improve what needs to be improved; I want to make sure there are enough therapists trained in DBT so this treatment I developed can carry on without me.

And this is very important to me also: I want to find ways of getting DBT and DBT skills to everyone in the world who needs them. My daughter, Geraldine, and I have been working on utilizing technology to disseminate DBT skills via computerized learning. Training and certifying therapists is equally important, and, through the DBT-Linehan Board of Certification, we are ensuring that patients have access to qualified and certified therapists and agencies.

One of my goals is to provide a scholarship fund to patients who need financial support to attend college. I am sure my daughter will help me make this happen.

You may be wondering how in the world I talked my daughter into helping me with this. As it turns out, she cares for people just as much as I do. My next goal is to get Geraldine to get Catalina involved as well.

Getting DBT into school curricula is going to be very powerful, helping not only kids in need to cope with their problems, but all kids. Emotion regulation, mindfulness, interpersonal effectiveness, and so on—all are skills each one of us could benefit from. Beginning at a young age is important.

DBT has spread far beyond the United States, becoming strongly established in Latin America, Europe, Asia, and the Middle East. And we now know that the treatment is also helpful for people with substance dependence, depression, post-traumatic stress disorder (PTSD), and eating disorders. No doubt there will be more applications as time goes on. We are already working on DBT skills for people with cancer, for instance.

You can see, therefore, that DBT's reach is now far greater than the problem for which I developed it: namely, helping salve the suffering of highly suicidal people.

So my last message to you is that I hope that you will develop the skills you need and that you will also help others have the skills they need to experience life as worth living—if I can do it, you can do it, too.

Amen

Acknowledgments

As many people know, having a daughter can be the best part of someone's life, and my daughter, Geraldine, has been that in mine. I want to thank Geraldine for walking this walk with me as I share the story of my life with you. Of all the people who helped make my memoir possible, Geraldine was the glue that kept us going.

I also would like to thank my unbelievable, fabulous family, my sister, Aline, and my brothers, John, Earl, Marston, and Michael. In particular you will find in this book everything there is to know about my brother Earl, who saved me as much as my daughter did. And whenever I thought I wasn't going to make it, I would call my sister, Aline, who believed in my ability that I could indeed write this book.

My son-in-law, Nate, has been my friend and companion to so many Husky games and shared the love for football with me. I thank him for being a kind soul and a loving son.

I give thanks to my Zen teacher Willigis Jäger and mentor Jerry Davison for their wisdom and friendship through the years, as well as my lifelong friends Sebern Fisher, Diane Perkins, Marge Anderson, and Ron and Marcia Baltrusis and my cousins Nancy and Ed.

My home away from home, the University of Washington, and specifically the Behavioral Research and Therapy Clinics, is where I have spent the majority of my waking life since 1977, conducting research, teaching students, and treating patients. UW has been a loving community that contributed to building a life experienced as worth living, and for this I'd like to thank so many. Of course, I am afraid of leaving a name out, but I will do my best:

At the Department of Psychology, Cheryl Kaiser, Sheri Mizumori, Ron Smith, Bob Kohlenberg, and Elizabeth McCauley for their friendship and support. My colleagues in clinical psychology for supporting my work and mission to educate and train students and conduct research, through which I was able to create DBT to save and improve lives.

The staff at the Behavioral Research and Therapy Clinics, who have been the pillars of support to me and our lab for many years: Thao Truong, Elaine Franks, Katie Korslund, Melanie Harned, Rod Lumsden, Jeremy Eberle, Matt Tkachuck, Heather Hawley, and Andrea Chiodo. As well, Angela Murray and Susan Bland, who were longtime assessors on our research studies. Angela moved to New York many years ago, but every year on my birthday she would bake and send me a birthday cake (Angela's delicious carrot cake). A special thanks to our volunteers and undergraduate students, who contributed to the numerous research projects and worked to sustain the DBT training program.

Some of my students, postdocs, and colleagues: Molly Adrian, Michele Berk, Yevgeny Botanov, Milton Brown, Eunice Chen, Sandee Conti, Sheila Crowell, Sona Dimidjian, Bob Gallop, Heidi Heard, Dorian Hunter, Cheryl Kempinsky, Cedar Koons, Debbie Leung, Noam Lindenboim, Beverly Long, Anita Lungu, Lynn Mc-Farr, Marivi Navarro, Lisa Onken, David Pantalone, Joan Russo, Nick Salman, Henry Schmidt, Cory Secrist, Liz Stuntz, Julianne Torres, Amy Wagner, Chelsey Wilks, Suzanne Witterholt, and Briana Woods.

Clinical supervisors: Our dedicated supervisors spend hundreds of hours as volunteers training and supervising our graduate students and postdocs in the DBT training program. We would not be able to provide much-needed treatment services to our clients without these supervisors. I want to thank Beatriz Aramburu, Adam Carmel, Jessica Chiu, Emily Cooney, Caroline Cozza, Angela

Davis, Lizz Dexter-Mazza, Michelle Diskin, Clara Doctolero, Dan Finnegan, Andrew Fleming, Vibh Forsythe-Cox, Bob Goettle, Michael Hollander, Kelly Koerner, Janice Kuo, Liz LoTempio, Shari Manning, Annie McCall, Jared Michonski, Erin Miga, Andrea Neal, Kathryn Patrick, Adam Payne, Ronda Reitz, Sarah Reynolds, Magda Rodriguez, Jennifer Sayrs, Sara Schmidt, Trevor Schraufnagel, Stefanie Sugar, Jennifer Tininenko, and Randy Wolbert for their commitment to our students and clients.

As well, I am deeply grateful to our donors for their generous support. Because of them, we are able to continue our mission to train clinician-scientists and serve highly suicidal, multiproblem clients, doing so regardless of the clients' ability to pay.

The National Institutes of Health: I could not have developed DBT without research sponsors such as NIH. I want to acknowledge the NIH's multidecade support for my research. In particular, my heartfelt thanks to Jane Pearson for being a champion of research on suicide prevention and treatment.

I'd like to acknowledge the DBT researchers and clinicians who want to advance the dissemination and implementation of DBT research through the United States and the world. I thank each of you: Martin Bohus, Alex Chapman, Kate Comtois, Linda Dimeff, Katie Dixon-Gordon, Tony DuBose, Alan Fruzzetti, Pablo Gagliesi, Melanie Harned, André Ivanoff, Sara Landes, Cesare Maffei, Shelley McMain, Lars Mehlum, Alec Miller, Andrada Neacsiu, Azucena Palacios, Shireen Rizvi, Roland Sinnaeve, Michaela Swales, Charles Swenson, Wies van den Bosch, and Ursula Whiteside.

The organizations I founded and the people who run them: I thank the leadership and staff of the DBT-Linehan Board of Certification, the International Society for the Improvement and Teaching of Dialectical Behavior Therapy, Behavioral Tech Research, Behavioral Tech, and the Linehan Institute.

This book was a long journey of understanding my own life so that I can describe it to you coherently. I'd like to acknowledge Roger Lewin for his ability to collect pieces of my life and help thread them into a complete story, my story. As well, I am fortunate and thankful to have my editor at Random House, Kate Medina, and her team, Erica Gonzalez and Anna Pitoniak, be such a strong cohort of powerful and caring women. Thank you for being a part of this and for always saying yes to the many deadline extensions I requested. Finally, I thank my agent, Steve Ross, who from the beginning recognized how important this book was to me.

My last hope is that this story helps others see that there is a way to get out of hell and to build a life worth living.

Appendix

....

REASONS FOR LIVING INVENTORY BY SUBSCALE*

SURVIVAL AND COPING BELIEFS

1. I care enough about myself to live.
2. I believe I can find other solutions to solve my problems.
3. I still have many things left to do.
4. I have hope that things will improve and the future will be happier.
5. I have the courage to face life.
6. I want to experience all that life has to offer and there are many experiences I haven't had yet which I want to have.
7. I believe everything has a way of working out for the best.
8. I believe I can find a purpose in life, a reason to live.
9. I have a love of life.
10. No matter how badly I feel, I know that it will not last.
11. Life is too beautiful and precious to end it.
12. I am happy and content with my life.
13. I am curious about what will happen in the future.
14. I see no reason to hurry death along.
15. I believe I can learn to adjust or cope with my problems.
16. I believe that killing myself would not really accomplish or solve anything.

* Table 1, in M. M. Linehan, J. L. Goodstein, S. L. Nielsen, and J. A. Chiles, "Reasons for Staying Alive When You Are Thinking of Killing Yourself: The Reasons for Living Inventory," *Journal of Consulting and Clinical Psychology,* 51, no: 2 (1983): 276–86.

17. I have a desire to live.
18. I am too stable to kill myself.
19. I have future plans I am looking forward to carrying out.
20. I do not believe that things get miserable or hopeless enough that I would rather be dead.
21. I do not want to die.
22. Life is all we have and is better than nothing.
23. I believe I have control over my life and destiny.

RESPONSIBILITY TO FAMILY

24. It would hurt my family too much.
25. I would not want my family to feel guilty afterwards.
26. I would not want my family to think I was selfish or a coward.
27. My family depends on me and needs me.
28. I love and enjoy my family too much and could not leave them.
29. My family might believe I did not love them.
30. I have a responsibility and commitment to my family.

CHILD-RELATED CONCERNS

31. The effect on my children would be harmful.
32. It would not be fair to leave the children for others to take care of.
33. I want to watch the children as they grow.

FEAR OF SUICIDE

34. I am afraid of the actual "act" of killing myself (the pain, blood, violence).
35. I am a coward and do not have the guts to do it.
36. I am so inept that my method would not work.
37. I am afraid that my method of killing myself would fail.
38. I am afraid of the unknown.
39. I am afraid of death.
40. I could not decide where, when, and how to do it.

Fear of Social Disapproval

41. Other people would think I am weak and selfish.
42. I would not want people to think that I did not have control over my life.
43. I am concerned about what others would think of me.

Moral Objections

44. My religious beliefs forbid it.
45. I believe only God has the right to end life.
46. I consider it morally wrong.
47. I am afraid of going to hell.

Index

·····································

Acceptance, radical, 159, 241,
    248–253, 263
Acceptance skills, 7, 89, 142,
    154, 169, 216, 219, 220,
    224, 225, 231, 232,
    238–240, 247, 263
Accumulating positive
    emotions, 183
Adaptive denial, 89, 186–187
Addis, Michael, 190
Agatha of Sicily, Saint, 48
Agnes of Rome, Saint, 47–48
American Foundation for
    Suicide Prevention, 191
American University, 161–162
Anger, 9, 203–205, 294–297,
    299–300
Anti-war movement, 149
Apparent competence, 39,
    40
Aramburu, Beatriz, 220, 221
Archives of General Psychiatry
    (journal), 292–293
Aristotle, 147

Assertiveness skills, 142–146,
    169
"Assessment and Treatment of
    Parasuicide Patients,"
    193
Association for Advancement
    of Behavior Therapy, 130,
    161, 220, 323
Association for Behavioral and
    Cognitive Therapies, 130
Atkins, David, 306, 307n

Bandura, Albert, 116–118, 127,
    131
Bar-Ilan University, Israel, 135
Basilica of the National Shrine
    of the Immaculate
    Conception, 140
Beaulieu, Rita, 180
Beck, Aaron "Tim," xii
Bedics, Jamie, 306, 307n
Beginner's mind, 275–276
Behavioral dysregulation, 168

Behavior therapy, 8, 9, 127–128,
130–136, 141, 161–163,
192, 195, 212–214, 220,
278, 289, 305
(see also Dialectical Behavior
Therapy)
Benediktushof (Benedictus
House), Germany,
256–272
Bernanos, Georges, 41
Biosocial theory of borderline
personality disorder,
301–303
Blessed Sacrament Church,
Seattle, 197–198
Bobo doll experiment, 116–117
Body, power of the, 203–204
Bohus, Martin, 63, 259, 330
Borchert, Bruno, 49, 105
Borderline personality disorder
(BPD), 5, 9, 46–47, 63,
138, 195, 289, 293–307, 299
Boundary violation, 208
Breathing, 154, 155, 278–279
Brockopp, Gene, 124
Byron, Lord, 288

Calvert, Brooke, 59, 60
Camano Island, Washington,
311–313
Catholic University of
America, Washington,
D.C., 57, 140–141, 145,

148, 150, 162, 164, 188,
192, 196
Cenacle Retreat Center,
Chicago, 101–103, 200,
232, 244, 267, 268
Cenacle Sisters, 101–103
Change skills, 142, 146, 169, 219,
225
Chicago, Illinois, 76, 77, 81
Chicago Institute for
Psychoanalysis, 105
Chiles, J. A., 341n
Church of Our Lady of the
Desert, Arizona, 273
Circular thinking, 97–98
Civil rights movement, 99, 177
Clarkin, John, 192, 306
Cleary, Allanah, 149–152, 161,
164
Clement I, Saint, 48
Clinical Behavior Therapy
(Davison and Goldfried),
131–132
Clinical outreach, 126
Cloud of Unknowing, The
(anonymous), 181, 197
Cognitive-Behavioral Treatment
of Borderline Personality
Disorder (Linehan), 38n,
40n, 298–299, 313
Cold pack therapy, 27, 33
Comtois, Katherine, 306, 307n
Connecticut River, 36–37
Consistency Agreement, 225n

Consultation-to-the-Patient
  Agreement, 225*n*
Continuous change, 230
Cook County Insane Asylum,
  Chicago, 83–85
Cope ahead skill, 187–188
Crivolio, Gus, 111–113

Dalai Lama, 10, 41
Dancing, 264–265, 275, 329–330
Dark Night of the Soul (Saint
  John of the Cross), 181
Davison, Gerald C. (Jerry),
  131*n*, 131–140, 161, 164,
  278, 298, 312, 323
DBT (*see* Dialectical Behavior
  Therapy)
DEAR MAN [describe, express,
  assert, reinforce, (stay)
  mindful, appear confident,
  negotiate], 143–145, 169
De Mello, Anthony, 248–249
Depression, 47, 60, 62, 63, 69,
  95, 113, 183, 335
Dialectical Agreement, 225*n*
Dialectical Behavior Therapy
  (DBT), 54, 139, 151,
  219–220
  acceptance skills, 7, 89, 142,
    154, 169, 216, 219, 220,
    224, 225, 231, 232,
    238–240, 247, 263
  adaptive denial, 89, 186–187

assertiveness skills, 142–146,
  169
beginnings of, 6–7
benefits of, 8
challenge for therapist,
  171–172
change skills, 142, 146, 169,
  219, 225
clinical trials of, 173,
  289–291, 305
cope ahead skill, 187–188
DBT-Linehan Board of
  Certification, 334
defined, 167–168
development of, xii, 3, 5, 44
distress tolerance skills, 153,
  154–155, 169, 170, 202,
  204, 216–217, 220, 241
emotion regulation skills,
  169, 170, 241
four categories of skills,
  169–170
irreverence, 221–223, 245
life skills and, 9–11, 241
living an anti-depressant life,
  182–183
mindfulness skills, 8, 11, 159,
  169, 170, 241, 271, 273,
  279–288
name of, 226, 227
opposite action, 146–147,
  202–203, 241
overall goal of, 67
sources of skills, 172–173

Dialectical Behavior Therapy (DBT) (cont'd)
spread of, 334–335
STOP skills, 217–219, 241
Strategic Planning Group, 304
therapists and, 220–221, 224–225
traumatic invalidation, 55
uniqueness of, 7–8, 168, 220
Zen and, 277–279
Dialectics, 302
defined, 226, 227
Diary of a Country Priest, The (Bernanos), 41n
Dimeff, Linda, 331
Distress tolerance skills, 153, 154–155, 169, 170, 204, 216–217, 217, 220, 241
DSM-IV (Diagnostic and Statistical Manual of Mental Disorders), 294, 295
Duncan, Sister Rosemary, 103
DX Oil Company, 25

Eating disorders, 126, 335
Edwards, Allen, 209
Edwards, Tilden, 196
Egan, James, 181
Egan, Joel, 181
Egan, Kelly, 181–182, 208–209
Electroconvulsive shock therapy, 22, 29, 30, 65

Emotion dysregulation, 168, 301
Emotion mind, 281–282
Emotion regulation skills, 169, 170, 241
Endorphins, 19
Engels, Friedrich, 302

Fallibility Agreement, 225
Family Connections, 46
Family interventions, 9, 168
Fisher, Sebern, 20, 25, 31, 33–38, 42, 64, 326
Foa, Edna, 247, 248
Four Great Vows of the Bodhisattva, 275
Frances, Allen, xi–xiii, 294–296, 302
Franks, Elaine, 327, 331
Free association, 115
Freud, Sigmund, 97, 115

George Washington University, 149
Goldfried, Marvin R., 131n, 131–132, 135, 161
Goodstein, J. L., 341n
Gordon, Judith, 233
Graduate Record Examination (GRE) scores, 109
Grand rounds, 302–303
Great Depression, 25, 53

Grimm, Beatrice, 264, 329
Group training, 9, 168
Gunderson, John, 307

Half-smiling, 204–205
Harborview Medical Center,
    Seattle, Washington, 278
Harrington, Mary, 150, 152–153
Hawk, Pat, 273–274
Heard, Heidi, 290, 293
Hendrix, Jimi, 177
Hohokam people, 273
Hoon, Peter, 135

"I Am Woman," 210–211
"I'll Be Seeing You," 60
Implicit bias, 99
Indiana Oil Purchasing
    Company, 67
Institute of Living, Hartford,
    Connecticut, 3, 5, 6,
    18–45, 65, 72, 91, 103, 107,
    113, 119, 137, 138, 162, 191,
    298–300, 325–331, 334
Intense exercise skill, 154–155,
    203, 217
Intermittent reinforcement
    schedule, 156–157
Interpersonal effectiveness
    skills, 169, 170, 176
Introject measure, 306, 307
Irreverence, 221–223, 245

Isaac Jogues, Saint, 47
"Is That God Talking?"
    (Luhrmann), 149n
Ivanoff, André, 189, 208, 266

Jäger, Willigis, 95, 206, 232,
    246, 255–266, 268–275,
    278, 279, 284
Jesuits, 114
Jiyu-Kennett, Roshi Houn, 232,
    235, 237
John of the Cross, Saint, 181
*Journal of Consulting and
    Clinical Psychology*, 307

Kabat-Zinn, Jon, 287
Kairos House of Prayer,
    Spokane, Washington,
    179–180, 232, 237
Kernberg, Otto, 293–294, 296,
    298–302, 306, 307, 324
Kipper, David, 135
Knox, Frank, 19, 34, 62
Koans, 199, 259–260, 262
Koerner, Kelly, 189
Kohlenberg, Bob, 207–208, 210,
    278
Koons, Cedar, 274
Korslund, Katie, 284
Kovacs, Maria, 194
Krasner, Leonard, 130–132,
    131n

Lake Washington, 164, 176

Langer, Ellen, 287

Laughlin, Patrick, 99, 100, 108–110

Lazarus, Arnold, 131

Leone, Sister Florence, 179–180

Letters to a Young Poet (Rilke), 139

Leventhal, Allan, 161–163, 164

Leventhal, Carol, 164

Life skills, 9–11, 241

Linehan, Aline, 5, 6, 15, 16, 24, 30, 32, 57, 60, 62, 65, 76, 93, 122, 153, 156, 164, 174, 175, 178, 264, 324, 328, 330
    mother, relationship with, 52, 54, 56, 66
    sister Marsha, relationship with, 11–12, 14, 46, 159, 315, 325
    wedding of, 118

Linehan, Brendon, 52

Linehan, Darielle, 76, 84, 93

Linehan, Earl, 6, 14, 16, 30, 45, 47, 52, 56, 62, 76, 84–87, 93, 113, 157, 292, 328, 330, 331

Linehan, Ella Marie (Tita), 14–18, 25, 42, 50–60, 63, 66, 68–71, 76, 81, 111, 118, 122, 175, 183–185, 229, 243–244, 257, 268, 269, 315, 330–331
    background of, 53
    daughter Marsha, relationship with, 16–17, 18, 24, 30–31, 51, 53–54, 56, 59, 66, 68–69, 184–185, 229, 243–244, 269

Linehan, John, 6, 14, 16, 50, 56, 62, 292, 328, 330, 331

Linehan, John Marston, 42, 53, 55, 58, 66, 71, 76, 81, 86, 89, 118, 175, 183, 311, 315
    background of, 13, 14, 25
    character of, 13, 51
    daughter Marsha, relationship with, 13, 25, 50, 77, 114

Linehan, Julia, 58, 63, 81

Linehan, Marsha
    alcohol use and, 67–68
    at Benediktushof (Benedictus House), 256–272
    borderline personality disorder (BPD) and, 46–47, 195, 295, 297–307
    boyfriends and, 75–76, 81, 121–123, 129, 138, 156–160, 200, 244
    brother Earl and, 84–87
    at Catholic University, 57, 140–141, 145, 148, 150, 162, 164, 188, 192, 196
    at Cenacle Retreat Center, 101–103, 200, 232
    childhood and youth of, 15–16, 47–50, 56, 58–64

circular thinking and, 97–98

Cleary, Allanah, and, 150–152

Cognitive-Behavioral Treatment of Borderline Personality Disorder, 38n, 40n, 298–299, 313

in Cook County Insane Asylum, 83–86

criticism of, 302–307

Crivolio, Gus, and, 111–113

Davison, Gerald C., and, 131–137, 278

Dialectical Behavior Therapy (DBT) and (*see* Dialectical Behavior Therapy)

drugs and, 19, 30, 41, 64, 69

education of, 4, 6, 13, 17, 45, 57, 59–60, 72–73, 75, 81, 82, 88–91, 97–100, 102, 104, 107–119, 121, 126, 128, 133–139

enlightenment experiences of, 102–104, 106, 113, 200–201, 232, 244, 252, 267, 268

family of, 13–17, 50–56, 58

father, relationship with, 13, 25, 50, 77, 114

finances of, 68, 89, 91

Fisher, Sebern, and, 20, 25, 31, 33–38, 42, 64, 326

Freud, Sigmund, and, 97, 115

Harrington, Mary, and, 152–153

Hawk, Pat, and, 274

at Institute of Living, Hartford, Connecticut, 6, 18–45, 46, 63, 65, 72, 103, 107, 113, 119, 137, 138, 162, 300, 325–328, 334

Jäger, Willigis, and, 255–256, 262, 264, 269–272, 273–275, 284

at Kairos House of Prayer, 179–180, 232, 237

leaves home, 66

Leventhal, Allan, and, 161–163, 164

Lisman, Steve, and, 135–139

Little Brothers and, 95–96

memory loss of, 30, 57, 65, 90, 116

mother, relationship with, 16–17, 18, 24, 30–31, 51, 53–54, 56, 59, 66, 68–69, 184–185, 229, 243–244, 269

moves to Chicago, 81

moves to Seattle, 174–179

music and, 29, 50

nature and, 175, 311–312

at Newman Catholic Student Center, 149–150, 152–153

NIMH-funded research and, 5, 193–195, 212, 289

Linehan, Marsha (*cont'd*)
O'Brien, John, and, 22, 24, 26, 28, 32, 34, 38–45, 68–71, 73–74
physical appearance of, 15, 16, 28, 30, 32, 59, 62
poem by, 23–24
reading by, 47–48
religion and, 23, 29, 48–49, 61, 93–94, 102–104, 113, 148–149, 197–198, 201, 333–334
Romb, Anselm, and, 91–93, 95, 104, 113, 196, 262, 271, 272
self-injury and, 19, 21–22, 25, 26, 35–36, 47, 66, 82–83, 85, 137
at Shalem Institute for Spiritual Formation, 196–197, 199, 200, 232
at Shasta Abbey, 232–245, 256, 261, 263, 267, 279
sister Aline, relationship with, 11–12, 14, 46, 159, 315, 325
smoking and, 33, 89, 185–186
in sorority, 59, 61
spirituality of, 11, 47–49, 92–93, 102–104, 123, 179–181, 196–197, 199–201, 206, 232–245, 271, 333–334

at State University of New York at Stony Brook, 133–139, 145, 223
suicidal thoughts and behavior, work on, 72–73, 125–126, 128, 136–138, 140–142, 167, 188–195, 212–224, 229–230, 289–291, 305, 306
suicide attempts by, 69–71, 113
at Suicide Prevention and Crisis Service, Buffalo, 124–126, 128–129
Swenson, Charles, and, 222, 294–298
talk at Institute of Living by, 3–6, 11, 327–331
tenure and, 207–211, 266
at University of Washington, 163–164, 167, 188, 192, 207, 209–211, 226
Vierra, Ted, and, 82, 93–94, 104, 113, 271, 272
at Weill Cornell Medical College, 293–294, 298, 302
Zen and, 7, 8, 11, 105, 231–245, 255–264, 267, 269–271, 273–278
Linehan, Marston, 6, 14, 56, 62, 71, 325, 328, 330, 331
Linehan, Mike, 6, 14, 56, 62, 71, 325, 328, 330, 331
Linehan, Tracey, 17

Lisman, Steve, 135–139
Little Brothers of the Poor,
    95–96
Loyola University, Chicago, 45,
    81, 82, 89–91, 97–102, 104,
    107–115, 118, 119, 121, 128,
    262
Luhrmann, Tanya Marie,
    148–149
Lungu, Anita, 221

Malawi, 150–151
Marshmallow experiment,
    116
Marx, Karl, 302
May, Gerald, 196, 201–202, 205,
    232, 253
May, Rollo, 196
McLean Hospital,
    Massachusetts, 307
Meditation (zazen), 257–258,
    261–262, 267, 278–279,
    286, 287
Merseth, Catalina, 333, 335
Merseth, Nate, 6, 321, 322, 330,
    333
Michels, Bob, 302, 303
Midwestern Psychological
    Association, 100
Miller, Henry, 288
Mindfulness-Based Stress
    Reduction, 287
Mindfulness (Langer), 287

Mindfulness skills, 8, 11, 159,
    169, 170, 241, 271, 273,
    279–288
Miracle of Mindfulness, The
    (Thich Nhat Hanh),
    286
Mischel, Walter, 116, 127, 131
Missionary Sisters of Our Lady
    of Africa (White Sisters),
    150
Monte Cassino School, Tulsa,
    Oklahoma, 13, 21, 56, 57,
    59, 64
Mother Teresa, 96
Mount Baker, 311
Mount Shasta, 235
Münsterschwarzach Abbey,
    Germany, 260–261
*Mysticism: Its History and
    Challenge* (Borchert), 49,
    105

"Nada Te Turbe," 265, 329
Nancy, Cousin, 17, 49–50, 58,
    59, 63, 64, 159, 160
National Alliance on Mental
    Illness (NAMI),
    324–325
National Defense Education
    Act fellowship, 110
National Institute of Mental
    Health (NIMH), 5,
    141–142, 193–195, 289

Neurofeedback in the Treatment of Developmental Trauma (Fisher), 38*n*
New England Educational Institute, 64, 159
Newman Catholic Student Center, Washington, D.C., 149–150, 152–153
New York Times, The, xi, 46, 103
Nielsen, S. L., 341*n*
Nixon, Richard M., 114

O'Brien, John, 22, 24, 26, 28, 32, 34, 38–45, 68–71, 73–74, 191
Observing-Limits Agreement, 225*n*
Obsessive compulsive disorder, 126
Old Saint Mary's, Chicago, 82, 93
Olmsted, Frederick Law, 298
Olympic Mountains, 176
Omega Point, 104
Opposite action, 146–147, 202–203, 241
Outcome measures, 212, 213

Paced breathing, 154, 155, 203, 217
Paired muscle relaxation, 154, 217

Parasuicidal behavior, 289, 290
Parasympathetic nervous system, 155
Payne Whitney, New York, 302
Peace movement, 149
People's movement, 149
Personality and Assessment (Mischel), 116
Personality disorders, 126
"Personal Story of the Development of DBT, The" (Linehan), 327
Phenomenological Agreement, 225*n*
Phenomenon of Man, The (Teilhard de Chardin), 104
Pielsticker, Margie, 50, 60, 63
Poor people's campaign, 149
"Postdoctoral Program in Behavioral Modification, A: Theory and Practice" (Davison, Goldfried, and Krasner), 131*n*, 132, 135
Post-traumatic stress disorder (PTSD), 126, 335
Presley, Elvis, 174
Principles of Behavior Modification (Bandura), 116
Proctor, Dr., 69, 73
Psychiatry, 126–127
Psychoanalysis, 115, 126–127
Psychodrama, 135

Psychodynamic therapy, 10,
141, 171
Psychotherapy, 8, 9, 11, 116, 167
Puget Sound, 164, 176

Quintianus, Senator, 48

Radical acceptance, 159, 241,
248–253, 263
Ratzinger, Joseph (Pope
Benedict XVI), 255
Reasonable mind, 281–282
"Reasons for Staying Alive
When You Are Thinking
of Killing Yourself: The
Reasons for Living
Inventory" (Linehan,
Goodstein, Nielsen, and
Chiles), 341
"Reasons for Staying Alive
When You Are Thinking
of Killing Yourself"
measure, 125
Reddy, Helen, 210
Redemptorist Renewal Center,
Tucson, Arizona, 273
Reserve Insurance Company,
81, 88
Rilke, Rainer Maria, 139, 312
Rodriguez, Geraldine, 6,
316–322, 331, 333–335
Rogers, Carl, 120, 215

Romb, Anselm, 91–93, 95, 104,
113, 196, 262, 271, 272
Rutgers University, 135

Safety cues, 187
Saguaro National Park, 273
Saratoga Passage, 311
Seattle, Washington, 176–178
Seclusion room, 32–34, 42
Self-injury, 19, 21–22, 25, 26,
35–36, 47, 55, 66, 82–83,
85, 126, 137, 193, 229, 291
Serene Reflection Meditation
(Soto Zen) tradition, 235
Sesshins, 257–259, 262
Shalem Institute for Spiritual
Formation, Washington,
D.C., 196–197, 199, 200,
232, 233, 256
Shasta Abbey, California,
232–245, 256, 261, 263,
267, 278, 279
Shearin, Ed, 208, 300
"Shepherd's Song, The," 265
Sherry, Jane, 58
Siegfried, Diane, 47, 59, 60,
62
Skagit Valley, 311
Skills (*see* Dialectical Behavior
Therapy)
Smith, Holly, 327, 331
Social behaviorism theory, 145,
146, 192

Social learning theory, 116–118, 127

Social phobia, 126

Soto School of Japan, 235

Spretnak, Charlene, 288

Staats, Arthur, 145, 146, 192

Stanford University, 131

State University of New York at Stony Brook, 130, 131, 133–139, 141, 145, 161–162, 223, 278, 312

Stolz, Stephanie, 141

STOP skills, 217–219, 241

Story of a Soul (Thérèse of Lisieux), 48

Strupp, Hans, 194

Subjective Units of Distress Scale (SUDS), 188

Substance dependence, 335

Suicidal thoughts and behavior, 7, 9, 24, 28, 34, 42–44, 47, 55, 69–71, 107, 125–126, 126, 128, 136–138, 289–291, 305, 306

Suicide Prevention and Crisis Service, Buffalo, New York, 124–126, 128–129

Sunoco, 13, 25

Supportive therapy, 215

Swenson, Charles, 222, 293–298, 302–303

Sympathetic nervous system, 155

T-group (sensitivity/encounter group), 120

Taizé songs, 264–265

Talk therapy, 126

Tante Aline, 25, 53, 63, 185, 229

Teilhard de Chardin, Pierre, 104–105

Telephone coaching, 9, 168

Temperature manipulation, 154, 217

Teresa of Avila, Saint, 329

Therapist consultation team, 9

Therapist teams, 224

Thérèse Couderc, Sister, 101, 103–105

Thérèse of Lisieux, Saint, 48, 61, 178, 179

Thich Nhat Hanh, 204, 286–287

TIP skills (see Distress tolerance skills)

Tolin, David, 5, 327, 330

Transaction, 228

Traumatic invalidation, 55

Trias, Elizabeth, 226, 227

Tulsa, Oklahoma, 13, 14

Turning the mind, 252–253

University of Chicago, 110

University of Illinois, 109

University of Tulsa, 72

University of Washington, 41, 57, 143, 188, 192, 207–211, 226, 278, 304

Valeška, Adolfas, 102
Vierra, Ted, 82, 93–94, 104, 113, 271, 272
Vietnam War, 114

Wagner, Amy, 182
Wake, Ann, 153
Walker, Ron, 108–110
Weill Cornell Medical College, White Plains, New York, 192, 293–295, 298–299
Weisstein, Naomi, 97, 98, 100
Wells, Sunder, 242
Whidbey Island, 311–312
Will and Spirit: A Contemplative Psychology (G. May), 196, 205
Willfulness, 202–203, 205
Williams, Mark, 292

Willing hands, 204–205
Willingness, 201–203, 205–206, 227, 232, 253
Wilson, Terry, 220
Windermyer, Jack, 149
Wise mind
origin of, 282–284
practicing, 285–286
recognizing, 284–285
Wolfe, Barry, 194

Yale University, 109

Zen, 7, 8, 11, 105, 199, 201, 231, 255–264, 267, 269–271, 273–278
Zielinski, Victor, 22, 105–106
Zimbardo, Philip, 287

MARSHA M. LINEHAN, PhD, ABPP, is the developer of Dialectical Behavior Therapy and a professor of psychology, adjunct professor of psychiatry and behavioral sciences, and director of the Behavioral Research and Therapy Clinics at the University of Washington. Her primary research interest is in the development and evaluation of evidence-based treatments for populations with high suicide risk and multiple severe mental disorders. Dr. Linehan's contributions to suicide research and clinical psychology research have been recognized with numerous awards, including the Gold Medal Award for Life Achievement in the Application of Psychology from the American Psychological Foundation, the Scientific Research Award from the National Alliance on Mental Illness, the Career/Lifetime Achievement award from the Association for Behavioral and Cognitive Therapies, and the Grawemeyer Award in Psychology. In 2018, Dr. Linehan was featured in a special issue of *Time* magazine, "Great Scientists: The Geniuses and Visionaries Who Transformed Our World."

ABOUT THE TYPE

....

This book was set in Fournier, a typeface named for Pierre-Simon Fournier (1712–68), the youngest son of a French printing family. He started out engraving woodblocks and large capitals, then moved on to fonts of type. In 1736 he began his own foundry and made several important contributions in the field of type design; he is said to have cut 147 alphabets of his own creation. Fournier is probably best remembered as the designer of St. Augustine Ordinaire, a face that served as the model for the Monotype Corporation's Fournier, which was released in 1925.